Mountain Islands and Desert Seas

Mountain Islands

COLLEGE STATION

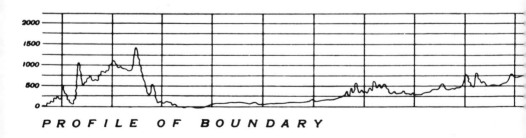

PROFILE OF BOUNDARY

and Desert Seas

A Natural History of the
U.S.-Mexican Borderlands

by FREDERICK R. GEHLBACH

TEXAS A&M UNIVERSITY PRESS

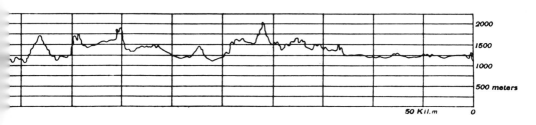

2000

1500

1000

500 meters

50 Kil.m   0

√

Library of Congress Cataloging in Publication Data

Gehlbach, Frederick R., 1935–
    Mountain islands and desert seas.

    Bibliography: p.
    Includes index.
    1. Natural history—Southwestern States. 2. Natural history—Mexico. 3. United States—Boundaries—Mexico. 4. Mexico—Boundaries—United States. I. Title. II. Title: U.S.–Mexican borderlands.
QH104.5.S6G43   508.78   81-40402
ISBN 0-89096-118-2   AACR2

Manufactured in the United States of America
FIRST EDITION

For my father and in memory of my mother, both of whom provided the theater for the evolution of a naturalist.

Contents

List of Illustrations

x Illustrations

California sister butterfly
Colorado hairstreak butterfly
Tripletail swallowtail butterfly
Birds
    Fledgling canyon wrens
    Yellow-eyed junco
    Acorn woodpecker
    Blue-throated hummingbird
    Elegant trogons
    Green jay
    Chachalaca
    Screech owl
    Juvenile Cooper's hawk
Mammals   *following page* 224
    White-throated woodrat
    Woodrat midden
    Desert pocket mouse
    Arizona gray squirrel
    Coatimundis
    Pygmy mouse
Fish, amphibians, and reptiles
    Leon Spring pupfish
    Comanche Spring pupfish
    Big Bend mosquitofish
    Tiger salamander
    Rough-footed mudturtle
    Bunch grass lizard
    Chuckwalla
    Yarrow's spiny lizard
    Fringe-toed lizard
    Tarahumara frog
    Rio Grande chirping frog
    Vine snake
    Ridge-nosed rattlesnake
    Ringneck snake

Preface

THIS book is a sampler of my twenty-six years of natural-history inquiries in the Borderlands, an area generally encompassing all U.S. and Mexican states along the International Border.[1] My investigations are concentrated within 100 miles of the Boundary and extend from the mouth of the Rio Grande to the western edge of the Sonoran desert region. Some of the effects of the last century of human explorations and exploitations are included because technological man is such a powerful influent. Still, the Borderlands retain most of their diverse blend of tropical and temperate, mountain and valley organisms and their mix of Anglo, Mexican, and Indian life-styles. A unique living landscape marks this broad belt across the waist of North America.

The historical perspective invites me to travel in the footsteps and reside at the campsites of naturalists associated with the First (1849–1855) and Second (1891–1896) U.S.–Mexican Boundary surveys. Like John Bartlett, U.S. Boundary commissioner from 1850 to 1853, I present a personal narrative of discovery.[2] This book summarizes my studies of landscape processes created by nature and altered by culture. Facts fascinate me and are recounted, but it is the explanation of repeated patterns that I seek. If anything contrasts natural-history research today with that of the nineteenth century, it is that pattern analysis has superseded fact finding.

Another Boundary commissioner, William Emory (1854–1855), produced three magnificent volumes on the discoveries of the first survey. Like Bartlett's writing, these references present valuable comparative material, and I make use of their illustrations and the personal

[1]The Borderlands region is delineated in E. R. Stoddard, "The Status of Borderlands Studies: An Introduction," *Soc. Sci. J.* 12 (1976): 3–8.

[2]J. R. Bartlett, *Personal Narrative of the Explorations and Incidents in Texas, New Mexico, California, Sonora, and Chihuahua, Connected with the United States and Mexican Boundary Commission during the Years 1850, '51, '52, and '53*, 2 vols. (New York: D. Appleton and Co., 1854).

contributions of many surveyors on that pioneering venture. The second survey report is especially important for its volume of landscape photographs, but it is less evocative because it is less personal. "If natural history research is for understanding nature . . . exposure of the learning process and the emotional leads in the pathways of scientific investigation is a necessary qualification."[3]

Edgar Mearns's treatise on plants and vertebrate animals, resulting from his tenure as survey surgeon and naturalist (1892–1894), is more intriguing. And from the same era, Vernon Bailey of the U.S. Biological Survey provides information for a useful historical perspective.[4] Through his writings, Aldo Leopold inspired any philosophical insights I might have, in a manner consistent with the holistic understanding that developed a few decades later. For me as for him, "field experiences . . . were [are] not only an opportunity for sustained observation but also for reflection, for putting together the pieces." I borrow Leopold's metaphor of the ecological theater and the evolutionary play.[5]

Furthermore, the written contributions of contemporary naturalists are important in my work. The dates of their publications, beginning in the 1950's, will indicate the overlapping of their time niches compared with the segregated works of their predecessors. Their narrow spatial niches are equally apparent, by contrast with the broader interests of the early generalists, although Joe Marshall's integrative approach to plants used by birds is a recent complement to Mearns's

[3] W. H. Emory, *Report on the United States and Mexican Boundary Survey*, vol. 1 and vol. 2 (vol. 2 in 2 pts.), 34th Cong., 1st sess., 1857–1859, House Exec. Doc. 135; U.S. Boundary Commission, *Report of the Boundary Commission upon the Survey and Remarking of the Boundary between the United States and Mexico West of the Rio Grande, 1891–1896*, pts. 1 and 2, 55th Cong., 2nd sess., 1898, Senate Doc. 247. Quote is from P. Dansereau, *Inscape and Landscape: The Human Perception of Environment* (New York: Columbia Univ. Press, 1975), p. 31.

[4] E. A. Mearns, *Mammals of the Mexican Boundary of the United States*, U.S. Natl. Mus. Bull. 56 (1907); V. Bailey, *Biological Survey of Texas*, N. Amer. Fauna 25 (1905); idem, *Mammals of New Mexico*, N. Amer. Fauna 53 (1931).

[5] A. Leopold, *A Sand County Almanac* (London: Oxford Univ. Press, 1949); idem, *Round River* (New York: Oxford Univ. Press, 1953). Quote about Leopold is from S. L. Flader, *Thinking Like a Mountain* (Columbia: Univ. Missouri Press, 1974), p. 152. See also E. P. Odum, "The Emergence of Ecology as a New Integrative Discipline," *Science* 195 (1977): 1289–93; G. E. Hutchinson, *The Ecological Theater and the Evolutionary Play* (New Haven: Yale Univ. Press, 1975).

monograph.[6] Often I reanalyze the modern information in light of my own questioning, so literature citations are as apt to furnish raw data for reinterpretation as to provide confirmatory evidence. The explanation of landscape patterns requires syntheses of observations from many sources.

Nearly all that I recount I know firsthand, although the published information may have originated elsewhere, as noted in the references. Most of my studies span more than one season or year in order to assess the vagaries of Borderlands climates. Places like the Guadalupe Mountains in Texas and New Mexico and the Canelo Hills in Arizona have received the equivalent of a full year of residence. Despite my fascination by life in all states of the Border, I must admit a predilection for fellow vertebrates and a particular familiarity with Texas, New Mexico, and Arizona.

The locales and species are selected from my nearly 800 pages of field notes and some 1,200 photographs as having been particularly instructive and inspirational to me. Common names of species and a few subspecies or varieties are those most frequently used, or they are standardized names as in birds. A few are names that mean the most to me personally, but none are novel. All are accompanied by their scientific equivalents in the index. As for the photographs, I have retrieved scenes and organisms that characterize my narrative, reflecting my sense of harmony with the living landscape. Drawings from the historic Bartlett, Emory, and Mearns documents were selected for their relevance to the experiences recounted.

I crossed the International Boundary for the first time in 1954 and relived the entire scene of my early experiences on a year-long journey in 1970–1971. The ensuing period has been devoted to additional investigations and to the writing of this book at the O'Donnell Cienega in the Canelo Hills and at Butterfly Hollow near Waco, Texas. Travel to a site was by vehicle and once there on horseback and foot; lodging was in structures like a century-old adobe farmhouse or tent for several days to three months at a time. I believe that naturalists must love and thus live with their subjects besides intellectualizing about them.

At first I journeyed alone or with others of the naturalist faith, es-

---

[6] J. T. Marshall, Jr., *Birds of Pine-oak Woodland in Southern Arizona and Adjacent Mexico*, Pacific Coast Avifauna 32 (1957).

pecially members of the Prairie Trek Expeditions and Jack Kaufmann, Tom Poulson, and Ted Hendrickson. In 1960 Nancy became my wife and coinvestigator, and my children, Gretchen and Mark, have been *compañeros* since 1964 and 1967 respectively. *Aficionados de la frontera* who aided us in a sustained way are George and Sis Bradt, Tony and Alice Echelle, Bill and Marina Hoy, Roger Reisch, and Wayne and Libby Shifflett. They made us second family and became sounding boards for my hypotheses. The Echelles and Bill Hoy read the entire manuscript of this book to its benefit.

Also, I received extra help from certain colleagues, students, and friends: Charles Ames, Ken Baker, Robert Baker, Richard Banks, Stanley Cain, Floyd Davidson, Raymond Davis, Don Delnicki, Larry Harrell, O. T. Hayward, Larry and Signe Henderson, Clark Hubbs, Jack Hudson, Pauline James, Spencer Johnston, Edgar Kincaid, Jeffrey Klopatek, Charles Lowe, Paul Martin, Larry May, Robert Miller, George Newman, Carroll and Joan Peabody, George and Holly Pilling, Harley Reno, Howard Rolf, Peter Sanchez, Philip VanCleave, Julian Watkins, Roland Wauer, and Paul Whitson. Sis Bradt provided the fire picture used in this book, and Braz Walker supplied the fish photos. Darla Millsap, Estellene Cox, Margaret Hughs, Iris Jeffries, and James Rogers aided as an instrumental secretary and four very cooperative librarians, respectively.

Expeditions were financed in part by Baylor University, Cornell University, the University of Michigan, National Park Service (which I served as collaborator for twenty years), and Sigma Xi. A John Simon Guggenheim Memorial Fellowship enabled me to weave this sampler's pattern, and a sabbatical leave from Baylor allowed some uninterrupted writing about the wild things and places I treasure most. I have tried to combine the delights of personal discovery with the documentation of natural patterns amid advancing culture, for I wish to foster conservation of the unparalleled natural diversity of the Borderlands.

Mountain Islands and Desert Seas

1. *The Living Landscape*

THE Border landscape is a carpet of interacting plants and animals deftly woven on a geologic loom. To understand the fabric of this carpet, fashioned by 26 million years of evolutionary weaving, and to comprehend its ten to twelve thousand years of shrinks and swells—the impact of the hand of man—I try to recognize general patterns in addition to details. Further, if I can learn something of the faint prehistory of the Borderlands, I will gain appreciation for the temporal and spatial continuity of its unique diversity. Yet latitude, longitude, and elevation capture most of my interest, since with modern transportation I can compress these spatial dimensions to suit my understanding. I have more difficulty recapturing time.

Cool-wet mountain islands and warm-dry desert seas give me the initial feel of the Borderlands. The living landscape depends primarily on the lay of the land plus climate and the nature of parent rock—the shape and materials of the loom. I shall make a brief mental excursion to recall such general impressions before considering details. And I will spend more time in Texas and its neighboring Mexican states, because this eastern sector represents nearly two-thirds of the trip from the Gulf of Mexico to the Colorado River, near the western limit of my Borderlands experiences. It is 1,250 river miles along the Rio Grande, el Río Bravo del Norte, from the Gulf to El Paso.

At the beginning of my journey the landscape is a flat plain, formed by being more exposed and then more flooded as glaciers tied up more or less water in ice during the last few million years. At Boca Chica, the mouth of the Rio Grande, I am 300 miles south of journey's end and about 100 miles north of the tropics. This southernmost Boundary region averages twenty-five inches of rainfall per year. Hurricanes and their floods dampen the otherwise semiarid climate. A subtropical aspect prevails, with only occasional freezes, and continues about 100 miles upriver to the Bordas Escarpment (Scarp), where I leave the floodplain for slightly higher ground.

Rio Grande Plain below Lomita (Emory)

Two large tributaries of the Rio Grande enter from Nuevo León and Tamaulipas, Mexico, on the western side of the Bordas Scarp. They have been important riparian pathways through broad grasslands. The Río San Juan is the first and empties into Gomez Reservoir before reaching the Great River. And the Río Salado disappears under one of two major Rio Grande impoundments, Falcon Reservoir. The only other large drainageway is Arroyo Colorado in Texas. It carries hurricane floodwaters out of the river floodplain northeastward into the Gulf of Mexico. Altogether, my impression of the first hundred miles of Boundary country is one of unnatural history, that is, of environmental change brought about by the acts—indeed, the very presence—of man.

This impression changes quickly as I climb over the Bordas Scarp. Irrigation agriculture and scattered tracts of natural history, locally called brush, are replaced by gently rolling hills with a desertlike appearance. The aridity continues through Texas and Coahuila, uninterrupted by major rivers, for 260 miles. Historically, this landscape changed when a traveler reached the great canyons of the Devils and Pecos rivers. But these two abrupt, topographic shifts are gone now.

The lower portions of these canyons are underwater in the name of U.S. – Mexican friendship, *amistad*, drowned by the second largest impoundment on the Rio Grande. I cannot find the Great River again until I get beyond Langtry, Texas.

Westward, however, the Rio Grande remains canyon country with one great earth slice after another along the wilderness between Langtry and Boquillas, Coahuila. Canyons that impeded the First Boundary Survey—Boquillas, Mariscal, and Santa Elena (San Carlos)—are spaced along an arc of the Rio Grande. North of the arc, in the Big Bend of Texas, high mountain islands float in flat desert or grassland seas. Timbered peaks of the Chisos, Sierra Chinati, and Sierra Vieja reach 7,000 to 8,000 feet. Southward, the Sierra del Carmen of Coahuila is 9,000 feet. Sea-level elevation of the deserts and grasslands is 2,000 to 3,000 feet, and it is so hot at midday in the summer that travelers head for the cool mountain islands like shipwrecked sailors.

I have climbed nearly half a mile without climbing any mountains in my journey from the mouth of the Rio Grande to its Big Bend. And I have entered a very arid region, averaging less than fourteen inches of precipitation per year. Locally the ranges include extinct volcanos and igneous mountains, where the hard remnants of molten earth, pushed up and worn down, produce a jagged skyline. Still others of these mountain islands are sedimentary rock, folded and faulted above the desert basins in the last few million years. The vertical exaggeration was even more spectacular at first, but as the mountains eroded the basins were filled with rock fragments. Nevertheless, a mile of vertical relief is impressive landscape flooring compared with the flat Rio Grande plains.

The free-flowing Rio Grande ceases to exist north of Presidio, Texas, on the west side of the Big Bend—except during flash floods. For instance, in 1851 a man drove mules along this riverbed between Presidio and El Paso and found only occasional pools of water, whereas in May, 1901, the river was almost a half-mile wide at Presidio.[1] The

[1] W. H. Emory, *Report on the United States and Mexican Boundary Survey*, vol. 1, 34th Cong., 1st sess., 1857, House Exec. Doc. 135, p. 50. The May, 1901, contrast is in a photo in the Proceedings of the International Boundary and Water Commission (1903), filed in the IBWC office in El Paso, Texas. A similar, horrendous flood occurred in September, 1978.

Original Boundary Monument, South of San Luis Springs (Emory)

dry stretch was natural a million years ago, when the upper Rio Grande drained westward before reaching the El Paso area and emptied into the playa region of northwestern Chihuahua. Then, perhaps 60,000 years ago, the river changed course and joined the older Río Conchos and lower Rio Grande system that had carved the canyons of the Big Bend. Today, the Conchos revives the Rio Grande at Ojinaga, Chihuahua, across from Presidio.

El Paso, Texas, and Juárez, Chihuahua, constitute the largest metropolitan complex in the Borderlands, with approximately 9 percent of the nearly nine million regional residents in 1970. This international city swallows up the Rio Grande and Boundary Monument 1, a man-made marker that replaces the natural river boundary between the United States and Mexico. Monument 1 is the first of 258 along the remaining 700 miles of political border. Originally, it sat alone in the river floodplain, but now it shares the site with other, taller markers, the smokestacks of metal smelters. To enter the western Borderlands I simply follow the row of political markers and sight on El Paso's smoke signals if I get lost. Except for the Potrillo, Florida, and Tres Hermanas mountains, I am awash in 100 miles of grassland and will not come ashore again until I reach the Carrizalillo Hills west of Columbus, New Mexico.

The view from the Carrizalillos or nearby Cedar Mountains reveals an archipelago of mountain islands. The Big Hatchets, Animas, San Luis and Peloncillo-Guadalupe ranges are the largest here in New Mexico's panhandle and adjacent Chihuahua. Eventually I will reach others—the Mule, San José, Ajo, Santa Rita, Huachuca, Cananea, Patagonia, Pinitos, Pajarito, and Baboquivari mountains along the Arizona-Sonora border. But now my view is blocked by the Animas–San Luis outlier of the vast Sierra Madre Occidental. The Continental Divide runs along these ranges. At 6,000 feet in San Luis Pass I stand on this backbone of North America and put one foot in the Pacific watershed, the other in the Atlantic watershed, the domain of the Rio Grande.

English, Spanish, and Indian cultures are reflected in the names of the mountain islands and in the Playas, Animas, San Bernardino, Sulpur Springs, San Pedro, San Rafael, Santa Cruz, and Altar valleys that serve as their erosional dumping grounds. These mountains and valleys are 1,000 feet higher than their Big Bend counterparts. The mountains reached present peak elevations of 8,000 to 9,000 feet through earth faulting that moved rock over a mile into the sky. Although individual earthquakes are often catastrophic to Boundary residents, as at Charleston, Arizona, and Bavispe, Sonora, in 1887, they have produced less than a thousandth of an inch a year of vertical displacement over the 26-million-year history of geologic loom construction.

Playas are flat, shallow lakebeds that occupy several of the valleys, especially the bolsónes, the valleys with no drainage outlets. Most playa lakes are ephemeral but hold water during the monsoon, the pronounced July–September rainy season characteristic of the Boundary between the Big Bend and the Colorado River.[2] Now they may be completely dry throughout a succession of drought years, yet at the height of glaciation in North America the playa lakes were respectable water bodies. Perhaps a hundred thousand years ago, a lake of 2,000 to 4,000 square miles inundated much of northern Chihuahua and adjacent New Mexico and Texas. The Palomas Basin in Chihuahua contains

---

[2] For background on the use of the term *monsoon* to describe the summer rainy season in the Borderlands, see P. S. Martin, *The Last 10,000 Years: A Fossil Pollen Record of the American Southwest* (Tucson: Univ. Arizona Press, 1963), pp. 3–5.

Mountain Islands—The Tule Mountains, Looking East (Emory)

the largest and most permanent of existing lakes, Lagunas de Santa María and Guzmán; the Mimbres River of New Mexico feeds this basin via underground drainage.

Three other small rivers cross the Border, sometimes above ground, sometimes below, depending on the season and man's use of their water. The first, the Río de San Bernardino, begins as small springs on the San Bernardino Ranch in southeastern Arizona and flows southward into the Río Bavispe in adjacent Sonora. The second, the Río San Pedro, returns water to Arizona as it flows out of Sonora to join the Gila River. The Santa Cruz River begins in the San Rafael Valley of Arizona and flows southward across the Border, around the southern end of the Patagonia Mountains in Sonora, and then back across the Border at Nogales, whereupon it is usually dry in its northward course to Tucson. All three rivers are particularly interesting in their metamorphosis from natural to unnatural history.

The Baboquivari Mountains, Arizona, mark the end of grassland seas in which timbered islands float and the beginning of a great desert ocean studded with barren, rocky peaks, as in the Ajo, Pinta, Tinajas Altas, and Tule mountains. Regional rainfall is only six inches a year. Except for the Río Sonoyta, coming from springs near Sonoyta, Sonora, and flowing west and then south toward the Gulf of California, there are no more perennial streams until the Colorado River makes a twenty-three-mile natural border between Yuma, Arizona, and San Luis, Sonora. Elevations drop precipitously to less than 100 feet at the Colorado River. The highest mountains are only 4,000 to 5,000 feet. In this most severe desert in North America, the summer monsoon disappears, and windblown sand dunes mingle with vast lava beds of the Pinacate region. Much remains a wilderness.

As I make the trek along the Border, I travel through a variety of natural communities. Those that contain the same or convergent life forms—species of similar appearance—can be lumped together in a manner analogous to grouping individuals with similar features as members of one species. Thus, two desert communities resemble each other in an easily identifiable manner, and each is quite distinct from a grassland or woodland. When I speak of desert, therefore, I use a synthetic concept, the sum of all desert communities I know. Yet different levels of synthesis are possible. Shrub desert is clearly a specific kind, different from succulent desert within the general idea I have of desert. Similarly, evergreen and deciduous woodlands are distinct, especially in winter, but enough alike in appearance that I do not confuse them with forest.

Charles Perry of the First Boundary Survey named local areas of similar plant life and observed that the living landscape—the scenery, as he put it—depends on plants. I agree, not only because plants stay put for me to recognize, but also because they are the living link with the life-giving sun. Besides noting the primacy of vegetation, Perry was an early observer of the continuum concept, the gradual blending of plants over environmental gradients. His modern interpretation did not stop there, for he also recognized the concept of dominance, the presence of larger, more populous, and more widely distributed— more obvious—species. As such, dominants are indicators of particular communities. My scheme of community identification, in which plant names or growth features are used descriptively, owes much to Perry's pioneering in 1851–1853.[3]

---

[3]C. C. Perry, "Botany of the U.S.–Mexican Boundary," in Emory, *Report*, vol. 2, pt. 1 (1859), pp. 9–26. To reduce complexity and jargon, I use the term *community* in the broad sense, applicable to plant associations, formations, and especially terrestrial biomes (see R. H. Whittaker, "Classification of Natural Communities," *Bot. Rev.* 28 [1962]: 1–239). Because of their smaller extent and lesser diversity, I do not find a need to use any special nomenclature for aquatic communities.

Certainly the most comprehensive twentieth-century arrangement of Boundary communities is Charles Lowe's. My scheme resembles his, too, but I prefer the name *shrub desert* to his *desertscrub*, because it denotes a shrub-dominated community. *Desertscrub* implies that stunted plants typify the desert, but they do not, at least not in undisturbed situations where species attain full growth. Also, Lowe does not recognize what I believe is a distinctive upland desert community, the succulent desert. Earlier, Forrest Shreve observed that this upland desert is quite different from lowland desert and showed that it alone gives distinction to the Chihuahuan and Sonoran desert regions.[4]

The succulent desert is just what the name implies, a dry, sparsely vegetated community dominated by succulent species. In the Chihuahuan desert region east of the Continental Divide this community is indicated by leaf succulent and semisucculent plants like lechuguilla, New Mexico agave, and narrowleaf sotol and to a lesser extent by non-succulent shrubs like slimleaf goldeneye. It grows typically on exposed mountainsides and canyon walls or on bajadas, those gradual rocky slopes extending from mountain walls to adjacent valley floors. The Sonoran desert region, that portion of the Borderlands from Arizona's Baboquivari Mountains and Gila River Valley westward into California, is characterized by succulent desert in another form. Here stem succulents such as saguaro and jumping cholla cactuses, plus foothill paloverde and brittlebush, are dominant species in similar positions on the landscape.

Dominant shrubs are not succulent or semisucculent but small-leaved, resinous, and sometimes drought-deciduous in the shrub desert. Moreover, they grow singly and may be widely spaced, in contrast to the tightly knit family groups or clones of many succulent desert shrubs. The widespread shrub desert indicator creosote bush does not tolerate crowding and may poison potential neighbors, an adaptation

---

[4]C. H. Lowe, "Arizona Landscape and Habitats," in *Vertebrates of Arizona*, ed. C. H. Lowe, pp. 1–132 (Tucson: Univ. Arizona Press, 1964); F. Shreve, "The Desert Vegetation of North America," *Bot. Rev.* 8 (1942):195–246. See discussion in F. R. Gehlbach, "Vegetation of the Guadalupe Escarpment, New Mexico–Texas," *Ecology* 48 (1967):204–219, and earlier observations of the Chihuahuan and Sonoran desert regions in D. D. Brand, "Notes to Accompany a Vegetation Map of Northwest Mexico," *Univ. New Mexico Bull.* 280 (1936):16. These regions are simply called Chihuahuan and Sonoran deserts today.

to the limited desert water supply. Conversely, the succulent desert dominant, saguaro cactus, often grows in family fashion in the scant shade of a paloverde, another adaptation to the same limiting scarcity of water. Shrub desert not only looks very different from succulent desert, but grows at lower elevations on deeper soils.

Bajadas reveal gradients of desert communities, the continuum recognized by Charles Perry. Succulent desert is at the top of the slope where large rocks predominate. Shrub desert begins to appear as the soil is composed of smaller rock fragments downslope. In the Sonoran desert region, saguaro, foothill paloverde, and triangle bursage blend with creosote bush and its codominant, white bursage, in the upslope to downslope continuum. In the Chihuahuan desert region, lechuguilla and narrowleaf sotol plus slimleaf goldeneye merge with creosote bush and tarbush or white-thorn acacia. Where surface or near-surface strata penetrate through the deep, silty soil of intermontane basins, succulent desert forms a mosaic with shrub desert, for it grows on the rock surrounded by or intermingling with shrub desert on the deeper soils.[5]

Deserts cannot be confused with grasslands, as the different names indicate, since shrubs are scarce and grasses abundant in natural grassland communities. However, desert grassland, the driest of three types of grassland, is invaded by desert shrubs like tarbush and creosote bush where grazing and drought have been severe. Mesquite, a shrub or small tree originally limited to drainageways and other naturally disturbed areas, also invades desert grassland with the help of drought and man. Edward Castetter recognizes no natural deserts in New Mexico, believing that the state's present deserts are made-over desert grassland.[6] But desert grassland remains above or adjacent to desert communities in mountainous terrain and is dominated by black

[5] Representative continuum analyses in the Chihuahuan and Sonoran desert regions, respectively, are in F. R. Gehlbach, "Vegetation of the Guadalupe Escarpment"; and R. H. Whittaker and W. A. Niering, "Vegetation of the Santa Catalina Mountains, Arizona: A Gradient Analysis of the South Slope," *Ecology* 46 (1965): 429–452. Distinctions between the soils of shrub and succulent deserts are given in T. W. Yang and C. H. Lowe, "Correlation of Major Vegetation Climaxes with Soil Characteristics in the Sonoran Desert," *Science* 123 (1956): 542.

[6] E. F. Castetter, "The Vegetation of New Mexico," *New Mexico Quart.* 26 (1956): 257–288. Cf. F. A. Gross and W. A. Dick-Peddie, "A Map of Primeval Vegetation in New Mexico," *Southwest. Natur.* 24 (1979): 115–122. See also chapters 7 and 13 of the present work.

grama, tobosa, and fluffgrass plus other species, depending on locale. All are less than two feet high and form clumps.

Plains grassland is slightly wetter and remains more pristine, where it remains at all. High valleys like the San Rafael in Arizona and Animas in New Mexico, generally above 4,500 feet, support this community. The relatively continuous cover of short grasses like galleta and blue or hairy grama provide the plains appearance. If one is familiar with the uninterrupted plains of the Texas panhandle, for instance, he may feel quite at home in plains grassland on the U.S.–Mexican Border. Quite different, however, is mountain grassland, which forms a landscape mosaic with tree-dominated communities in mountain canyons or on protected slopes. This is a community of tall bunchgrasses like mountain or bull muhly, and pinyon rice grass, all more than two feet in height.

Compared with grassland and desert, communities that grow closely packed shrubs or tree-sized wood look very different and develop differently. These communities—woodland, forest, and chaparral—gain additional wood because they grow under more favorable moisture conditions. Either they border streams or arroyos in the lowlands, or they climb the cooler mountains. As I climb a mountain, the air temperature drops about one degree Fahrenheit every 250 to 330 feet. On a summer day that is ninety degrees in the desert or grassland, I can reach an ideal thermal position—seventy-two degrees—by climbing around 5,200 feet. Furthermore, tree growth is favored by a threefold increase in mean annual precipitation over the spread of my climb.

Deciduous woodland occurs where precipitation runoff is concentrated along drainageways. This community is typified by trees that average less than fifty feet in height and shed their leaves in winter. Mesquite bosques are such woodlands along the arroyos of ephemeral drainage in desert and grassland areas. Littleleaf or Arizona black walnut, velvet ash, Arizona sycamore, and various willows and cottonwoods are deciduous woodland indicators around more permanent streams in mountain canyons. Berlandier ash, sugarberry, and cedar elm are particular dominants on the Rio Grande floodplain below the Bordas Scarp. Moisture lovers all, trees of deciduous woodland have an open to partly closed canopy and short to medium stature that contrasts with the closed canopy of fifty-foot and taller trees in forest communities.

Growing along dry or wet stream courses up and down mountain canyons and through adjacent valleys, deciduous woodland forms another kind of mosaic pattern in the landscape carpet. Within this woodland I can experience a gradual blending of mesquites into walnuts into ashes and sycamores, boxelders and bigtooth maples—a floristic relay over increasing elevation. Moreover, evergreen trees may intermingle with these deciduous trees of a canyon bottom and produce a between-community continuum. The landscape carpet is complex, like an oriental rug, but not unintelligible if one takes the time necessary to study and identify its component parts.

Evergreen woodland of lower mountain slopes also follows drainageways across lowlands but usually at higher elevations than deciduous woodland. It too forms tree-ribbon highways that permit plant and animal dispersal from one moist mountain island to another. Evergreen woodland is dominated by green- or gray-leaved trees the year round—oaks like Emory, gray, and Mexican blue plus alligator juniper, madrone, and Mexican pinyon, for example. With its short to medium stature and generally open canopy, it is unmistakable woodland. Again, in the lower Rio Grande Valley, dominants are regionally distinct. Species like the Texas palm, ebony, anacua, and tepeguaje lend a subtropical air to that landscape.

There are two remaining communities dominated by woody plants in the Borderlands. The first is chaparral, distinguished by densely packed, evergreen shrubs less than twenty feet tall on the average— manzanita, buckbrush, mountain mahogany, and scrub oak, to name a few. Chaparral grows sparingly in the Big Bend of Texas and becomes increasingly common westward, especially along the California–Baja California border in foothills. Despite familiarity of the name due to its widespread use in describing almost any brushy area, naturalists recognize only the distinctive evergreen shrub community of arid slopes as true chaparral.

Spanish-speaking people of the Borderlands also note the dominance of vegetation and attach the suffix -al ("place of") to a plant name appropriate to community description.[7] Thus, *chaparral* comes from *chaparro*, which refers to shrubby vegetation like scrub oak in California or black acacia in the Rio Grande Valley. However, a tree-size ever-

[7] Lowe, "Arizona Landscape and Habitats." See also E. U. Clover, "Vegetational Survey of the Lower Rio Grande Valley, Texas," *Madroño* 4 (1937):41–66, 77–100.

Mount Emory, Chisos Mountains, and Rio Grande (Emory)

green oak is called *encino*, hence the familiar term *encinal* that denotes evergreen woodland. Woodland in general is known as *bosque*.
Mesquite is Spanish, too, so *mesquital* is a shorter term for mesquite
bosque. Other plant and community names in Spanish are not so familiar to Anglo naturalists—*zacate* ("grass") and *zacatal* ("grassland"), for
instance—but I relish such flavorsome names.

Chaparral and encinal are expected natural communities of mountain slopes. Above is the most restricted community of all, the coniferous forest. As I climb, the temperature drop and moisture increase
bring changes in evergreen structure, especially in the conifer or needle-leaved aspect. First, pinyons give way to larger species such as
Chihuahua and Apache pines. These, too, may be associated with oaks
and junipers in canyon evergreen woodland and result in the pine-oak
woodland appellation sometimes given in Arizona. Then the change
brings ponderosa pine and finally southwestern white pine, Douglas
fir, white fir, and Engelmann spruce, in approximate ascending order.[8]
From the ponderosas on up I am in coniferous forest, the coolest, wettest, and most heavily vegetated of Borderlands communities.

Time now to return to the foot of the mountain, a particular

[8] A good example is in D. A. Sawyer and T. B. Kinraide, "The Forest Vegetation at
Higher Altitudes in the Chiricahua Mountains, Arizona," *Amer. Midl. Natur.* 104 (1980):
224–241.

mountain, to review the landscape carpet in position. I shall choose the Chisos range of Texas, where I have made the vertical trek many times.[9] I start on Emory Peak, at 7,000 feet in coniferous forest, but if I had picked a less massive range I might have begun in evergreen woodland at the same elevation. Smaller mountains are more arid, in part because they are less massive. For example, the Huachuca Mountains, Arizona, are 350 feet lower and just a third the areal extent of the nearby Chiricahuas; therefore coniferous forest is displaced a thousand feet higher on Huachuca slopes.[10]

Surely more mass contributes to cooler environments in the summer growing season, since bulkier mountains should take longer to heat up and cool down. This, in turn, should reduce evaporation of the monsoon rains and favor assemblages of cool-wet-adapted organisms like coniferous forest. Anyhow, I am glad to call the mountain mass phenomenon the Merriam Effect, because I wish to remember C. Hart Merriam's pioneering in landscape interpretation, even though I do not use his historic life-zone system to describe communities.[11] And I like to recall such construction features as mountain mass, for I am then reminded of the geologic loom and its constant remanufacture in time. I do not wish to lose the perspective of millenia I cannot experience.

Actually, the Chisos Mountains are barely large enough to support coniferous forest, which is there restricted to protected canyon sides and bottoms. In Boot Canyon below Emory Peak—named for William Emory of the First Boundary Survey—I am inside a small ponderosa stand. Above me on exposed slopes is evergreen woodland, more tolerant of drying than coniferous forest. Below along the stream is a string of Arizona cypress, more in need of moisture. The mountainside is a continuum, with evergreen woodland blending into coniferous forest, which grades into deciduous woodland downstream. Local deciduous woodland is denoted by Graves oak and bigtooth maple.

[9] Gehlbach, "Vegetation of the Guadalupe Escarpment"; idem, "Plant Formations in the Natural History Interpretation of Southwestern Desert Regions," *Natl. Parks Mag.* 40 (1966):16–18.

[10] Martin, *The Last 10,000 Years*, fig. 4. See also C. H. Lowe, Jr., "Biotic Communities in the Sub-Mogollon Region of the Inland Southwest," *J. Arizona Acad. Sci.* 2 (1961):40–49.

[11] No matter the era, naturalists should read C. H. Merriam, *Life-zones and Crop-zones of the United States*, U.S. Biol. Surv. Bull. 10 (1898).

I leave the stream course at Boot Spring and swing off into typical evergreen woodland with its characteristic dominants, Emory and gray oaks, Mexican pinyon, and alligator juniper. Mountain grassland, thick with tall bunchgrasses, is scattered here and there where deeper soil has accumulated. The trail leads steeply downward to 5,400 feet through this woodland-grassland mosaic to the Chisos Basin, a human settlement and later lesson in unnatural history. I walk to the head of Green Gulch, the top of a bajada, and look down at shrub desert 3,000 feet below. I gauge the gradient of rocks to gravel to silty soil over which I will travel and the drying effect of the sun on south- and west-facing slopes in contrast to the more shaded, moister north- and east-facing slopes. I am descending the north face of the Chisos, a comparatively cool experience, and prepare for the ten-degree rise in temperature toward the base of the mountains.

The thousand-foot drop demonstrates the blend of tree-dominated evergreen woodland into shrub-dominated succulent desert. I would be surprised if the continuum did not exist. Mexican pinyon and alligator juniper are dominants first, then, lower down, pinyon plus gray oak and slimleaf goldeneye. Pinyon disappears around 5,000 feet, where red-berry juniper remains the only tree. Narrowleaf sotol, lechuguilla, and goldeneye replace this juniper below 4,000 feet, and at 3,500 feet they bow out to shrub-desert indicators, white-thorn acacia and creosote bush. Lechuguilla hangs on because rocks punctuate the silty soil, and, at the Grapevine Hills, the continuum itself is replaced by a community mosaic. Shrub desert occupies the flats, succulent desert the hills.

My hike down from Emory Peak takes only six hours, while the landscape carpet I walk upon required the last five thousand years to weave. The loom was some 26 million years in the making before that. The natural communities I experience are climax communities, the most long-lived under present physical conditions. All developed through succession—carpet weaving—in which species came and went, readjusting to one another, resulting in community change over time. Succession began on the geologic flooring, influenced by climate, but later changed direction on naturally and culturally disturbed sites like landslides and pastures. Whatever the place, succession replaces a few prolific species with a more diverse array of slower-reproducing species. The pace may be historic or geologic.

Successional changes in the passing century are prominent

themes in the Borderlands, since man leaves such clear impressions of his landscape alterations. Prehistoric changes are more difficult to document. Some evidence comes from fossils here in the Chisos region, where Philip Wells found packrat middens like those that house packrats today but built eleven to forty thousand years ago.[12] In them are fragments of evergreen woodland trees as much as 2,500 feet below their present lower limits. Because packrats don't travel more than a few hundred feet for housing material, the prehistoric middens must have been made in woodland instead of the desert in which Wells discovered them.

Fossils of organisms with representatives living today are particularly useful in reconstructing prehistoric landscapes, because their lifestyles and hence landscape requirements are known. If, for example, most of the bones at a site represent northern species, a cooler climate is suggested. If more are southern in current distribution, then warmer conditions may be inferred, or if a north-south mixture of species is present perhaps the ancient environment was less seasonal or more spatially diverse than the present one.

Very small but abundant pollen grains trapped in streamside or pond-bottom sediments for thousands of years are further important evidence of community change. If pine, spruce, or fir pollen occurs where creosote bush or grass grows and such tree pollen is far from any montane source, perhaps coniferous forest once occupied the site. And, conversely, if the pollen of nonwoody species predominates in an earth layer below a living forest or woodland, an earlier grassland or desert may be indicated.

Equally good evidence of temporal change is furnished by disjunct or relict populations of living plants and animals, for instance maples here in the Chisos, on other mountain islands, and even in a few central Texas and Oklahoma canyons. These trees are intermediate between the western bigtooth maple and eastern sugar maple, though more like the latter, and isolated in sugar maple–like habitat.[13] Thus, I

---

[12] P. V. Wells, "Late Pleistocene Vegetation and Degree of Pluvial Climatic Change in the Chihuahuan Desert," *Science* 153 (1966):970–976. See also Wells's "Macrofossil Analysis of Wood Rat (*Neotoma*) Middens as a Key to the Quaternary Vegetational History of Arid America," *Quaternary Res.* 6 (1976):223–248.

[13] E. L. Rice, "The Microclimate of Sugar Maple Stands in Oklahoma," *Ecology* 43 (1962):19–25. Current studies in which Robert Gardner and I employ a cluster analysis of leaf flavonoid compounds and a discriminant function analysis of six features of leaf

can infer that a wetter climate once prevailed in the Borderlands, allowing sugar maples to spread west through what is now inhospitable country and interbreed with their bigtooth relatives. Regional dryness then fashioned the present, remnant populations.

To move backwards some 26 million years to the near beginning of today's natural communities, I move my mind without moving my feet, a welcome change after I have traveled nearly five thousand feet in seven miles. Five thousand years ago, for instance, I might have been sitting in evergreen woodland instead of the open desert here on the Grapevine Hills. I lack local evidence, but Paul Martin's thesis of warm-wet conditions conducive to woodland, rather than Ernst Antevs' concept of a warm-dry climate supportive of desert, fits my experience and that of others in the Borderlands.[14] Moreover, the pollen of pinyon-juniper woodland that existed along the Rio Grande five thousand years ago and fifty miles downstream substantiates the warm-wet thesis in this area.[15]

The change from low-elevation woodland to grassland and desert began eight to ten thousand years ago. Shrub deserts dominated by creosote bush did not even exist until about ten to eleven thousand years before the present, and, as I contemplate further, I am struck by the comparative recency of the present aridity.[16] Eleven to forty thousand years ago the Chisos—indeed all the Border country—were different, as the packrat middens reveal. Grasslands were limited, for woodlands spread downward on mountainsides and across the high valleys. Continental ice sheets came no closer than about nine hundred

shape show the conspecificity of Arkansas (sugar maple) and Arizona (bigtooth maple) reference samples.

[14] Martin, *The Last 10,000 Years*; E. Antevs, "Late Quaternary Climates in Arizona," *Amer. Antiquity* 20 (1962):317–335. See, for example, T. R. Van Devender and R. D. Worthington, "The Herpetofauna of Howell's Ridge Cave and the Paleoecology of the Northwestern Chihuahuan Desert," in *Symposium on the Biological Resources of the Chihuahuan Desert Region, United States and Mexico*, ed. R. H. Wauer and D. H. Riskind, pp. 85–113, U.S.D.I., Natl. Park Service Trans. and Proc. Ser. 3 (1977).

[15] L. Johnson, Jr., "Pollen Analysis of Two Archaeological Sites at Amistad Reservoir, Texas," *Texas J. Sci.* 15 (1963):225–230.

[16] T. R. Van Devender, "Holocene Woodlands in the Southwestern Deserts," *Science* 198 (1977):189–192; P. V. Wells and J. H. Hunziker, "Origin of the Creosotebush (*Larrea*) Deserts of Southwestern North America," *Ann. Missouri Bot. Garden* 63 (1977):843–861.

miles, but a few mountain glaciers existed two hundred miles to the north in New Mexico. Cool-wet climates prevailed and allowed woody vegetation to grow two to four thousand feet below present lower limits.

Animals adapted to cool-wet conditions were more widespread then, but, with the exception of some presently extralimital and extinct species, boundary communities looked a lot like modern ones before Anglos arrived. Ten percent of the vertebrates of those faunas now live in wetter regions to the north and east. An additional 6 percent of the reptiles became extinct, a figure I can understand, but I am startled by the 19 to 22 percent extinction among birds and mammals, chiefly large species, that lived here more than ten thousand years ago.[17] I must return for explanations, but for the present I am satisfied that around half the faunal difference in that prehistoric landscape is attributable to community position, not basic structure.

During the 3 million years before present time, four cool-wet periods called pluvials alternated with four warm-dry interpluvials in the Pleistocene Epoch of Borderlands prehistory. Pluvials were associated with glacial advances, interpluvials with glacial retreats. Pluvial lakes expanded and contracted accordingly. Forests and woodlands came, and grasslands went with the pluvials, vice versa with the interpluvials, like alternating electric currents. Actually, plant and animal species advanced and retreated, causing communities to march to and fro over the region.

But the structural resemblance of Pleistocene communities to those of today is the result of earlier evolution in a different ecological theater. Sometime in the Pliocene and Miocene epochs—back at least 26 million years in certain cases—desert, grassland, and evergreen woodland species evolved, formed community-style interdependencies, and spread with the help of drying climates. Dominant plants often originated in the Mexican highlands. In recognition of the Sierra

---

[17] Calculated from data in tables 1 and 2 in A. H. Harris, "Wisconsin Age Environments in the Northern Chihuahuan Desert: Evidence from the Higher Vertebrates," *Symposium on the Biological Resources of the Chihuahuan Desert Region*, pp. 35–52. Note also the conclusion in F. R. Gehlbach, "Amphibians and Reptiles from the Pliocene and Pleistocene of North America: A Chronological Summary and Selected Bibliography," *Texas J. Sci.* 17 (1965):56–70.

Madrean influence and time of origin, the term Madro-Tertiary geoflora is given to their ancestry. This fossil flora supplanted an older Arcto-Tertiary geoflora that dominated earlier landscapes and was ancestral to coniferous forest and perhaps deciduous woodland.[18]

Displacement of cool-wet communities of Arcto-Tertiary origin by warm-dry ones of Madro-Tertiary derivation was triggered by basic changes in continental climate. As the Sierra Madres of Mexico and the Rocky Mountains rose to their present heights in Miocene through Pleistocene time, they became barriers to moisture-laden winds from the Pacific Ocean. So the lowlands dried out and were occupied successively by evergreen woodland and grassland until the end of the Pleistocene, when deserts formed and displaced them locally. Mountains, originally clothed in forests, remained wet refuges, but in time coniferous forest was relegated to the high peaks, while deciduous forest was degraded to deciduous woodland and confined to watercourses. Evergreen woodland finally resettled mountainsides or intermediate portions of regional moisture gradients, and the landscape carpet became essentially as I have found it.

[18] R. A. Darrow, "Origin and Development of the Vegetational Communities of the Southwest," in *Bioecology of the Arid and Semiarid Lands of the Southwest*, ed. L. M. Shields and L. J. Gardner, pp. 30–47, New Mexico Highlands Univ. Bull. 212 (1961). See also P. S. Martin and P. J. Mehringer, Jr., "Pleistocene Pollen Analysis and Biogeography of the Southwest," in *The Quaternary of the United States*, ed. H. E. Wright, Jr., and D. G. Frey, pp. 433–451 (Princeton: Princeton Univ. Press, 1965).

2. Valley Jungles

TUESDAY, October 17, 1970, dawned hot and muggy on the south Texas coast, as it usually does before a cold front or "great blue norther" hits. I could feel what William Emory and other Boundary surveyors might have felt before many a storm in this hurricane land, for I had just come from the cultural emptiness that is Indianola, Texas. John Bartlett landed at Indianola the last day of August, 1850, and so initiated the first of many Boundary survey trips overland from this once famous port. Then in 1854, near the end of the First Boundary Survey, Emory witnessed a hurricane that leveled the town of Matagorda, Texas, and devastated nearby Indianola.

The norther feeling grew more ominous as I drove south to camp at Boca Chica, mouth of the Rio Grande and eastern terminus of the Borderlands. I reflected on last night's Indianola sunset and the cattle egrets, which had been absent in the nineteenth century. These birds invaded the Borderlands in the mid-1950's on their own steam from Africa via the American tropics, aided by man's growing livestock industry. On the Texas Gulf Coast these cattle followers—eaters of kicked-up grasshoppers—constituted 70 percent of all breeding wading birds in the early 1970's.[1] The approaching storm reminded me of the historical Borderlands, while the cattle egrets suggested the cultural changes that reshape natural landscapes.

That natural and unnatural histories are intertwined in transforming the Borderlands is imprinted upon the beaches at Indianola and Boca Chica. I simply cannot walk these sandy shores for any distance without acquiring a barefoot undercoating of tar and oil. This was not true before the 1960's. Oil has leaked naturally from beneath Gulf of

---

[1] Data from *Texas Ornithol. Soc. Newsletter* 21 (1973):8. See also H. C. Oberholser, *The Bird Life of Texas*, ed. E. B. Kincaid, Jr. (Austin: Univ. Texas Press, 1974), 1:114–115; and C. E. Bock and C. W. Lepthien, "Population Growth in the Cattle Egret," *Auk* 93 (1976):164–166.

Mexico waters for millenia, but only recently has it been allowed to spill unnaturally from wells and tanker ships and wind up on beaches. Significantly, the Pemex spill in the Gulf between Campeche, Mexico, and Texas, June, 1979, to March, 1980, is the world's worst to date. More people who require more oil to run more vehicles to the recreational beaches—and to run their society—have brought about the change.

Perhaps a reconditioned landscape will restore the Atlantic Ridley to its rightful place on the beaches. Once I might have watched an *arribada*, or daytime arrival, of nesting Ridleys. Historically these two-foot marine turtles returned to their birthplace beaches between South Padre Island and Veracruz, Mexico, each spring to dig holes in the sand, lay about 110 eggs each, and then disappear for a year in the waves. *Arribadas* may have contained forty thousand Ridleys, but the species dwindled to nearly zero on south Texas beaches by the 1920's.[2] Overhunting of these turtles, particularly their eggs, caused their decline.

In 1966, however, with Padre Island National Seashore firmly established, a few Ridley lovers gathered eggs in Tamaulipas near Rancho Nuevo, incubated them in the island's sand, and released seventy-nine hatchlings. A thousand more two-inch hatchlings were released the next year, and the first Atlantic Ridley to come ashore on South Padre Island in two decades struggled up the beach and laid its hundred eggs in May, 1974. Was it a 1966 or 1967 hatchling? Perhaps. No one knows how fast a Ridley grows to reproductive maturity, but knowledge of other marine turtles and migratory vertebrates in general shows that to return to one's birthplace to reproduce is familiar instinctive behavior. Man is fortunate that wild creatures can help rectify his unnatural history in this manner.

By the time I camped at Brazos Island State Park and set out a grid of live mammal traps, the telltale line of black clouds was in the north. But the wind had not shifted from the south when I tired of reflecting on Ridleys. With the thermometer nearly ninety degrees, a sleeping

[2]C. H. Ernst and R. W. Barbour, *Turtles of the United States* (Lexington: Univ. Kentucky Press, 1972), p. 240. There is a single 1950 nesting record on Padre Island in J. E. Werler, "Miscellaneous Notes on the Eggs and Young of Texas and Mexican Reptiles," *Zoologica* 36 (1951):37–48.

bag was out of the question. Twinkling stars, the sound of waves, and the absence of men and mosquitoes lulled me to sleep. At midnight the storm with its fifty-degree north wind forced me inside my sleeping bag inside the car. At dawn I awoke to the peculiar sound of surf on car wheels instead of sand. Within a few minutes the traps were picked up—freedom for a hispid cotton rat and seven crabs—and I headed for Brownsville, as the valley jungle of the lower Rio Grande drank some rain.

Spanish explorers sometimes called the lower Rio Grande the Río de las Palmas in recognition of the Texas palm that lined its banks. Just how far upriver palms grew is uncertain, although Arthur Schott of the First Boundary Survey reported that they extended about eighty miles from the Gulf. Nearly a century later Elzada Clover noted palms in a much more limited area, from a point about ten miles below Brownsville upriver only three or four miles.[3] Today, native palm groves are rare. I know of but two in the southmost bend of the Río de las Palmas. Because of this and because evergreen woodland dominated by the Texas palm lends a subtropical air to the eastern Borderlands, palm-grove communities are unique living museum pieces.

The demise of natural palm jungles in Texas and adjacent Tamaulipas, Mexico, results directly from cutting and burning the Rio Grande floodplain for agriculture. I believe no other natural terrestrial community of the Borderlands is so seriously endangered. Yet cutting Texas palms is only the end of community structure, not of the species, since it is often grown from seed in cultivated groves from which trees are sold for ornamental purposes. Other tree species associated with palms in the once junglelike atmosphere are not so fortunate. Man-made palm groves lacking cedar elms, ebonies, anacuas, and tepeguajes are unacceptable living museums, since the simplistic, palms-only vegetative structure supports an equally simplistic native fauna.

Fortunately the National Audubon Society protects the largest of the two palm jungles I briefly studied in the Rio Grande Valley. Many palms are burned here, apparently from ground fires, but mature trees

[3] Schott's observations are quoted in E. U. Clover, "Vegetational Survey of the Lower Rio Grande Valley, Texas," *Madroño* 4 (1937):41–66, 77–100.

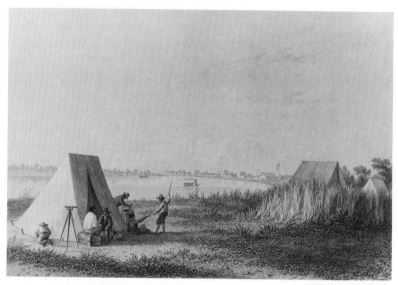

Brownsville, Texas (Emory)

are not seriously injured. I suspect fires had been set by a former owner to clear undergrowth for planting exotic species in the former nursery. But fire may have been a natural factor once, feeding on dead palm fronds and clearing the ground surface for the germination of palm seedlings. I think this because in February, 1971, I found an average of three seedlings per hundred lineal feet of plowed field adjoining the palm grove.

Palm fronds blown from the trees provide excellent ground cover for small creatures of this subtropical evergreen woodland. The inch-long Rio Grande chirping frog runs beneath the fronds, pursued by its foot-long predator, the black-striped snake. Both are tropical species like their palm host and penetrate the U.S. Borderlands only in its valley jungles. The frog becomes quite edificial as native habitat disappears. It now inhabits suburbia wherever dampness prevails and especially likes the public restrooms at Santa Ana National Wildlife Refuge. The public doesn't tolerate the black-striped snake there, and when this innocuous native is harassed it waves its tail, displaying the salmon-red underside. Does this frighten people the way I think it frightens natural predators?

Dead palm fronds clinging to palm trunks also provide snug retreats, especially for bats. The southern yellow bat roosts abundantly among the dead fronds at the Audubon Society's sanctuary, and the rare subtropical race of the northern yellow bat is present, together with the more familiar evening and pallid bats.[4] Lately, even the pestiferous, exotic roof rat has joined this unique roosting and nesting community. Hooded and black-headed orioles also ornament the palm-crown environment, but both birds have become increasingly rare since mid-twentieth century.

As the hooded and black-headed orioles declined, the equally bright altamira oriole began to increase in the late 1950's. At the Santa Ana Refuge, for example, altamiras had three nests by 1961, nineteen by 1965, twenty-four the following year, and have stabilized at some fifteen to twenty breeding pairs since then. This larger bird is less choosy about nesting places, even suspending its two-foot hanging basket from telephone wires on occasion. And it is more successful in defending its more pendulant hence harder-to-enter nest against the increasing hordes of cowbirds, especially bronzed cowbirds that specialize in parasitizing orioles.

Between January 29 and February 1, 1951, the lower Rio Grande Valley experienced its most disastrous recorded freeze. The citrus crop was devastated, and subsequently much of it was replaced by more freeze-resistant pastures, cotton, grain, and vegetable crops. Cowbirds were favored by the change to a more pastoral landscape, and about the same time hooded and black-headed orioles began their precipitous decline. Despite the suggested cowbird influence, my analysis of the Audubon Society's Christmas bird counts at the Santa Ana Refuge and Bentsen–Rio Grande State Park, 1953–1973, reveals that the increase in altamira orioles best explains the decrease in numbers of their kin.[5]

Yet altamira orioles must be only a proximate factor in reducing hooded and black-headed oriole populations. Ultimately the great

[4] R. J. Baker, T. Mollhagen, and G. Lopez, "Notes on *Lasiurus ega*," *J. Mammal.* 52 (1971):849–852.

[5] Multiple stepwise regression analysis (MSR) of individuals per party hour gives the following significant ($P<0.05$) determinants of decline of the hooded plus black-headed orioles: altamira oriole, $r^2 = 0.30$ ($F = 8.2$), and bronzed cowbird, $r^2 = 0.10$ ($F = 6.0$). Multiple correlation (R) = 0.63 ($P<0.01$, 18 $d.f.$). See also Oberholser, *Bird Life of Texas* 2:816–818, 828.

freeze, man's landscape alterations, and the subsequent explosion of cowbirds must have been involved. Surely natural history caused man to change his citrus successor to valley jungles into cowbird habitat, from which altamira orioles benefited in contrast to hooded and black-headed orioles because of their greater tolerance of unnatural history and their greater resistance to cowbird parasitism. Simply put, altamira orioles have gained the competitive edge—at least temporarily.

Because any synergy of natural and unnatural limiting factors is difficult to unravel, the foregoing thesis is not completely satisfying to me. Besides, I expect tropical species like these orioles to experience considerable flux on their northern frontier by comparison with their home base in Mexico. Again I look at the Audubon Society's annual Christmas bird counts, this time comparing Santa Ana and Bentsen–Rio Grande with Gómez Farías, Tamaulipas, and El Naranjo, San Luis Potosí, to the south in Mexico. I find fourteen species that reside permanently at all four locales, and together their northern populations show significantly more variability.[6]

Perhaps some cyclic change will reverse the present oriole scene. After all, other birds have come and gone, some to return again after a recorded leave of absence. The elf owl, for example, reappeared in 1960 after sixty-six years of absence. This smallest of owls increased in numbers and expanded its breeding range into higher elevations and latitudes in the western Borderlands about the same time as it returned to these valley jungles. Early naturalists associated the elf owl with saguaro cactus, rarely with riparian timber, in Arizona. But since midcentury it is equally widespread in evergreen woodland.[7]

---

[6]The years 1973–1977 offer concurrent data for figuring coefficient of variation from individuals per party hour of the plain chachalaca, common ground dove, white-tipped dove, groove-billed ani, pauraque, fawn-breasted hummingbird, tropical kingbird, great kiskadee, green jay, long-billed thrasher, tropical parula, and black-headed and altamira orioles. Texas data average 0.79, Mexican data 0.56 (a nested analysis of variance [ANOVA] of the arc sine–transformed data tests latitude versus locale and shows latitude alone as significant with a significant species effect, $F = 4.1$, $P<0.004$).

[7]P. James and H. Hayse, "Elf Owl Rediscovered in Lower Rio Grande Delta of Texas," *Wilson Bull.* 75 (1962):179–182. On the former restricted range in Arizona see C. Bendire, *Life Histories of North American Birds with Special Reference to Their Breeding Habits and Eggs*, U.S. Natl. Mus. Spec. Bull. 1 (1892), pp. 413–414; F. M. Bailey, *Birds Recorded from the Santa Rita Mountains in Southern Arizona*, Pacific Coast Avifauna 15 (1923); and H. S. Swarth, "The Faunal Areas of Southern Arizona: A

The clearing of natural brush, as Texans call their native woody vegetation, has taken three-quarters of these valley jungles since the 1930's.[8] Small mesquite-choked tracts, usually less than one hundred acres, are poor reminders of the once heavily wooded lower Rio Grande shoreline. In 1850 William Emory remarked on the junglelike growth. My notes in 1970, describing Texas Route 281 between Brownsville and the Santa Ana Refuge, mention mostly cultivated fields. But brush increases in the Carazos Ranchito area, where small mesquite-granjeno stands are prominent, and then decreases toward Los Indios. Cultivation also characterizes the landscape along Mexico Route 2 between Matamoros and Camargo, south of the Great River.

Both south and north of the floodplain, ranching is man's main occupation, so plains grassland with *lomas*, or hillocks, of live oak or ebony occasionally resembles the historic landscape. On the Texas side, John Bartlett saw pronghorn antelope and mustangs driven by a prairie fire in his 1853 journey from Fort Ringgold on the Rio Grande to Corpus Christi. Gone are the antelope, mustangs, and most grass fires, hence mesquite and other woody species have increased and changed the nature of my view. Short trees were always present but not so thick before fire suppression, and mesquite-dotted grassland became mesquite-choked brush in the last half of the nineteenth century.[9]

Scrawny mesquite is not scarce in these eastern Borderlands, but individuals more than a foot in diameter are rare. So are other deciduous woodland dominants in virgin condition—huisache, sugarberry, cedar elm, and Berlandier ash. Perhaps only a hundred acres of origi-

Study in Animal Distribution," *Proc. California Acad. Sci.* 18 (1929):267–383. Cf. J. D. Ligon, *The Biology of the Elf Owl*, Micrathene whitneyi, Misc. Publ. Mus. Zool. Univ. Michigan 136 (1968). See also chapter 6 in the present volume.

[8] W. R. Marion, "Status of the Plain Chachalaca in South Texas," *Wilson Bull.* 86 (1974):200–205. Cf. W. H. Emory, *Report on the United States and Mexican Boundary Survey*, vol. 1, 34th Cong., 1st sess., 1857. House Exec. Doc. 135, p. 59.

[9] J. H. Bartlett, *Personal Narrative of the Explorations and Incidents in Texas, New Mexico, California, Sonora, and Chihuahua, Connected with the United States and Mexican Boundary Commission during the Years 1850, '51, '52, and '53*, vol. 2 (New York: D. Appleton and Co., 1854), p. 524; J. M. Inglis, *A History of Vegetation on the Rio Grande Plain*, Texas Parks and Wildl. Dept. Bull. 45 (1964). See also M. C. Johnston, "Past and Present Grasslands of Southern Texas and Northeastern Mexico," *Ecology* 44 (1963): 456–466.

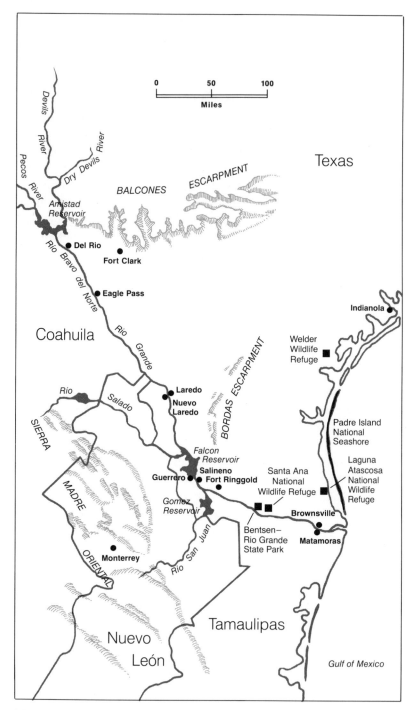

MAP 1. Eastern Section of U.S.–Mexican Boundary

nal deciduous and evergreen woods are protected in the two-thousand-acre Santa Ana National Wildlife Refuge. Yet some giant trees border Santa Ana's resacas, the marshy disjunct channels of the Rio Grande. One mesquite is 3.5 feet through, and a particular Berlandier ash is 5.5 feet in diameter at the standard survey height of 4.5 feet above ground. Although topped by many hurricanes, this *viejo* lives on crown sprouts of less than ten inches in diameter.

The U.S. champion ebony is symbolic of the natural and unnatural history of these eastern Borderlands. Purposely, man protects the tree's life by fencing it on the preserve. Inadvertently, he dooms it, because flood control and the pumping of ground water for irrigation reduce the tree's life support. Other species are dying too, presumably from the same drying out of Santa Ana's soils. After Falcon Dam, a major flood-control device, was completed, Raymond Fleetwood watched the death of a sugarberry stand in one ten-year period between floods. However, the August, 1971, hurricane that once again flooded Santa Ana gave its living landscape a stay of execution.

Surely Santa Ana's human visitors deserve to see large trees, to smell and feel the American subtropics. Ebony is but one species among nine that dominate the climax vegetation of the evergreen woodlands. Trees of the canopy average fourteen inches in diameter and 50 feet in height along my 300-foot transects. Tepeguaje outnumbers ebony slightly but is smaller in diameter by five inches on the average. Anacua, cedar elm, and sugarberry follow ebony and tepeguaje. Coma, soapberry, and brasil are next. Often only a hundred feet away, but always closer to a resaca, the deciduous woodland is very different, with Berlandier ash in the lead. Both woodland types share sugarberry, cedar elm, and tepeguaje, and this confirms the continuum theory of vegetation.

To really feel the subtropics at Santa Ana, though, I must sense beyond the sights and smells of trees and heavy, Gulf-moisturized mornings. Certainly the dawn clamor of plain chachalacas, the midday "poor-boy" song of the black-headed oriole, and the dusk "go-where" of pauraques are subtropical experiences. Is *subtropical* a quantifiable concept? This question led me to compare breeding birds in the evergreen woodland at Santa Ana with those in a similar community at the Río Corona in Tamaulipas, Mexico, 200 miles to the south. I found intriguing differences, which I interpreted to mean that Santa Ana is truly in and of the temperate zone, while the Río Corona represents the northeastern limit of the New World avifaunal tropics.[10]

I recorded an average of thirty-nine breeding species in two twenty-acre study plots on the Río Corona, whereas I averaged only twenty-three species in a plot of the same size at Santa Ana. The Río Corona count is essentially the same as the forty-species average per plot in breeding avifaunas of southern Mexico to Costa Rica, and, similarly, twenty-three is only one bird short of the twenty-four-species average per plot in floodplain forests of the southeastern United States. Fifteen of the twenty-three species at Santa Ana are geographically tropical, reaching their northeastern breeding limits in south Texas. Plain chachalacas, pauraques, and altamira orioles are examples. All fifteen also nest in my Río Corona plots and there are joined by twenty-four additional species, like the rose-throated becard, which rarely nests at Santa Ana, the red-crowned and yellow-headed parrots, which occasionally wander there, and the mottled owl, which has not been recorded in the United States.

Undeniably there is tropical influence at Santa Ana, but a basic structural difference exists between its avifauna and that along the Río Corona. Somehow more different species can nest per unit area at the Corona. In part it must be that fewer individuals per species occupy the habitat. I found an average of 1.9 individuals per species versus 2.4 at Santa Ana. There is only so much space for birds in evergreen woodland, and it can be occupied by fewer individuals of more species, as at the Río Corona, or more individuals of fewer species, as at Santa Ana. The latter is a temperate-zone characteristic, whereas the comparative paucity of individuals per species is a tropical phenomenon.

In addition to the latitudinal factors that affect Santa Ana's avifauna, there is also the influence of man. Modern man evaluates resources monetarily. Aesthetic and scientific values of his society remain subordinate to utilitarian considerations, if they remain at all. Without dollar values to compete with the pricing of game birds, mere "bird-watcher birds" are often sacrificed. At Santa Ana, for instance, resaca marshes are drained and deepened, and their sedges and cat-

[10] F. R. Gehlbach, D. O. Dillon, H. L. Harrell, S. E. Kennedy, and K. R. Wilson, "Avifauna of the Río Corona, Tamaulipas, Mexico: Northeastern Limit of the Tropics," *Auk* 93 (1976):53–65.

tails plowed up to create open ponds that foster pintails, blue-winged teal, and ring-necks instead of masked and black-bellied whistling ducks, least grebes, and jacanas. The value of such nongame birds has not been figured, whereas, by one calculation, a pintail or teal in the hand is worth $3.29 to the duck hunter.[11]

What is the worth of the hook-billed kite that nested at Santa Ana in June, 1964, the first time in the United States, and did not return until December, 1975? Refuge visitation increased significantly during the first six months of 1976, compared with the same period in 1975 before the kite came back.[12] Was this due to kite watchers? Could it be translated into a monetary evaluation of these snail-eating birds? My curiosity shifted from birds to birders in 1977–1978, when I made a survey at Santa Ana to discover what the birders came to see, what they spent, and hence what their birds were worth by comparison with game.

First I asked what particular species the birders most wanted to find and confirmed the hook-billed kite as the principal drawing card, with 41 percent of the first-place votes. Green jays, altamira orioles, clay-colored robins, fawn-breasted hummingbirds, black-headed orioles, red-billed pigeons, great kiskadees, rose-throated becards, and chachalacas were the next-most-favored species. Ocelots and jaguarundis were named as the most desired mammals in response to a question about other wildlife. Even giant toads and tropical butterflies made that list. Above all, I was happy to see such fundamental varmints as bobcats and coyotes among the desiderata.

My sample of 155 birders came from thirty-four states and two Ca-

---

[11] J. Hammack and G. M. Brown, Jr., *Waterfowl and Wetlands: Toward Bioeconomic Analysis* (Washington, D.C.: Resources for the Future, 1974), p. 32. A general comparison of methods for arriving at game and nongame bird values is in R. M. DeGraaf and B. Payne, "Economic Values of Non-game Birds and Some Urban Wildlife Research Needs," *Trans. 40th N. Amer. Wildl. and Natur. Res. Conf.* 40 (1975):281–287. See also D. W. Ehrenfeld. "The Conservation of Non-resources," *Amer. Sci.* 64 (1976): 648–656; and A. Leopold, *A Sand County Almanac* (London: Oxford Univ. Press, 1949), p. 210, for alternative evaluations.

[12] In a Mann-Whitney rank test of persons registered in each of the first six months of 1975 (average 6,951) versus those of the same period in 1976 (average 8,849), $U = 30$ ($P<0.05$). The kites nested in May–June, 1976, and fledged one of two offspring (see D. L. Delnicki, "Second Occurrence and First Successful Nesting Record of the Hook-billed Kite in the United States," *Auk* 95 [1978]:427).

nadian provinces, a fact that revealed the national if not international reputation of Santa Ana's resources. On the average the birders traveled 3,350 miles round trip, spent $950 in so doing, stayed three days in the area, and spent $130 locally. Assuming average expenditures reveal average value, I simply summed the monies spent for travel, food, and lodging, multiplied by 41 percent (the percentage that had reported the kite as their objective), and found the hook-billed kite to be worth $148 per bird for the three individuals on the refuge at the time. That was forty-five times the value of a local pintail or teal and five times more valuable per bird than Santa Ana's own game specialty, the white-winged dove.[13]

Yet there is another, more important difference. Individual ducks and doves are consumed by the hunters who spend money in their behalf. Once shot, they have no further value. Hook-billed kites and other species of the birding game are nonconsumable resources, by contrast. Once seen, they are reported and become available to a multitude of birders. Thus, their average values can be multiplied by the number of their seekers. My ten-month survey disclosed a total expenditure of $168,330; attributing 41 percent of this total to hook-billed kites would make the average value of an individual $23,005.

Of the thirty-one birders I personally interviewed, only five had seen a hook-billed kite, but all agreed that their general birding was good or the best they had experienced. All said they did not begrudge the price they had paid for the trip thus far and would be willing to pay it again. The birders averaged sixty-seven species per three-day refuge visit, so they spent $16 to list an average species. But consider the "return on investment." The $168,330 generated during my survey was 2.6 times the concurrent operating cost of the refuge!

Sometimes studies are not strictly planned in the manner of this economic analysis, because unforeseen events—opportunities—can foil a naturalist's most systematic endeavors. Serendipity may countervail. But if baseline knowledge is available, any change of conditions may be measured against a known situation. That is why inventories of a preserve's communities and their constituents are so valuable. What

[13]C. Cottam and J. B. Trefethen, eds., *Whitewings—Life History, Status and Management of the White-winged Dove* (Princeton: Van Nostrand Publ. Co., 1968), p. 286. I increased the species' published value by 78 percent to account for inflation between 1967 and 1977.

Chisos Mountains, Texas, from the north, during cloudy weather in April. Shrub desert in foreground.

San Pedro River Valley, Arizona, from east slope of Huachuca Mountains, Arizona, in April. Evergreen woodland along drainages in desert grassland in valley; Sierra San Jose, Sonora, right background.

Left: Evergreen woodland of Texas palms near Brownsville, in February. *Right*: Evergreen woodland with alligator juniper and sacahuista, Montezuma Canyon, Arizona, in July.

Left: Deciduous woodland, Cave Creek Canyon, Arizona. Arizona sycamores, wet after August rain, in foreground. *Right*: Deciduous woodland near head of Babocomari Wash, Arizona, in June. Fremont cottonwoods and sacaton grass denote the drainage.

Plains grassland, San Rafael Valley, Arizona, in August. Santa Rita Mountains in background.

Left: Apache pine and silverleaf oak in the continuum from deciduous into evergreen woodland, Cave Creek Canyon, Arizona, in August. *Right*: Coniferous forest, dominated by ponderosa pine, and mountain grassland, near Rustler Park, Arizona, in August.

O'Donnell Cienega, Arizona, in June. The cienega is the dark patch below the horizontal green band of deciduous woodland along O'Donnell Creek. Plains grassland in foreground is mostly dormant.

O'Donnell Cienega, Arizona, in August, following growth stimulus of summer monsoon.

acreage is occupied by what natural community, where the species are, their population sizes, and seasonal fluxes constitute the minimum, basic information.

In December, 1970, for example, I had surveyed the rodent fauna of Santa Ana's major communities and marked my trap lines for later work on seasonal changes. Then came the 1971 hurricane, a natural but rarer cyclic event that flooded most of the refuge, as its 1958 and 1967 predecessors had done. So I retrapped the same spots in the same way to discover the impact of flooding instead of seasonality. My pre-flood effort had consisted of 300 trap-nights—one trap set one night is a trap-night—and on a few nights all my traps had held captives. I remember feeling lucky that Santa Ana gave up its mammalian secrets so readily.

The white-footed mouse was the most abundant and widespread of local rodents, just as Frank Blair had found it two decades earlier. The house mouse was equally widespread and was the second most numerous preflood species. Blair's data are more interesting here, for he trapped as close as four miles from the refuge yet caught no house mice. Only four house mice were among the 263 rodents taken along the lower Rio Grande by William Lloyd in 1891.[14] My hypothesis in that preflood winter was that house mice had increased together with man's technological skill in flood control.

Floodwaters lapped at Wayne Shifflett's front door, as he left the refuge manager's house by boat in August, 1971. Indigo snakes and large rodents rode floating logs and perched in the branches of his front-yard ebonies. When I arrived in December all resacas were brimful, although soils in adjacent woodlands were dry already. Maybe I would find next to nothing in my postflood survey. If I were to catch a rodent, I thought it might be a resaca rice rat since this subtropical species takes to the trees to build its globular nests during floods.[15]

[14] W. F. Blair, "Mammals of the Tamaulipan Biotic Province in Texas," *Texas J. Sci.* 3 (1952):230–250; data from the field catalogue of William Lloyd, 1890, deposited in the U.S. Fish and Wildlife Service Laboratory, Natl. Mus. Nat. Hist., Washington, D.C. My findings are summarized in "Winter Populations of Small Mammals at the Santa Ana National Wildlife Refuge," U.S. Fish and Wildl. Serv. Rept. (1972). Chi-square (χ^2) analysis of total captures of white-footed and house mice, with an expected catch in the postflood regime equal to that in the preflood environment, gives 0.22 ($P>0.05$) and 4.6 ($P<0.05$), respectively.

[15] D. L. Benson and F. R. Gehlbach, "Ecologic and Taxonomic Notes on the Rice Rat (*Oryzomys couesi*) in Texas," *J. Mammal.* 60 (1979):225–228.

Surely most pygmy mice, fulvous harvest mice, spiny pocket mice, and hispid cotton rats had drowned. How long would it take before any refugees would repopulate the woodlands, prairies, and marshes?

My first fifteen-trap line in evergreen woodland was a shocker—eight white-footed mice and a spiny pocket mouse. Then I moved to plains grassland overgrown with mesquite and caught five white-footed mice and two pygmy mice. The average capture rate of 52 percent preflood became 54 percent. Moreover, rice rats and harvest mice were just as numerous as before and in the same places. Cotton rats were apparently the only natives affected by the flood, for I now found them primarily in the marshes instead of in mesquital, where I had caught them the previous December.

House mice were apparently gone after the flood. I had taken them in every natural and edificial site earlier and had found them second in abundance to rice rats in resaca marshes during dry periods. In fact, I failed to catch house mice in any habitat after the flood, even in the refuge worksheds where white-footed mice reigned supreme. Were they absent or so scarce that they did not encounter my transect trap lines? I believe house mice are ill adapted to withstand major floods, in contrast to the native rodents. It seems unlikely that any species took refuge in surrounding crop fields behind levees and reinvaded Santa Ana between August and December. If the natives had done this, certainly the house mouse would have also.

Modern flood control, beginning with Falcon Dam in 1953 at the close of Blair's study, probably initiated the death march of Santa Ana's riparian trees and its invasion by house mice. Surely periodic flooding is the critical physical factor required to maintain naturalness in subtropical, floodplain woodlands. Now managed flooding must be substituted if valley jungles are to be preserved. Controlled floods should be scheduled during the late summer and fall hurricane season to coincide with remaining natural cycles of vegetative growth and faunal reproduction. Seasonal flooding occurred accidentally in September, 1976, but such reprieves cannot keep natural landscapes in the midst of unnatural history. Thoughtful management is required.

Lesser sirens may outwit man who controls floodwaters, for they employ a peculiar adaptive strategy in the face of drought. Like the better-known African lungfish, these eellike, aquatic salamanders burrow into the muddy bottom of a drying marsh and secrete a mucous cocoon that completely envelopes them except for the mouth. The cocoon retards water loss, the amphibian's biggest nemesis, while it becomes inactive and metabolizes stored fat until the marsh fills with water again. Large individuals can remain inactive for two to three years. Of course this survival strategy did not evolve in response to human impact on resacas but probably in response to natural drought. That sirens thrive at Santa Ana is fortuitous, then, although some that do not burrow deeply enough to escape the plow that controls cattails are cut up like so many chunks of sausage.

Sirens are said to "wail," presumably like the mythical sirens of antiquity that lured Greek sailors to their deaths. Carolus Linnaeus, that eighteenth-century namer of beasts, must have heard about the wailing when he invented the generic name. Few people at Santa Ana or elsewhere have ever heard a siren wail, because one must wade the marshes and have a hydrophone and high-gain amplifier in hand. The wail is really a drawn-out series of clicks, if it resembles a wail at all. Siren clicks are given in response to other sirens and may announce a resident's territory in a manner similar to bird song. Also, sirens "yelp" when bitten by each other, and this sound is more easily heard by the unaided ear.[16]

To quest for Santa Ana's sirens may not seem exciting, but this beast with external gills and only two front legs has been around some 70 million years, essentially unchanged since late Cretaceous time, when the very rocks that underlie the refuge were made. Can I trap living antiquity? There are great kiskadees fishing in the resaca and malachite, banded purple wing, and zebra butterflies to condition me to subtropical "Cretaceous seas." I suppose the art of trapping any animal is exciting in itself, because one never knows what traps will hold. Expectation may be the trademark of the naturalist. I use unbaited, funnel-type fish traps in shallow, weedy water. Why sirens enter unbaited traps is a recurring mystery.

On consecutive nights in December, 1973, I used twenty-five traps in a thousand-square-foot plot to determine the density of one

[16] F. R. Gehlbach and B. Walker, "Acoustic Behavior of the Aquatic Salamander, *Siren intermedia*," *Bioscience* 20 (1970):1107–08; F. R. Gehlbach, R. Gordon, and J. B. Jordan, "Aestivation of the Salamander, *Siren intermedia*," *Amer. Midl. Natur.* 89 (1973):455–463.

resaca population. The first night I trapped 18 sirens, which I branded individually. Small numbers were burned into the skin, just as symbols are burned into a cow's hide. Sirens, by the way, have the thickest hides of any salamander and are not debilitated by careful branding. On the second night I caught 12 sirens, including 2 marked ones. Dividing the product of the number marked the first night times the number captured the second by the number of recaptures, I estimated 108 sirens in the study plot or about 1 per ten square feet.

Such mark-recapture analysis is standard procedure among naturalists. The method's accuracy is tested by plotting the cumulated total of marked individuals against time. At some point the curve levels off. Then enough specimens have been marked to gain the closest approximation to total population size without having to catch every single siren. That is highly unlikely anyway. Other assumptions include thorough mixing of marked and unmarked sirens, no movement into or out of the population, and the likelihood that branding does not interfere with subsequent capture.

Chachalac, Chachalac, CHACHALAC—on and on, louder and louder in the dawn, just a few hours after I've spent most of the night wading through resacas trying to catch and watch nocturnal sirens. I must tape-record the morning conversation of Santa Ana's "roosters" sometime, but not today. This tropical, pheasant-sized bird makes a horrendous noise at dawn, for it is highly social and quite bilious. In fact, the species once was crossed with domestic fowl for cockfighting purposes in the lower Rio Grande Valley.[17] I learn a good lesson in peck-order behavior by watching the chachalacas on Santa Ana's main road, where they concentrate at grain spread to attract them. A dominant bird shepherds two or three others, and the group's lesser members displace their equivalents in other groups. Despite the disharmonious music of the artificial feeding, chachalaca behavior is so nicely exhibited that I don't mind the unnaturalness.

When a largely natural preserve is surrounded by unnatural landscape, it seems inevitable that the preservers are accused of harboring varmints that sally forth to raid man's crops or livestock and return to

[17] S. D. Casto, "The Fighting Chachalaca," *Texas Ornithol. Soc. Bull.* 6 (1973):25.

relative immunity. Coyotes provoke such accusations most frequently, since these crafty musicians are most successful among varmints in living with or in spite of man. Periodically farmers around Santa Ana ask its managers to control coyotes on the refuge, for too many melons or chiles are being eaten. A trapping campaign often follows.

In 1967 a particularly indiscriminate campaign caught a number of coyotes, an ocelot, several bobcats, skunks, opossums, and a badger. Ocelots were not seen again for a decade, although I noted one shot by a rancher near Falcon Dam in 1971 and another photographed by a naturalist at Laguna Atascosa National Wildlife Refuge in 1974. Meanwhile, ocelots were endangered by the fur trade; I calculated a 40 percent decline in Mexico alone and 34 percent throughout the species' tropical American range, in 1968–1970.[18] Ironically, 1967 was the year after Santa Ana became a Registered Natural Landmark in recognition of its exemplary subtropical biota.

Another small spotted cat, the margay, seems to be absent from this region. Aside from the 1852 specimen taken by the First Boundary Survey at Eagle Pass, Texas, upriver from Santa Ana Refuge, there are no margay specimens within 300 miles of the Border. A four-thousand-year-old fossil jaw from the Texas Gulf Coast is supposedly a margay, but I doubt it. The specimen is hardly distinguishable from a domestic cat, and there are no other fossil records anywhere in the United States.[19] Indeed, all other wild cats—jaguars, cougars, bobcats, ocelots, and jaguarundis—are known from the Gulf Coast in historic time and from Pleistocene fossil evidence. Could Samuel Cooper, who collected the Eagle Pass margay, have bought or found a pet from southern Mexico, thinking he obtained a native animal?

Just outside Santa Ana's eastern fenceline stands a lone Montezuma bald cypress tree in a field of broccoli or cabbage. Other *sabinos*, Mexico's national tree, are scattered upriver. The Rio Grande

[18] N. Myers, "The Spotted Cats and the Fur Trade," in *The World's Cats*, vol. 1, ed. R. L. Eaton, pp. 276–326 (Winston, Oreg.: World Wildl. Safari Publ., 1973), calculations from data in table 3.

[19] C. D. Eddleman and W. A. Akersten, "Margay from the Post-Wisconsin of Southeastern Texas," *Texas J. Sci.* 18 (1966):378–385. Note the negative evidence in B. Kurten, "The Pleistocene Felidae of Florida," *Bull. Florida St. Mus.* 9 (1965): 215–273.

grew Montezuma cypress only between the mouth of the Río Salado and Roma, according to William Emory, but I believe they were simply most abundant there and escaped notice downstream by reason of relative scarcity.[20] Surely the river transported cypress seeds. Today in the United States the species is present in a natural stand near Salineno, Texas, and nowhere else. Here the unofficial champion is five feet in diameter and thirty-five feet tall. Its mature companions number twelve, and I found no seedlings or small saplings in January, 1973, although each tree's round cones were full of seed.

Is reproduction lacking? Has the controlled Rio Grande changed so drastically that seeds cannot germinate? I know the river rises and falls as Falcon Dam is opened and closed to the demands for irrigation water. Historically the river fluctuated wildly, of course, but probably not so frequently. Must cypress seeds germinate and seedlings grow in the slow-velocity regime between natural floods? To test this possibility, I brought 80 seeds inside a greenhouse with a small pool and slowly running stream. I placed 20 in muck at the pool waterline, 20 in the pool directly, another 20 in the stream, and a like number in damp pot soil for controls. Another 100 I sectioned to check viability, which proved to be 40 percent.

Within a week the seeds in the pool sank and began to rot in the anaerobic environment. The damp-pot seeds also rotted eventually, as did all but one of those in muck. This sprouted a month and a half after planting, along with four of the seeds placed in running stream water. By comparing these results against germination potential—eight seeds expected to sprout, twelve to rot—I find statistical significance in favor of the stream environment.[21] The tests substantiate my slow-river hypothesis. Perhaps the frequent high-water cycles wash cypress seeds downstream to drown in deep water before they can germinate.

Did anyone figure the endangered Montezuma cypress into the cost-benefit calculus of Falcon Reservoir? When the dam was completed in 1953, cypress stands at the mouth of the Río Salado drowned. I crossed the Salado near Guerrero, Tamaulipas, twenty years later and

[20] Emory, *Report*, vol. 1 (1857), p. 67.

[21] If the expected germination is eight, for the observed four seedlings the simulated stream gives $\chi^2 = 3.3$ ($P>0.05$), and the observed one in the muck gives $\chi^2 = 10.0$ ($P<0.01$). Thus the results do not deviate significantly from the expected in the stream, while they do in the muck, indicating the unfavorable nature of this environment.

noted a large cypress population with perhaps two-thirds dead or dying. Six feet of exposed mud flats attested to periodic drawdowns of Falcon Reservoir and suggested that man's landscape tinkering could spell doom for this most magnificent tree of the eastern Borderlands. Oxygenless mud was piled around trees that would have been swept free of such encumbrance by natural floods before the mid-twentieth century. Golden-fronted woodpeckers swarmed in the dead cypress limbs that late February day. Spring had arrived, and they would benefit.

I often camp in an ebony grove just below Falcon Dam, a convenient walk from my cypress trees and near the only U.S. nesting population of brown jays. Here the spiny pocket mouse reaches its northwestern limit, and blue spiny lizards do push-ups with rivals in the rock riprap. I see the concrete apron of Falcon Dam and hear the "mo hope" call of the Inca dove. Black-headed orioles and red-billed pigeons furnish other music, while Julia butterflies and fawn-breasted hummingbirds at anacahuite blossoms are living rust on white and yellow. Then I retrieve my fish traps, built into a beaver dam overnight, and admire the persistence of one mammal that was trapped nearly to extinction in Boundary-survey days.

It is always Halloween at this place, because the ringed kingfisher's rattle sounds like a Halloween noisemaker to me. This big cousin of the medium-sized belted and tiny green kingfisher divides up fishing space with its relatives in an interesting manner. It chooses broad, deep river reaches. The green kingfisher sticks to narrow, shallow rivulets, while the belted kingfisher, the least abundant and a winter visitor only, prefers the still water of ponds and sloughs. Each species dives into water of a depth appropriate to its body weight and hence inertia, a fine way to subdivide the Rio Grande's stage space.

In the 1950's the ringed kingfisher, *martín pescador*, was only casual in these Borderlands. By the late 1960's, it was seen regularly here, and in April, 1970, it nested. That first cavity, 200 feet from the Rio Grande, had foot furrows indicating active use when Albert McGrew discovered it.[22] McGrew waited until adults came by with

---

[22] A. D. McGrew, "Nesting of the Ringed Kingfisher in the United States," *Auk* 88 (1971):665–666.

Green Kingfisher Pair (Emory)

minnows and entered to feed nestlings, but he never saw the family. Apparently the young were ready to leave the nest hole and, like many birds, were stimulated by their parents to leave a bit early after being discovered by the arch predator. I wonder if this also happens in response to natural predators.

Did the control of the Rio Grande permit the ringed kingfisher to move northward to the Border? Perhaps, because this bird's local livelihood depends on a river whose features have been changed considerably in the last two decades. What particular attribute of the new river is responsible? The answer may be the more continuous flow of comparatively deep water. Reservoirs drown free-flowing streams, but by holding silt behind a dam they clear up downstream portions and may create suitable habitat with the channel-clearing help of beavers.

Stimulated by a rustling in the leaf litter, I ponder the gains and losses of natural diversity in this evergreen woodland. The disturbance continues, an olive sparrow scolds, and a giant "pill bug" appears. I am approached by two leathery, erect ears like Piglet's. The ears atop the pill bug stop, a long pointed nose appears, I change position for a better look, and a mad scrambling bids me follow on the run. If I stop, the creature stops, stands erect, and if I am quiet commences its "sniff-rooting" in the leaf litter. I am at home with the armadillo.

During the First Boundary Survey, armadillos were confined to valley jungles between Fort Ringgold and Brownsville in the United States. Edgar Mearns found them commonly at Fort Clark in the 1890's, and Vernon Bailey noted their occasional presence as far north as Austin, Texas, in 1902. By the 1950's armadillos had moved into southern Oklahoma, adjacent Arkansas, and Louisiana. In but twenty years more they moved another 200 miles northward. If I stop to recall that armadillos were not present in Texas at all until the last three thousand years, I figure they walked and waddled about a third of a mile per year in their journey out of Mexico.[23] Then in the twentieth century, they increased the pace to six miles a year.

[23] S. R. Humphrey, "Zoogeography of the Nine-banded Armadillo (*Dasypus novemcinctus*)," *Bioscience* 24 (1974):457–462; S. F. Baird, "Mammals of the Boundary," in Emory, *Report*, vol. 2, pt. 2 (1859), p. 49; V. Bailey, *Biological Survey of Texas*, N. Amer. Fauna 25 (1905), pp. 53–54; E. A. Mearns, *Mammals of the Mexican Bound-*

Why the northward push and speedup recently? A warmer climate may be one answer, but armadillos have not kept up with the northward advance of warm temperatures. Instead, the clearing of land for agriculture, started slowly by hand in Mexico and expanded exponentially with machine manipulations in the United States, must be part of the explanation. Although armadillos commonly inhabit woodlands and second-growth forests, they are rare or absent in virgin forest. They prefer to forage in the open, especially where the soil is freshly tilled, and they love a watered landscape such as an irrigated field or suburban lawn. So I suggest they have run as fast as they can in response to man's recent and massive disturbance of natural landscapes.

---

ary of the United States, U.S. Natl. Mus. Bull. 56 (1907), p. 157; E. L. Lundelius, Jr., "Late Pleistocene and Holocene Faunal History of Central Texas," in *Pleistocene Extinctions: The Search for a Cause*, ed. P. S. Martin and H. E. Wright, Jr., pp. 287–319 (New Haven: Yale Univ. Press, 1967).

3. *Poison, Poison*

PRESIDIO, TEXAS—the name evokes the immediate vision of a cold drink! This town is famed for its 100-degree summer temperatures. More than 100 consecutive days of over 100 degrees is not unusual, but Presidio can't match the Gran Desierto on the western end of the Borderlands for heat, as I am later to discover. However, Presidio excels in melons, cotton, and DDT or methyl parathion, so omnipresent that even the jackrabbits may act a little crazy because of it. I know this because pesticide research at Presidio is a classic in teamwork by naturalists, an exemplary study of unnatural history.[1]

Nearly 5,000 acres are under cultivation in the Rio Grande Valley at Presidio and Ojinaga, Chihuahua, across the river. Irrigation agriculture is the mode, and the Rio Grande is potentially nutritive, since Ojinaga dumps raw sewage into it. Pesticides are another way of life here—mostly DDT and methyl parathion—about 44,000 pounds in 1965, triple that amount by 1968. The U.S. and Mexican governments have jointly sprayed some ninety miles of the Rio Grande Valley.

When sprayed on cotton to control pestiferous insects, DDT is expected to accumulate in these plants, since it is washed into irrigation water, enters the soil, and is absorbed by plant roots. Even native plants that grow outside the cotton fields take up poisons. Leatherstem is a good example, accumulating methyl parathion in particular. Both kinds of pesticides rapidly decrease in amount from the centers of cotton fields to the peripheries, yet persist up to fifteen miles away.

Physical factors contribute to dispersing the poisons. Cultivated

[1] H. G. Applegate, W. Hanselka, and D. D. Culley, Jr., "Effect of Insecticides on an Ecosystem in the Northern Chihuahuan Desert," in *Food, Fiber, and the Arid Lands*, ed. W. G. McGinnies, B. J. Goldman, and P. Paylore, pp. 393–404 (Tucson: Univ. Arizona Press, 1971).

fields at Presidio are at the lowest elevations in the region, hence act as gigantic air-exchange devices. Cool night air moves in through arroyos, heats up during the day, and rises out over the surrounding shrub desert. As it moves, the air picks up dust particles from freshly turned agricultural earth. Dust devils, *remolinos*, the miniature tornadoes that swirl and dance across summer landscapes, are major vehicles of transportation. Moving dust is easily seen, but what cannot be seen are the millions of pesticide particles adsorbed on the surface of each tiny dust particle.

Western, checkered, and little-striped whiptail lizards served the pesticide research team in demonstrating some results of pesticide drift and relocation. Specimens taken in shrub desert up to nine miles away from cotton fields contained DDT and methyl parathion in their tissues. Concentrations of the poisons increased during the growing season with continued aerial spraying until August, when a decrease occurred in females. But then up to five times the body tissue amounts were discovered in the lizards' eggs. The pesticides had simply shifted position from mother to egg, as fat energy was utilized for egg production. From eggs to the next lizard generation—the transfer of persistent pesticides may continue. If lizard eggs fail to hatch or hatch into deformed young, as we know happens in some birds, perhaps there will be no next lizard generation.

Whiptail lizards are familiar to anyone who walks awhile in the desert. Would they be missed? Suppose we add small mammals, say jackrabbits, to the list of the missing. Would the decrease in natural diversity then become apparent? What about kangaroo rats and pocket mice? The fate of pesticide-poisoned whiptail lizards is conjectural, but I can add a different hypothesis concerning small mammals in the shrub desert community.

Silky and desert pocket mice, Merriam kangaroo rats, and black-tailed jackrabbits were captured by the study teams. Some individuals were marked for reidentification and released. Curiously, individuals were recaptured most often in study plots with high pesticide concentrations. One would expect no difference in recapturability unless something was different about the mammals or their community. The team could find no differences in population sizes, food availability, soils, or climate. But they did find that the small mammals had higher body loads of pesticides in the plots with higher pesticide concentrations.

Methyl parathion in the brain tissue of black-tailed jackrabbits was significantly higher in such plots. Also, age-class structure of the jackrabbit population showed that addition of yearlings to replace old adults did not occur in the second year of study. Perhaps methyl parathion in the brain interferes with the normal behavior of jackrabbits, so these animals blunder into traps. This would explain the higher incidence of recaptures. And, if a live trap is replaced with a live coyote, the lack of recruitment of yearlings is explained. What will then become of the coyotes?

Proponents of the use of persistent pesticides often argue that the opponents' evidence comes only from plants and small animals, not humans. Thus the study team investigated man, the jackrabbit's distant cousin. Two area residents were examined, one with normal exposure to the local poisons, the other without. At the start the exposed fellow had stored a tenth of a part of DDT per million parts of urine. His unexposed counterpart—his control in the experiment—had no DDT in his urine. Two weeks later the first man's share of DDT had increased elevenfold, the second had acquired three-tenths of a part per million parts urine. A month after that, the first man had twenty-three times the original amount of DDT, the second, six times his original amount. Can this go on until man himself blunders into a trap?

A third human subject, a pesticide spray–plane pilot, stored a third to three times his original amount of DDT just during the course of a day's work. He once complained of nausea following a mission. His doctor diagnosed the condition as methyl parathion poisoning and gave him atropine; he recovered. How many other Presidio and Ojinaga residents were affected? We don't know, but jackrabbits should make us cautious, since they are enough like the beagle dogs and white rats used in medical research to furnish an outdoor laboratory example.

Presidio is just one of many well-studied examples of large-scale agricultural use and the resulting widespread ramifications of pesticides. But what about small-scale use—the guy with the bug bomb in his hand? Can the average urbanite poison the Borderlands? Most likely he can, as Howard Applegate concluded in Big Bend National Park, where samples of soil, plants, and animals were collected eighty miles downwind of Presidio.[2] Of nine sampling sites in the park, the four most used by people had the highest pesticide concentrations. Surprisingly, the Chisos Basin campground, 3,000 feet above the desert lowlands and shielded by a 2,000-foot mountain rim, was among the four. It should be isolated from pesticide drift.

Is it possible that the DDT and methyl parathion found in the Basin campground were applied by people with bug bombs? Amounts needed to reach existing soil concentrations of DDT were calculated using the following assumptions: that pesticide concentrations were characteristic of the total camping area, not just the particular samples taken, that an acre of soil three inches deep weighs a million pounds, and that a pressurized spray can contains nine-tenths of one percent DDT. Then the size and typical visitor use of the Basin campground and two other camping areas, three of the four most highly poisoned sites, were figured. The Basin site was estimated to contain thirty-eight pounds of DDT, which would require 4,367 spray cans or 1.4 cans per camper during a June-to-August season. Boquillas campground indicated 0.3 cans used per person, and Castolon, 1.9 cans in the same prime camping period.

If I hadn't had considerable experience in the Chisos Basin, I would hesitate to accept the figure of 1.4 cans per camper. But I remember this area, Boquillas, and Castolon too, from a time before the modern flood of campers and spray cans. Even in the 1950's, flies were unnaturally bothersome in the Basin campground because of the horse concession nearby. And gnats are a natural pestiferous feature of the summer monsoon. Now campers spray themselves, their equipment, and campside vegetation from March to September; so I believe 1.4 cans per person is a reasonable estimate, particularly when park rangers and concessioneers are included in the Basin's suburban population. When will people "meet the parks on the parks' terms, rather than expect to significantly modify the parks to the terms of the users . . ."?[3]

Among the known recipients of pesticides are bats, the most nu-

---

[2] H. G. Applegate, "Insecticides in the Big Bend National Park," *Pesticide Monitor. J.* 4 (1970):2–7.

[3] National Parks Centennial Commission, *Preserving a Heritage* (Washington, D.C., 1972), p. 102.

merous mammals in the world besides rodents. But bats are some ten times more susceptible to lethal DDT poisoning than rodents and perhaps ten times less able to compensate for their loss of individuals. A mouse can produce ten to twenty offspring per year, whereas a bat produces only one or two. Moreover, mice move only a few hundred feet at most in their nightly foraging, while bats fly several miles, can feed on insects over sprayed cropland, and hence can be poisoned outside refuges like Big Bend National Park. So I am not surprised that certain bat populations are declining in the Borderlands, and I believe it legitimate to suspect pesticide poisoning along with natural factors.

The once spectacular evening flight of eight million Brazilian free-tailed bats from Carlsbad Caverns, New Mexico, has all but ceased. Between 1934 and 1973, this population lost 98 percent of its members. Another colony of 25 million free-tails near Clifton, Arizona, declined 99.9 percent between 1963 and 1969.[4] Although pesticides are not proven culprits in either case, proximity of both colonies to sprayed fields and winter migrations into Mexico, where DDT is still widely used, suggest such a hypothesis. Western pipistrelle bats in the same Arizona cave suffered no concurrent decline, but this smaller species does not migrate or travel far to feed and may not encounter pesticides as readily as the Brazilian free-tail. In any case insect consumption by the fewer free-tails in Arizona dropped from an estimated forty tons a night to a mere ninety-six pounds, and I wonder if spraying crops for destructive insects increased accordingly?

Brazilian free-tails remain among the most numerous of bats— murciélagos—in Big Bend National Park, and their population dynamics may predict the future of all bats in that refuge. Happily, these particular free-tails show no significant decline in numbers. Of course their summer home is farther from sprayed croplands than the summer haunts of free-tails at Carlsbad Caverns and Clifton, Arizona, but the Big Bend free-tails also migrate into Mexico each winter. Perhaps if pesticides have decimated the Carlsbad Caverns and Clifton colonies,

[4]Carlsbad Caverns data are from K. N. Geluso, J. S. Altenbach, and D. E. Wilson, "Bat Mortality: Pesticide Poisoning and Migratory Stress," *Science* 194 (1976): 184–186. These authors show that fat laced with DDT is mobilized during migration, and the poison reaches the brain. E. L. Cockrum ("Insecticides and Arizona Bat Populations," *J. Arizona Acad. Sci.* 5 [1969]: 198) presents the Arizona example.

only U.S. agribusiness is to blame, since the Big Bend population seems unaffected by its international experience.

Big Bend National Park has the richest bat fauna of any comparable area in my purview. Between 1967 and 1971, David Easterla recorded eighteen species, including the Mexican long-nosed bat not known elsewhere in the United States. Although he worried about bat population declines in Big Bend, I cannot find general evidence of it.[5] Among fifteen species abundant enough for individual trends analyses, I do note that the Mexican long-nosed, ghost-faced, and California myotis bats may be declining by comparison with the overall bat population. However, all three are peripheral in Big Bend, and I expect them to show strong population flux in contrast to species that do not reach their range limits there.

Unfortunately, Easterla's study spans too short a time to distinguish human impact from natural population cycles in a region where drought can last a decade or more and reduce plant life, insects, and bats in their turn. Even an eleven-year investigation of bat numbers on the Mogollon Rim in New Mexico shows no trends of the Carlsbad Caverns–Clifton, Arizona, type.[6] I would guess that a minimum of two decades is required to distinguish culturally induced from naturally determined population flux, if the severe drought of 1947–1956 and the ensuing wet decade represent average climatic flux.

I know of but one local study with the temporal scope necessary to relate small-vertebrate population cycles to climate. Between 1951 and 1972, William Milstead trapped lizards at Black Gap, just north of Big Bend National Park.[7] There, at the height of the 1947–1956 drought, average annual rainfall was only six inches. By 1962 it had

[5]D. A. Easterla, *Ecology of the 18 Species of Chiroptera at Big Bend National Park, Texas*, Northwest. Missouri St. Univ. Studies 34, nos. 3 and 4 (1973). A multiple stepwise regression (MSR) of total number of bats on each species' numbers in 1967–1971 gives significant ($P<0.05$) r^2 additions of 0.91 and 0.08 for the Brazilian free-tailed and pallid bats; multiple correlation (R) = 0.99. The regression coefficient of total bats per visit per year versus years is 0.375 (F = 0.5, $P>0.05$).

[6]C. Jones and R. D. Suttkus, "Notes on Netting Bats for Eleven Years in Western New Mexico," *Southwest. Natur.* 16 (1972):261–266. The regression coefficient of total bats per visit per year versus years is 0.557 (F = 4.1, $P>0.05$).

[7]W. W. Milstead, "The Black Gap Whiptail Lizards after Twenty Years," in *Symposium on the Biological Resources of the Chihuahuan Desert Region, United States and*

Western Whiptail Lizard (Emory)

risen to ten inches, about normal, but in 1970–1971 it averaged eighteen inches. Accompanying the spectacular climatic shift were changes in numbers, distributions, and food habits of three instructive whiptail lizards.

Western whiptails lived in the valleys, little-striped whiptails on hillsides, and rusty-rumped whiptails on hilltops in 1951–1952. The population of the western, most amenable to trapping, averaged eighteen lizards per acre. In the following drought years, the western almost completely replaced its two cousins, which had virtually disappeared by 1962, when western whiptails had increased to seventy-four per acre and spread into both upland sites previously dominated by the others. Also, the western's diet had changed from mostly termites, associated with the dead vegetation of 1951–1952, to mostly caterpillars, which ate the new growth of 1962.

Drought must have favored the comparatively dry-adapted western whiptail, and it was on the increase while little-striped and rusty-rumped whiptails were decreasing in 1951–1952. Further, I suspect that things had just begun to cycle around to the characteristic three-species landscape by 1962. By 1971–1972, there were only fourteen western whiptails per acre. Now adversely affected in the wetter uplands, this species was confined to desert valleys during the third census, and the other two had returned to their upland haunts. Moreover, the western's diet shifted a third time to mostly grasshoppers, which had become abundant on green plants with the arrival of the supranormal rainfall.

Mexico, ed. R. H. Wauer and D. H. Riskind, pp. 523–532, U.S.D.I., Natl. Park Serv. Trans. and Proc. Ser. 3 (1977). See also W. G. Degenhardt, "A Changing Environment: Documentation of Lizards and Plants over a Decade," pp. 533–555, in the same volume.

A community's recovery from stress, either natural or cultural, is called secondary succession. This is the replacement of disturbance-tolerant, short-lived, highly prolific species by the less tolerant, long-lived, and less prolific species that eventually compose a climax community. When succession follows natural impacts like drought, fire, and landslide, pioneering species are likely to be natives. After human impact and particularly with continued human activity, pioneers are often exotics. In the Chisos Basin, for example, Paul Whitson found exotic pioneers like Johnson grass, Russian thistle, and horehound. Native pioneers such as cane bluestem and blue three-awn grasses are there too and appear to replace the exotics during succession on the basin's eighteen-year-old water-line scar. Similarly, I found that Russian thistle gave way to native grasses on a four-year-old pipeline scar in the Guadalupe Mountains to the north.[8]

Continual disturbance to the soil through compaction and drainage alteration results in pioneer species' holding their own. Some like Johnson grass produce inhibitory substances—poisons—that prevent establishment of other plants. Road shoulders are good examples of constantly disturbed sites. Whitson found only 28 percent of the ground covered by vegetation on one Chisos Mountains road shoulder, whereas plant cover increased to 82 percent beyond the influences of maintenance. He was struck by the abundance of desert species like mariola and creosote bush on the shoulder, since they are not characteristic of the surrounding evergreen woodland. Probably road fill containing seeds of these species had been brought into the Chisos from the shrub desert below.

Basin trails are in a constant state of disturbance, too. Trail impact comes directly from hiker and horseback rider plus the accelerated erosion of summer thunderstorms. The upslope side of a trail is often hard and steep; the downslope side, soft by comparison; and a trail's drainage ditches are even softer with accumulated soil. Trail margins provide a desertlike environment, occupied by acacias and broomweed in the midst of evergreen woodland. Back from the margins a variety of

[8] P. D. Whitson, *The Impact of Human Use upon the Chisos Basin and Adjacent Lands*, Natl. Park Serv. Sci. Monogr. Ser. 4 (1974); F. R. Gehlbach, "Biomes of the Guadalupe Escarpment: Vegetation, Lizards, and Human Impact," in *Biological Investigations in the Guadalupe Mountains National Park, Texas*, ed. H. H. Genoways and R. J. Baker, U.S.D.I., Natl. Park Serv. Trans. and Proc. Ser. 4 (1979), pp. 427–439.

plant species lives above the trail, comparatively few species below it. Presumably the constant washing of silt on the downslope margin creates too much disturbance for anything but pioneering species.

Paul Whitson discovered the interesting horse-trail syndrome, wherein riding horses consistently walk on the softer downslope trail margin, and trail maintenance crews support this habit and so destroy the landscape. As the downslope side erodes and the trail becomes slanted, maintenance personnel add soil from the upslope side. Uprooted rocks are simply heaved downhill. The result is a wider and smoother trail until the horses' sharp hooves again promote erosion of soft soil on the downslope side and the maintenance cycle is repeated. Aerial photos of the Laguna Meadow trail above the Chisos Basin show a pathway almost half as wide as paved roads in the basin.

Particularly destructive too is the horse and human tendency to short-cut trails at sharp turns called switchbacks. Switchback trails normally allow a diagonal traverse of a steep slope, easiest for man and beast and least erosive for the mountainside. This is the way deer do it and Apaches did it but not modern man in a hurry to get to the top. When corners are cut, the diagonal trail begins to straighten out, to run up and down hill instead of across, and every footfall and rainstorm causes rocks and soil to tumble downslope, accelerated by the steepened angle.

Besides the mechanical effects of horses' hooves on trails, the indirect damage of horse manure must be reckoned with. Many kinds of plant seeds are dispersed in livestock manure. Mesquite seeds, especially, are planted and fertilized in this manner, passing unharmed through the digestive tracts of grazing animals that have eaten the succulent bean pods. Digestion may even aid germination by scarifying the hard seed coat of the bean, releasing the enclosed plant embryo. So mesquite joins mariola and creosote bush among native desert plants indirectly planted in the Chisos Basin. I think of this as I suck the sweet sugars of a red-ripe mesquite pod, plucked from a plant two thousand feet above its natural elevational limits in the Chisos Mountains.

My personal interest in the unnatural history of mountain trails stems from an early realization that whenever I trod the backcountry of a Borderlands park, I often walked on footprints and hoofprints, if not horse manure. Thus in July, 1964, I made a study of trailside vegetation in Boot Canyon, Big Bend National Park, and North McKittrick Canyon in the proposed Guadalupe Mountains National Park.[9] I wanted to provide a baseline for future studies and to contrast similar plant life in geographically close but environmentally distinct areas. Boot Canyon at 6,800 feet with a rhyolitic rock floor is potentially cooler and wetter than North McKittrick at 5,200 feet on limestone. And Boot Canyon experienced five times more annual visitation in those pre–Guadalupe Park days.

First, I established the vegetative similarity I sought. Trails in both canyons traversed deciduous woodland with an evergreen component furnished by such widespread dominants as alligator juniper, gray oak, and Texas madrone. Floristically, however, the trails were distinct. Graves oak was the overriding dominant in Boot Canyon; bigtooth maple, in North McKittrick. Fully 84 percent of the thirty-eight recorded species grew along only one trail or the other. To ascribe differences to differential human impact, I could look at species in common, but even then the cooler-wetter Boot Canyon site might enhance trailside growth and ameliorate the effects of more hooves and feet.

I was astonished when I computed ratios of seedling-sapling trees to mature ones, a reproductive index, and dead trees to live ones, an index of mortality. The six dominants in North McKittrick exhibited a combined two-to-one reproductive advantage over the five in Boot Canyon. Among the three in common—bigtooth maple, gray oak, alligator juniper—individual advantages were up to three times greater in McKittrick except for a slight reverse showing in gray oak. The mortality index was less dramatic, with 1.2 times more dead trees in Boot Canyon than in McKittrick. Could severe human impact override the more favorable growing conditions in Boot?

Easily trampled and eaten herbaceous plants should clarify the situation, and I recorded the same two dominant grasses along both canyon trails—bull muhly and pinyon rice grass. However, all grass cover was half as dense and the dominants half as frequently encountered in my cross-trail plots at Boot. The reduced grass cover plus

[9] F. R. Gehlbach, "Plant Ecology of the Boot Canyon and McKittrick Canyon Trails, Trans-Pecos, Texas: A Research Report on Vegetation Dynamics and Human Impact," Natl. Park Serv. Rept. (1965). More trailside data on live and dead trees are in tables 10–13 and 16–18 of P. D. Whitson, *Impact of Human Use upon the Chisos Basin.*

larger reproductive index in the warm-dry-adapted gray oak, relative to the cool-wet-adapted Graves oak, suggested that Boot Canyon might be desiccating at the hand of man. Grossly greater impact there could come from trampling down and removing grasses, crushing leaf litter, and compacting the soil, all of which inhibits the percolation of rainwater and causes runoff.

Today, nearly a decade after McKittrick Canyon has been open to the public, I should rerun my investigation to determine whether trailside vegetation has suffered the Boot Canyon syndrome. But I cannot bring myself to do it, because I knew that canyon before the "improvements" that come with public ownership. I feel about it as Aldo Leopold did about the delta of the Colorado River in the western Borderlands: "It is the part of wisdom never to revisit a wilderness, for the more golden the lily, the more certain that someone has gilded it. To return not only spoils a trip, but tarnishes a memory." [10]

Meanwhile I had another trailside experience in the south fork of Cave Creek Canyon, Chiricahua Mountains, Arizona. I wish now I had begun a trail study above the campground there in the 1950's before birdwatching became so popular, for in the 1970's I walked a trail that seemed to widen in response to the probability of finding elegant trogons along it. In the 1950's I don't remember motorcycles on the trail or other swimmers in the creek, and I didn't worry about a swimming suit in those days. It was extra baggage. Things have changed a lot.

I decided to validate impressions of the widened trail one early August day in 1976. Two pairs of elegant trogons nested in the south fork above the campground, each commanding a lineal half-mile of territory. I reasoned that birders would concentrate their walking in the first or trailhead territory, going only as far as necessary to add the species to their lists. Also, because a good swimming hole was in the first territory, others would focus impact there, while weekenders escaping the Douglas, Arizona, smog would do likewise. So I postulated that the south-fork trail would narrow and its leaf-litter carpet and edge vegetation become richer with increasing distance from the trailhead at the campground.

In two hours Mark and I did what any two land managers could do

[10] A. Leopold, *A Sand County Almanac* (London: Oxford Univ. Press, 1949), p. 141.

to judge human impact along trails in reserves. At 300-foot intervals over a two-mile stretch, excluding rocky or steep grades, we measured trail width, counted herbaceous plant species within a foot radius of the sides of the trail, and graded leaf litter in the trail as none to much on a scale of zero to three. My hypotheses were supported. The trail averaged three feet, nine inches wide between the campground and upper limit of the first trogon territory and only one foot, eight inches thereafter. Simultaneously, trailside plant species doubled in number, as did the amount of leaf mulch.[11]

To make matters more interesting for naturalists but worse for the south-fork trail, four eared trogons flew out of the Sierra Madre Occidental and joined a wintering elegant trogon in the area, October–December, 1977. The new arrivals, the first in the United States, triggered a migration of birders that surely should have earned the eared trogon a monetary value similar to the hook-billed kite's in the eastern Borderlands. Birder ranks swelled to about 800 in the month after discovery and reached 100 per day on at least one weekend.[12] I was bemused by the onrush of those seeking additions to their life lists, attracted by eared trogons seeking their own winter food supply. What a difference in impact between the birders and the birds!

Trampling is a kind of poison—pollution—whether by man or horse, because it is destructive or harmful to a landscape. By "poisoned landscape," I mean one that lacks certain species or supports fewer individuals than normal. Natural populations are below carrying capacity because man's population is above carrying capacity. Furthermore, poisoning results in the degradation of community superstructure, as in the decline of leaf litter, and may foster exotic plant and animal replacements for native species. Some degree of poisoning may be

---

[11] Both number of trailside plant species and amount of leaf litter in the trail are negatively correlated with trail width ($r = -0.51$, -0.69, respectively, $P<0.01$, 25 $d.f.$). An MSR of plant species on trail width and litter gives r^2 additions of 0.26 ($F = 8.6$, $P<0.05$) and 0.01 ($F = 0.04$, $n.s.$), respectively. For further reference see R. F. Burden and P. F. Randerson, "Quantitative Studies of the Effects of Human Trampling on Vegetation as an Aid to the Management of Semi-natural Areas," *J. Appl. Ecol.* 9 (1972): 439–458.

[12] D. A. Zimmerman, "Eared Trogon—Immigrant or Visitor?" *Amer. Birds* 32 (1978): 135–139.

acceptable—even naturalists help to make trails—but there are limits if the natural landscape is to survive.

A deer trail is a natural disturbance that accommodates me without major alterations to it. Yet I am a social trampler, whose herds grow too large and make highways of deer trails. I do want others to lead or follow me, for I cannot experience natural history to the fullest without sharing it. Social animals are like that. How many of us should be here together? Others on horseback? Certainly not on motorcycles if preservation is our goal. The number of people and kinds of activities must be limited if a region's natural appeal is to include eighteen species of bats or eighteen western whiptails per acre—or a pair of elegant trogons per twenty acres of canyon bottom.

Each natural community has its own carrying capacity of humans, its tolerance for poisoning, above which diversity declines. That bug bombs are inappropriate in preserves is painfully obvious, though ignored, but too many people is the primary cause of landscape deterioration. Man must begin to regulate his own numbers in wild areas, closing some for recovery and simply curbing human floods in others. Although I don't like "closed-door" or reservations-only concepts of wildlands management, I realize that "open doors" may result in no natural history at all. The most critical discovery to be made in this century is the human carrying capacity of each natural community.[13] And a singular challenge is man's management of man with that in mind.

[13] J. A. Wagar, *The Carrying Capacity of Wild Lands for Recreation*, Forest Sci. Monogr. 7 (1964), is a source of some techniques available to ascertain human carrying capacity.

4. *The Devil's Waters*

A few miles downstream from Presidio, Texas, as the Rio Grande runs, is the mouth of Alamito Creek, a stream of cool water with hot springs, like several others in the region. Here the Great River receives a small contribution of pesticide-free water. The provider is a desert stream essentially pristine throughout its course in the grazing lands from the Davis Mountains to the Rio Grande. Perhaps this is because Alamito Creek—"little cottonwood"—flows below ground most of the way, appearing as a permanent surface stream only when it nears the Border. Monsoon thunderstorms may swell the flow, though, and the creek can be a raging torrent. Conditions for life in such Border waters are extreme. One must be adapted to swift currents, tumbling boulders, and hot, shallow water if one is a fish or turtle there.

So it is not surprising that this ecological theater has many stage settings but only a few adaptable actors. What does surprise me is the presence of two species, the rough-footed mud turtle and the Mexican redhorse, found nowhere else in the United States. Similarly, in the United States, the Conchos pupfish lives only here and at one spot in the Devils River, while the Mexican stoneroller minnow is abundant only in Alamito and Cienega creeks. Four other fishes are widespread in the eastern Borderlands—the roundnose minnow, red shiner, common mosquitofish, and green sunfish. As in Tornillo Creek to the south, some fishes may come and go according to the season and different water levels, using the Rio Grande as a retreat from locally unfavorable conditions.

The Mexican stoneroller was the most common fish in my April, 1971, and April, 1973, seine-haul samples from the mouth of Alamito Creek. This two-inch, cigar-shaped minnow made up three-quarters of all fish in the net. Stonerollers live in eighty-five- to ninety-degree water, fed by the hot springs here and quite unlike the seventy-five- to eighty-degree water upstream. The hot water seems optimal for the inch-long Conchos pupfish, which does not occur upstream. Common mosquitofish and green sunfish are less abundant. Although diversity is high (1.37) in this four-species community, it is not as high as in headwaters pools with four species (1.66), probably because of the overwhelming numbers of stonerollers.

I compute species diversity as a field-guide characteristic of community type.[1] This index figures number of species together with their individual abundances and is a handy attribute to use in comparing communities. Higher values denote more species or greater similarity of their abundances or both. Thus, finding four fishes, each represented by three individuals in a community sample gives a diversity of 2.00, whereas finding four species with the same total number of individuals (twelve) but abundances of six, three, two, and one gives 1.73. A catch of two species, each represented by six individuals—again a total of twelve—provides a diversity of only 1.00, and a catch of two with the unequal representation of eight and four individuals gives 0.92.

Communities with a diversity of resources support more species than simpler communities of similar space. As a rule of thumb, a tenfold increase in space about doubles the number of species.[2] But relative abundances are determined by species interactions such as predator-prey relations and competition plus seasonality, with its effects on reproduction and retreat. Therefore, to arrive at a satisfactory comparison of creek-mouth, midcourse, and headwaters pools on Alamito Creek I must sample areas of similar size in the same fashion at the same time of year. When I do, higher diversities truly reveal more complex communities and, locally, the probability of finding different and unique species of the Borderlands.

Upstream, my next stop on Alamito Creek is Casa Piedra, where Mexican stoneroller and roundnose minnows occur alone and species diversity is lowest (0.59). Both fishes have bright orange fins, and males have white skin tubercles about the snout in springtime. With their red eyes and distinctive brown band through the dorsal fin, male

[1] Species diversity here and henceforth is calculated using the Shannon-Weiner function: $H' = - \Sigma p_i \times \log_2 p_i$, where p_i is the number of individuals of each species in a sample. In assessing a fish fauna, I seine with a four-by-ten-foot seine of one-eighth-inch mesh, and I present average diversity values derived from at least two different years.

[2] R. H. MacArthur and E. O. Wilson, *The Theory of Island Biogeography* (Princeton: Princeton Univ. Press, 1967). Land-bridge islands in that book are analogous to mountain islands in the present volume.

stonerollers are a particular treasure. Populations are dense in the one-
to six-foot-wide multichannel stream. I catch about twenty-five stonerollers by seining in fast-flowing, gravelly channels or about the same
number of roundnose minnows in a shallow pool. The roundnose is a
plumper minnow, not as well adapted to current, so space and perhaps
food competition between this species and the stoneroller are minimal.

Also, young fish of both species are segregated from the adults, an
equally effective way of avoiding competition. Individuals less than an
inch long are in water less than an inch deep. Adult stonerollers frequent deeper riffles and channels; adult roundnose minnows inhabit
pools, although water more than two feet deep is scarce since flash
floods quickly fill stream-scoured pools with fresh gravel. Where
the creek first appears above ground, deeper pools are available but
are quickly occupied by green sunfish and red shiners. These two
are somewhat larger species, up to four inches in length, and I find
that fish size is positively correlated with depth of water in the
Borderlands.[3]

Nearby at Plata a series of small cienegas (also spelled ciénagas) or
spring-fed marshes drain into the creek. These cienegas, mostly modified into stock-watering ponds, are the habitat of the rough-footed mud
turtle, whose entire U.S. population probably numbers less than 200.
Although widespread on the central tableland of Mexico, rough-footed
mud turtles are known from only five ponds in Texas and apparently do
not live permanently in the mainstream of Alamito Creek. Its high
domed shell and two yellow chin stripes mark this five-inch turtle as
distinctly as its cienega habitat. A nebulous discovery, chance rediscovery, and the subsequent confirmation of its relict status mark the saga
of the rough-footed mud turtle in the U.S. Borderlands.

Vernon Bailey found the first rough-foot at what he called Lloyd's
Ranch, thirty-five miles southwest of Marfa, Texas, in January, 1890.[4]

[3]The Pearson correlation, r, of mean standard length with mean water depth is
0.63 ($P<0.001$, 47 $d.f.$) for eight pool, four riffle, and two channel samples of sixteen fish
species in Alamito Creek and Devils River, Texas, plus Aravaipa and O'Donnell creeks,
Arizona.
[4]Unpublished field notes of V. Bailey in the U.S. Fish and Wildlife Service Laboratory, Natl. Mus. Nat. Hist., Washington, D.C. (William Davis kindly supplied me with a
typescript of the Texas notes in 1963). See also T. C. Maxwell, "Three Men in Texas Or-
nithology," *Bull. Texas Ornithol. Soc.* 12 (1979):2–7.

The specimen I have seen, but the ranch apparently did not exist. Even Hart Greenwood never heard of the place, and he has lived in the vicinity since 1908. Furthermore, rough-foots are not in the area of Cienega Creek, a tributary of Alamito, as best I can tell. Maybe Bailey made a mistake, for he was more interested in birds and mammals than reptiles. I was perplexed in 1971 when I tried to find the missing mud turtles, which had not been seen by naturalists in the United States since 1950.

I knew William Davis and his students had picked up a second rough-foot south of Marfa in 1941.[5] They found it in seepage water below a stock pond on the Harper Ranch. So, after I had checked Alamito and Cienega creeks, Ted Harper directed me to three cienegalike ponds on his property. There I found the rough-foot in 1971 and 1973. Six individuals were taken as vouchers, three of which were preserved and three kept alive to study changes in appearance during growth and perhaps to initiate a captive breeding population. Twelve others were marked by filing a notch in the shell and released for later recovery and reidentification, but I was concerned that ranchhands were using the turtles for occasional pistol practice. Fortunately the daily activity cycle of this *tortuga* does not coincide with that of the vaquero.

How does one find and catch a secretive aquatic creature like a rough-footed mud turtle? Neither my family nor I saw anything at the cienega ponds before dark. A diurnal predator would have been discouraged, but I suspected rough-foots were mainly nocturnal as other mud turtles are. So I became nocturnal—and still saw nothing. Not discouraged, though, I tied some bones left from my supper on string and established four bait stations for the carnivorous mud turtles. Then about 9 P.M. I began to see four- to five-inch females, slightly larger males next, and finally, by 11, youngsters three inches or less. A dominance hierarchy prevailed, with the largest displacing the smallest at my supper tables. The turtles bit and shoved at one another until a subdominant individual gave way.

Females about equaled males in abundance, and the juveniles

---

[5] Bryan Glass supplied details of the rediscovery of the rough-footed mud turtle. My notes were given to Roger Conant for his use with J. F. Berry in *Turtles of the Family Kinosternidae in the Southwestern United States and Adjacent Mexico: Identification and Distribution*, Amer. Mus. Novitates 2642 (1978).

equaled adults. This suggested that the population was relatively stable, neither growing, as when juveniles outnumber adults, nor declining, as when adults are more common. Population size could have been estimated, if marked turtles had been recaptured on my second visit. But the water was cool in April, 1973, and I caught only 4 unmarked turtles. I was forced to estimate population size visually in one shallow 50-by-125-foot pond and assume other ponds held about the same number of turtles per unit of surface water. By adding my educated guesses for each of the five inhabited ponds, I came up with 150 to 200 rough-foots.

Adults were five to seven years old, except for a single nine-year-old senior citizen. Juveniles were two to four. I counted annual growth rings on the lower shell scutes of each individual in a manner similar to counting growth rings in tree trunks, and I tried to exclude narrow, seasonal rings in the process. The distinction between adults and juveniles was based on what I knew about the age of reproductive maturity in nearby populations of yellow mud turtles. And then I theorized: if adult females lay an average of four eggs annually, as yellow mud turtles do, and if adult mortality approaches 20 percent and egg plus juvenile mortality approximates 73 percent each year—not unreasonable assumptions—the population could be stable.[6]

"What good are those turtles?" a vaquero asked one morning. "Are they worth anything?" I gave a practical answer, something about the role of mud turtles as scavengers that help to keep stock ponds clean, but secretly agreed with Aldo Leopold's philosophy: "The last word in ignorance is the man who says of an animal or plant: 'What good is it?' If the land mechanism as a whole is good, then every part is good, whether we understand it or not. If the biota, in the course of aeons, has built something we like but do not understand, then who but a fool would discard seemingly useless parts? To keep every cog and wheel is the first precaution of intelligent tinkering."[7]

Jack Brown Spring feeds the small pond in which I captured rough-footed mud turtles. A thick sedge and rush cienega surrounds

---

[6]The matrix algebraic model for stability (eigenvalue = 1) is $2/3x^4 (1 + x^1 + \ldots + x^5) - 1 = 0$, where x is the survival rate for years two through nine, and $x/3$ is the survival of turtles into the second year.

[7]A. Leopold, *Round River* (New York: Oxford Univ. Press, 1953), pp. 146–147.

the spring, and towering over all are large Rio Grande cottonwoods. The vegetational diversity offered by the cienega and trees in a shrub desert typifies oasis-style environments at many places in the Borderlands. Birds are abundant, and certain species typical of these green carpet spots. At dawn the western-kingbird chorus ushers in chattering vermilion flycatchers and lyrical summer tanagers and hooded orioles. At dusk the kingbirds afford an overture for elf and screech owls. Coyotes, javelinas, and mule deer water at the pond. I played hide and seek with a pink coachwhip snake in a pile of old adobe bricks one morning.

The mud turtle ponds and cienegas are only a few miles from Alamito Creek, where cottonwoods joined by willows form acre-sized groves. These woods provide delightful shade for men and cows at noonday and nesting places for white-winged doves and the owls and songbirds. The little screech owl—*el tecolotito*—is my favorite, as I have watched its antics and followed its predatory trails from New York to the mouth of the Rio Grande and westward to the Pacific. Here on Alamito and Cienega creeks I found screech owls under especially intriguing circumstances.

In April and May screech owls are vociferous, because they are nesting and vigorously, vocally defending territories. *Tecolotito* does not screech but comes forth with whistles or whinneys of various modes. East of the Devils River, Texas, the whinneys are quavering and all on the same pitch or descending. Westward from the Devils River the primary call is like a bouncing ball—whistle notes that get faster and shorter in duration toward the end. The quavering-whinney and bouncing-ball calls are distinctive, belonging to eastern and western races of one species, according to Joe Marshall. He found mixed pairs near Langtry and Boquillas on the Rio Grande in 1962, and I discovered two more on Alamito and Cienega creeks in April, 1973. But I note both eastern and western screech owls along the Devils River without interbreeding.

No screech owl gives both kinds of calls or intermediate ones in the Big Bend overlap zone. Moreover, the red plumage and greenish yellow bill of the eastern, quavering owl are lacking in the western, bouncing-ball owl, at least in the Borderlands. I believe this is evidence of infrequent hybridization between two different species, with rigorous selection against their offspring. If eastern and western screech owls mated regularly and produced enough progeny to breed with screech owls to the west, red and greenish yellow color genes would be transmitted into the western Borderlands. Also, I would expect to hear intermediate calls. So, instead of suggesting the impending evolution of two species from two subspecies of screech owls, as did Joe Marshall, I believe that two species already exist and hybridize infrequently in the Big Bend region of Texas.[8]

Alamito Creek and its native biota disappear some twelve miles above Plata. San Esteban Lake stands silted in on the creek farther north, dry testimony to the folly of damming a flash-flooding stream. These creeks typically carry such a load of geologic loom-building materials that any dam serves as a warehouse for silt, gravel, and rocks, rather than as a reservoir for water. Shrub desert grades into plains grasslands near San Esteban Lake, and pronghorn antelope plus more cattle per section of land are indicative of the community change.

Terlingua and Tornillo creeks, both flowing through the Big Bend, are other permanent streams with unusual fishes. Today both are reduced to small areas of permanent surface water at their mouths, for overgrazing eliminated the once extensive grasslands of their watersheds. This, in turn, reduced the water-holding capacity of the soil, causing fast runoff, flash flooding, and channeling instead of the original controlled discharge. In 1885 Terlingua Creek was a running stream, alive with cottonwoods and beavers. Grass on the Tornillo Creek flats was so high before the 1900's that ranchers cut it with mowing machines. But cattle came to the lower Big Bend country in 1885. Six thousand head increased to thirty thousand by 1891 and declined to fifteen thousand by 1895, following the 1890–1893 drought.[9]

Despite its limited water supply, Tornillo Creek supports an average of four fish species, the same as Alamito Creek, and its mean spe-

[8] J. T. Marshall, Jr., *Parallel Variation in North and Middle American Screech Owls*, Monogr. Western Found. Vert. Zool. 1 (1967), pp. 8–11.

[9] R. H. Wauer, "A Case History of Land Use and Some Ecological Implications: The Chisos Mountains, Big Bend National Park, Texas," *Proc. 2nd Nat. Res. Mgmt. Conf.*, 1975, Southwest Regional Office, U.S. Natl. Park Serv., pp. 70–83; R. C. Tyler, *The Big Bend: A History of the Last Texas Frontier* (Washington, D.C.: U.S. Natl. Park Serv., 1975), pp. 121, 127, 133.

cies diversity (1.25) is similar to Alamito's (1.21).[10] But Tornillo is a spawning stream and nursery for fishes from the Rio Grande, unlike Alamito, where hot-spring water at the mouth apparently precludes many species. In May to September the Tornillo fauna swells to six to nine species, and diversity rises (2.11) as the Rio Grande makes its seasonal contributions. The Mexican stoneroller is here and the Chihuahua shiner, another local specialty found in the United States only in Tornillo and Terlingua creeks plus the adjacent Rio Grande.

The Rio Grande killifish is a third species whose increasing abundance may account for the concomitant decline of the stoneroller. Stonerollers were the most abundant Tornillo Creek species prior to appearance of the killifish in 1956. Now they constitute only 5 to 17 percent of the fauna. If the killifish was released as bait by fishermen inadvertently, its apparent effect of stressing the indigenous stoneroller is a good example of how man reweaves the landscape carpet without really trying. Because introduced fishes have upset natural fish communities elsewhere along the Border and since local minnows make good bait too, I think it should be illegal to use non-native fishes as bait.

Within a three-mile reach of the Rio Grande east of Tornillo Creek lives the Big Bend mosquitofish, whose history includes the purposeful introduction of an exotic competitor.[11] Clark Hubbs once held the last three living individuals of this inch-long species in his hand and is largely responsible for its tentative recovery. The story began in 1929, when Carl Hubbs described the species from specimens discovered in Boquillas Spring. Additional specimens were not found until 1954 at Graham Ranch Warm Spring. Meanwhile Boquillas Spring had dried up and common mosquitofish had been introduced by the National Park Service at Graham Ranch Warm Spring, Big Bend National Park, Texas.

[10]C. Hubbs and R. H. Wauer, "Seasonal Changes in the Fish Fauna of Tornillo Creek, Brewster County, Texas," *Southwest. Natur.* 8 (1972):46–48. My computations are from the data in this paper. See also C. L. Hubbs, "Fishes from the Big Bend Region of Texas," *Trans. Texas Acad. Sci.* 23 (1940):3–12.

[11]C. Hubbs and J. G. Williams, "A Review of Circumstances Affecting the Abundance of *Gambusia gaigei*, an Endangered Fish Endemic to Big Bend National Park," in *First Conference on Scientific Research in the National Parks*, ed. R. M. Linn, pp. 631–635, U.S.D.I., Natl. Park Serv. Trans. and Proc. Ser. 5 (1979). This account continues the story through 1976.

Common mosquitofish are aggressive competitors following most transplants. They severely reduce native relatives like the Big Bend mosquitofish by preempting food and space, exterminate them outright by predation on their fry, or insidiously endanger them through hybridization. When a mosquito problem exists, natural-area managers may elect biological controls like the mosquitofishes instead of chemical warfare. But when a native mosquito eater is present, introduction of an exotic is redundant at the very least. It is possible that the National Park Service did not recognize the potential they already had in the endemic Big Bend species. Maybe "desk jockeys" did not even know it was there.

Within two years of their introduction, common mosquitofish had virtually eliminated Big Bend mosquitofish. Twenty-five of the natives, all that could be found by seining, were placed in holding tanks while Graham Ranch Warm Spring was poisoned with rotenone to eliminate the swarming exotic species. Of the twenty-five, fifteen were released in other Big Bend ponds, where they died, six were kept at park headquarters and died, and the final four were taken by Clark Hubbs. One of these died, too, but the three remaining specimens were carefully cultured. They and their descendants were returned to two pools specially maintained for them at Graham Ranch a year later. There populations of around a thousand thrived for awhile.

Development of Graham Ranch as a campground included the planting and irrigation of Rio Grande cottonwoods. Unfortunately, the common mosquitofish had not been eliminated completely in 1956. By 1960 irrigation water apparently overflowed, connecting the original pond with the new pools reserved for Big Bend mosquitofish, and the exotic got the upper hand once again. So with fifteen Big Bend mosquitofish, Hubbs resumed his native fish culture. A new pool was built at Graham Ranch, too high for any more irrigation connections, and was stocked with the natives in 1960. Others were transplanted to remote ponds elsewhere in Big Bend National Park. Finally, irrigation practices were modified, and in November, 1970, when I last saw them, the beleaguered Big Bend mosquitofish seemed out of danger.

The Big Bend is the upper gateway to an international river wilderness with but three easily accessible land entries over the 150 miles downriver to Langtry, Texas. Even so, there are threatened plants and animals along the way, because today's wildland is not beyond human reach as was yesterday's frontier. The land is charted now and bordered by people with designs on its resources, whether nonconsuming recreationists or an increasing number of permanent settlers who must wrest a living from the desert.

One November day at La Linda, Coahuila, I watched a drifting sunrise and drifting smoke from a fluorspar plant. The wild river aroma was moderated. What would it be like when I got the chance to make a personal trip by boat through this landscape of falcon cliffs and candelilla? Would pesticides or falconers eliminate the peregrine falcons, perhaps the most concentrated population in the Borderlands? Would *candelilleros* cut the last wax plant? It is easy to be elated about a sunrise on a crisp winter day and forget emergencies.

Here and there Rio Grande cottonwoods, velvet ashes, and Goodding willows were cut from the *vega*, or riverside deciduous woodland. And most slopes above the cuts were bereft of candelilla, a soda straw–like plant from which wax is made by *mexicanos*. The *candelilleros*, as they are called professionally, cut both the wax plant and *vega* trees illegally, like moths taking tiny patches out of the landscape carpet. David Riskind suspects that the distribution of velvet ash in the *vega* is related to that of candelilla on the slopes above, for along the lower portion of the wild river, where candelilla is too scarce for a worthwhile harvest, the ash is still abundant.[12]

Local *vega* consists of seep willow, tree tobacco, salt cedar, and the giant and common reeds, in addition to larger woody species like the cottonwoods, willows, and mesquites. Huisache is the distinctive sight and smell of March. In many places the vegetation is impenetrable to man but excellent cover for small animals. *Vega* used to provide a highway along which subtropical species like the indigo snake and jaguarundi moved northward from their native "brush" on the lower Rio Grande. Most such travelers seem to have stopped around Del Rio, Texas, where *vega* was broken and narrow historically. Today I wonder if any make the trip past Falcon Reservoir, since it and Amistad Reservoir have flooded major *vega* pathways of the middle Rio Grande.

[12] David Riskind sent personal notes on a section of the Rio Grande, Maravillas Canyon to Langtry, that I have not seen.

Ammonite, Devils River (Emory)

A spectacular canyon and typical *vega* once graced the mouth of Texas' Río San Pedro—now known as the Devils River. Three-foot ammonites, predatory mollusks of Cretaceous seas, decorated the limestone, and wonderfully named Goodenough Spring poured forth less than a mile above the Devils–Rio Grande junction. Amistad Reservoir began to drown this scene in 1968. Rising waters extinguished another endemic spring fish, but a few live specimens were snatched from Goodenough Spring as it went under. Is amistad mosquitofish a fitting epithet for this recently described species?[13] Surely man's *amistad,* "friendship," with natural history did not figure into the cost-benefit calculus of dam builders.

Deterred from crossing the Devils River canyon, the First Boundary Survey struck the river at its junction with the Rio Grande and

[13] A. Peden, "Virtual Extinction of *Gambusia amistadensis* n. sp., a Poeciliid Fish from Texas," *Copeia* (1973):210–221.

well above the cleft, near the headwaters, near a place later called Beaver Lake. Vernon Bailey camped at Beaver Lake in July, 1902, and described what I saw in July, 1957, and as recently as March, 1975—an old slough in the riverbed nearly filled with the gravel of many flash floods. Neither Bailey nor I saw beavers there, although they were abundant downriver, as a functioning beaver trapper told Bailey and as I confirmed more than half a century later. Moreover, the overgrazing of livestock noted in 1902 had not stopped, for I observed the river valley and surrounding hills nearly bare of grass and other palatable vegetation, much as Bailey had described that 1902 landscape.[14]

Grass is a vital component of succulent desert and evergreen woodland, in addition to various grasslands, particularly if Montezuma quail are to thrive. Between 1849 and 1851 these plump camouflage experts with the harlequin facial pattern were abundant in the Devils River country and west beyond the Pecos, but by the time of Bailey's visit they were on the way out locally. By 1945, for instance, they were gone from the overgrazed Chisos Mountains, Texas, but present in the Sierra del Carmen across the Rio Grande in Coahuila, where grass remained in good condition. Today no more than a few hundred survive in Texas, most near Rocksprings on the Edwards Plateau and in the Davis Mountains.[15]

Montezuma quail prefer to sit unnoticed in the grass until almost stepped upon. Then they fly explosively but briefly to a new grass clump to hide. They are not the runners other quail are and do not form large coveys, but remain in family groups of about ten or fewer. They need grass, too, because of the lilies and sedges that grow with it, for they feed on the bulbs of these perennial plants in winter. When

[14] V. Bailey, field notes.
[15] S. W. Woodhouse, "Birds," in *Report of an Expedition down the Zuni and Colorado Rivers by Capt. L. Sitgreaves*, U.S. Congress, Senate, 32nd Cong., 2nd sess., 1853, Sen. Exec. Doc. 59; F. M. Bailey, *Birds of New Mexico* (Santa Fe: New Mexico Dept. Game and Fish, 1928), p. 225; T. D. Burleigh and G. H. Lowery, Jr., "Birds of the Guadalupe Mountain Region of Western Texas," *Occ. Papers Mus. Zool. Louisiana St. Univ.* 8 (1940):85–151; J. Van Tyne and G. M. Sutton, *The Birds of Brewster County, Texas*, Misc. Publ. Mus. Zool. Univ. Michigan 37 (1939). These sources describe abundance of the Montezuma quail in 1915, decline by the 1930's, and last sightings in 1939 and the early 1940's. The Chisos–Sierra del Carmen comparison is in W. P. Taylor, W. G. McDougall, C. C. Presnall, and K. P. Schmidt, "The Sierra del Carmen in Northern Coahuila," *Texas Geog. Mag.* (1946):11–22.

Devils River above Second Crossing (Emory)

overgrazing opened up the soil to annual weeds and the Devils River slopes to bare rock, local landscapes lost still another feature of natural history: *el codorniz pinto*, the Montezuma quail.

But they lost—I lost—much more than a single species. We lost whole communities like Beaver Lake and sizable chunks of the most spectacular floodplain woodland anywhere in the Borderlands. With overgrazing came soil erosion and then the chain of events that has been repeated too many times—faster runoff, siltation, increased frequency and severity of floods, gravel scouring, and filling of river pools, plus the washing away of river terraces with their centuries-old woodlands. Finally, settlements like Del Rio are flooded, as in 1954, and concrete dams like Amistad go up to control floods that could have been controlled by proper use of the living landscape in the first place. Will we ever learn to protect watersheds and stop building permanent dwellings in floodplains?

Drawn by its remaining natural diversity, I frequently visit the Devils River. The floodplain woodland cannot be matched, for its live oaks average thirty-seven inches in diameter and sixty feet in height. One monster with a straight trunk is sixty-six inches through and eighty feet high; another that branches below the four-and-a-half-foot diameter measurement level is eighty-four inches and sixty-five feet. The other major tree is the native pecan, whose succulent nuts I much prefer over the paper-tasting papershell varieties. Pecans outnumber live oaks three to one but are not so large. I measure a forty-eight-inch specimen, sixty feet high, but the average diameter is only fifteen inches. Trees of lesser importance include the sugarberry, American sycamore, and soapberry. Most are hosts for ball moss, a flowering relative of Spanish moss, and hence northern parula warblers reach their western breeding limits along the Devils River.

I wrestle with two concepts of protection for the remaining free-flowing Devils. Its present human tenants are jealous guardians who believe they own the river in addition to the woodland and desert. Trespassers are intimidated at the point of a gun, so illegal entries are minimal and general visitation reduced to the commercialization at Baker's Crossing. Yet overgrazing continues. If government were to husband this landscape for the public, grazing would cease, but human feet would replace hooves and, I fear, trample the shady groves with equal force. If the soil is mostly gone already, what would the elimination of grazing accomplish? Is the land best left in private hands?

One July day in 1957 my camp south of Juno was close to, if not the same as, Vernon Bailey's after he left Beaver Lake in 1902. My notes recall the feeling that my extraordinary luck was somehow related to the touch of mammalogist Bailey on this land. The rattle of a green kingfisher first stirred my senses that day. Bailey did not mention this bird in his field notes, but he did observe the equally loud golden-fronted woodpecker, another specialty of the area. In fact, Bailey's observation of a family of these birds and one of screech owls in a live oak with a hundred-foot spread was duplicated by my observations in the 1950's and 1960's.

Summer mornings are for birds, just as the hot afternoons are conveniently devoted to fishes and the cooler evenings to small mammals and reptiles. This particular morning the eastern and western mix of the Devils avifauna is apparent. Canyon and Carolina wrens, eastern and western wood pewees, and red-shouldered and zone-tailed hawks are nesting or with recently fledged young. The eastern element, further demonstrated by nesting acadian flycatchers, yellow-throated vireos, yellow-throated warblers, and the northern parula, is particularly striking. These species are at their western limits of breeding range. Equally important is the dense population of zone-tailed hawks—four pairs in the ten river miles between Juno and Baker's Crossing in 1974–1975. Their nests are forty-five to fifty-five feet up in fifty-five- to sixty-five-foot live oaks and pecans.

A midafternoon swim with a face mask introduces the unusually diverse Devils River fish fauna. Fish watching is as sporting as birdwatching though less common. Native fishes need more advocates. I spy the red-spotted Rio Grande darter, discovered here on the First Boundary Survey and confined to this and neighboring creeks. Then I find a Devils River minnow and proserpine shiners, other regional endemics. Mexican tetras and Rio Grande perch are abundant and beautiful, representing two tropical fish families in this largely temperate fauna. I may find a dozen species, including the gray redhorse—delicious—perhaps the same kind of fish Vernon Bailey had for supper at Beaver Lake in July, 1902.

Springtime fish species diversities increase from the headwaters to the tailwaters along the Devils River, and they average up to five times larger than those of smaller streams like Tornillo and Alamito. I record six to seven species upstream at Beaver Lake and diversities of 1.23 to 1.80, about like those in desert streams of the Big Bend. However, down around Baker's Crossing I find ten to twelve species and higher diversities (2.52 to 3.29). The juxtaposition of pool, riffle, and channel environments, plus a wider river—more space—permits more species to coexist. Also, the downstream river is less stressful to aquatic creatures, because it holds more water in the dry spring season. This, I believe, promotes more equal population sizes, for a drought-resistant species or two cannot get the upper hand.[16]

But desert streams are prone to flash flooding after thunderstorms. Then ecologic stage settings change drastically, as pools lose water space to gravel fill and shallow riffles become deep channels. How do the actors fare? Fortunately, Larry Harrell was here in October, 1974, just after a tremendous flood hit the Devils, the ninth

[16] Cf. R. J. Horwitz, *Temporal Variability Patterns and the Distributional Patterns of Stream Fishes*, Ecol. Monogr. 48 (1978):307–321.

largest in its recorded history. He had surveyed the fish fauna earlier in the summer and could answer my question. I rather expected his report of a general decline in species diversity and dissolution of species associations. After all, the fauna had been severely stressed. Less expected, however, was his observation that six preflood dominant fishes remained dominant and in the same rank order after the flood. All shifted positions on stage yet retained their comparative superiority in numbers and weight among the total of twenty fishes studied.[17]

After cooling down in the river—the air temperature is 100 degrees plus—I set out live mammal traps, though I have been pretty well skunked in my mammalian surveys of the river floodplain. The First Boundary Survey found raccoons, ringtails, and fox squirrels, and I see numbers of these. The fox squirrel, also collected by Bailey, reaches its western limits of range in this area and seems to be replaced by the similar-looking and similar-acting Apache (Nayarit) squirrel in the western Borderlands. Bailey found hog-nosed and striped skunks, the rock squirrel, southern plains woodrat, white-ankled and white-footed mice, and Merriam's pocket mouse, named for C. Hart Merriam, who developed the concept of life zones. But I catch only woodrats and white-footed mice plus wayward skunks.

As I trudge along the edge of a cattail slough this July evening in 1957, a slim, gray shape darts out of some common buttonbushes and into the marsh ahead of me. It looks large and low slung, perhaps three feet long including the long tail. So I plunge into the cattails, too, hoping to force the shape into the river or onto a more exposed portion of the floodplain, where I can get a good look at it. What luck—the shape darts out just ahead at the riverside. We identify each other for what seems a satisfactorily long time, the gray jaguarundi, the secretive tropical cat that barely reaches northward into Texas, and I, the arch predator, just as curious and excited.

I doubt that I have ever been more thrilled by a Borderlands experience, although I later saw jaguarundis at Santa Ana National Wildlife Refuge on the Rio Grande. Few people have observed an uncaged jaguarundi. Frank Armstrong knew the cat at Brownsville, Texas, where

[17] H. L. Harrell, "Response of the Devil's River (Texas) Fish Community to Flooding," *Copeia* (1978):60–68.

Jaguarundi (Emory)

in 1891–1892 he and William Lloyd of the U.S. Biological Survey collected specimens.[18] The First Boundary Survey obtained a jaguarundi at Matamoros, Tamaulipas, across the Rio Grande from Brownsville. Unlike the ocelot, the jaguarundi, or *leoncillo*, never ranged northward from the lower Rio Grande or Texas coast in modern time, but, like his tropical cousin, *el leoncillo* vanishes as his *vega* environment is destroyed.

Jaguarundis intrigue me more than any other wild cat of the Borderlands, because they come in two plain color phases, gray and reddish brown, have unspotted kittens, and lack the light ear spots characteristic of ocelots, bobcats, jaguars, and young cougars. Why two distinct colorations? Clarence Cottam told me he watched a gray and brown pair at the Welder Wildlife Refuge near Corpus Christi in the fall of 1973. Is color sex-linked? Why should the kittens be unspotted when all other native cats have spotted young? Surely body spots camouflage cats, young or old, and ear spots may look like supranormal eyes to adversaries of angry or frightened cats with flattened ears. The jaguarundi has some secrets left to tell me.

[18] F. B. Armstrong's experiences are quoted in V. Bailey, *Biological Survey of Texas*, N. Amer. Fauna 25 (1905), p. 168. I do not admit the jaguarundi to the Arizona fauna on any basis other than "escapee," since there are no substantiating records for the state and none at all from northern Sonora or anywhere in Chihuahua. The dubious Arizona record is in E. L. Little, Jr., "A Record of the Jaguarundi in Arizona," *J. Mammal.* 19 (1938):500–501.

I think about this quite often—about the marsh where I saw the cat eighteen years ago and about how hot it is today, March 27, 1975, as I seek the shade of a riverside sycamore. It is ninety-two degrees. The marsh is almost gone now, the victim of man and nature. Will these sycamores remain and with them the yellow-throated warblers that sing above me? Mark and Gretchen are swimming in the river. A hot breeze stirs. High cirrus clouds, hot wind from the south. I read the signs. Within twenty-four hours it is freezing—a sixty-degree temperature drop, a Borderlands specialty of spring or fall—and we too, the constant-temperature generation, are gone.

5. *The Arch Predator*

A thin blue streak on the horizon signals dawn. The sky is leaden in the wake of the late winter cold front. The landscape of the growing light is a grassy plain with breaks of evergreen woodland overlooking the Pecos River canyon near its junction with the Rio Grande. Dry side canyons wander off on several sides, and near one of these, Mile Canyon, a herd of bison begins to graze. There are perhaps a hundred animals here at the southern terminus of their winter range, a retreat from snow-covered plains north of the Borderlands. The adult males are impressive with their three- to four-foot horn spans and massive heads draped in thick, woolly winter hair.

Near a grove of Mexican pinyons and alligator junipers an eastern meadowlark whistles. A hundred yards up the draw that feeds Mile Canyon, another answers. Then along the draw, among trees and rocks, come other whistles. The larks are ensconsed. Several shaggy heads pause to listen and smell the north wind, but they are a thousand yards away between the draw and the canyon. Yet the magnificent males on the fringes of the herd do not graze. A band of scrub jays bursts from the draw shrieking, as a half-dozen small woolly forms emerge, moving toward the herd. The males snort, stamp, and wheel toward the herd. Now the woolly forms become men, their bison hides tossed and waving, and they join the shrieking jays.

The bison stampede. The herd turns to thunder, the dry plain to dust, as the men wave the beasts on toward Mile Canyon with their hairy flags. Most of the *cíbolos* reach the canyon and pour through a natural chute over the edge, plunging seventy-five feet to their death on the rocks and the bones of other bison before them. The slaughter lasts only twenty minutes. Then more predators—women, children, and old men—emerge beneath the lip of the bison jump. They are quickly joined by the hide wavers, who know a pathway to the canyon bottom. All feast, and the women cut and carry meat into Bonfire Shel-

Confluence of Rio Grande and Pecos River (Emory)

ter for drying. After the day's butchering, more than half the fallen herd remains. It is left to dire wolves and coyotes in the night.

Eight thousand years pass. Pinyons nearly disappear, and redberry junipers replace the alligator junipers. Modern bison with hidden horns replace the giants with four-foot racks. Evergreen woodland contracts and disappears locally; the giant bison disappear universally and forever, along with mammoths, horses, camels, and dire wolves. Indians of the late Archaic period replace the predators of the great beasts—the paleo-Indians that killed more than 100 head of bison during several hunts at their cliff in Mile Canyon. Still they kill at the jump, a total of 800 bison once, but the modern species is the evolutionary product of adjustment to the Indian and does not go extinct—at least, not yet. Wolves still follow the herds, but they are gray wolves. California condors scavenge the remains. The coyote persists.

I sit on the cliff overlooking Bonfire Shelter, where they butchered giant bison ten thousand years ago. Or I walk the dry arroyo at the Lehner Ranch in Arizona, finding bits and scraps of mammoth ribs, the remains of a dozen elephants that were human prey about the time of the slaughter in Texas. And I visualize a Borderlands as rich in large mammals as Africa today. The fossil evidence lies at my feet. Most giant species survived climatic changes of the last glaciopluvial, plus the warm-dry environments that followed, but didn't make it into historic time. Suddenly, between ten and twelve thousand years ago, the American megafauna vanished, and man came to dominate the landscape.

As I conjure the scene of the giant bison and paleo-hunter, based on the evidence below, I must agree with Paul Martin that aboriginal man overkilled the large animals of the latest Pleistocene in just a few thousand years following his arrival in North America.[1] Consider him a novel predator and hence potent, socially and technically, a practitioner of mass killing. No four-legged carnivore can kill dozens to hundreds of wild prey at once. The American megafauna was unadjusted to human impact, not only to the mass slaughters, but to the indirect predation. Think of fire drives that burned food and dispersed animals— or hunting camps at waterholes that forced animals to wander far for water if they were not killed on the spot.

Men do not choose small game if they can get meat or trophy in the form of bison or mammoth. Because such large animals have a lengthy immature period and then few offspring, their reproductive rates are low. Females may have one calf per year after age five, as does the modern bison, or a single calf every three or more years after age twelve, as do modern elephants. The replacement rate of large species' populations is naturally low, and, when environments change, large animals are more extinction prone than small ones with mouselike or rabbitlike reproduction hence larger numbers and greater genetic variation. Man's invasion of North America was a decided environmental change, of course. Paul Martin suggests that if one person out of four in a population of one per square mile killed sixty bison-size animals annually extinction of the prey would follow. And he believes the

[1]The bison jump scene is adapted from D. S. Dibble and D. Lorrain, *Bonfire Shelter: A Stratified Bison Kill Site, Val Verde County, Texas*, Texas Mem. Mus. Misc. Papers No. 1 (1968). P. S. Martin's overkill thesis is summarized in "Palaeolithic Players on the American Stage: Man's Impact on the Late Pleistocene Megafauna," in *Arctic and Alpine Environments*, ed. J. D. Ives and R. D. Barry, pp. 669–700 (London: Methuen & Co., 1975). Evidence for indirect killing through exclusion is in W. J. Judge and J. Dawson, "Paleoindian Settlement Technology in New Mexico," *Science* 176 (1972): 1210–16.

American range was stocked with antelope- to mammoth-size game at about this capacity when man arrived.

Natural predators typically select young, old, or infirm prey, avoiding or being less efficient at taking individuals in their prime defensive-reproductive years. Thus, prey populations are not jeopardized. Moreover, this is selectively advantageous to predator populations, since for a wolf or cougar to stab its prey to death with its teeth it must make physical contact and would risk injury or death at the hooves and horns of mature prey in good health. Conversely, man kills all age classes indiscriminately at bison jumps or actually selects prime meat or trophies, the reproductive individuals. Man's long-range and indirect weaponry allows this. Physical contact between the human predator and his prey is avoided. Personal danger and hence restraint are minimized. Add the use of fire, cliff, fence, and bulldozer to spear or gun—even trap or poisoned bait—and man becomes the arch predator, the only animal capable of causing its prey to go extinct.[2]

The front passes, and the lead sky turns to turquoise while I sit and dream of that ancient scene. Men butcher bison below me, but they are too few to use all the meat. Wolves and coyotes eat about the fringes of the slaughter and are not molested unless they come too close. Millenia pass before my eyes, and the great game herds dwindle to nothing. The waters of Amistad Reservoir drown Bonfire Shelter, for men no longer need it. Instead they need water, as the woodland becomes grassland and turns into desert in the century of Boundary surveys. Fenced cattle have replaced free-ranging bison and cannot leave the grass alone by migrating in the natural manner of hoofed animals. Of the original scene, only the coyote remains.

We differ little from our prehistoric ancestors in our propensity to exterminate large animals, particularly the carnivores. Only the rate and cost of extinction increase because of our more sophisticated weap-

---

[2]G. S. Krantz, "Human Activities and Megafaunal Extinctions," *Amer. Sci.* 58 (1970):164–170, compares prey survivorship under human and nonhuman predatory pressure. L. D. Mech's *The Wolves of Isle Royale*, Fauna of the Natl. Parks No. 7 (1966), is one of many good studies of prey selection (see also p. 92 in Dibble and Lorrain, *Bonfire Shelter*). Similarly, studies of prey populations controlled by predators and vice versa are many (e.g., F. W. Clark, "Influence of Jackrabbit Density on Coyote Population Changes," *J. Wildl. Mgmt.* 36 [1972]:343–356).

ons and unsophisticated ways. Whereas the Indian bothered little with the wolf or coyote, these animals are intolerable to us. The cost of raising beef or wool is high when livestock must be fed hay that must be irrigated with reservoir water. What is that cost in terms of predator control—say coyote meat? Gerald Cole figured $80.88 each to kill 1,864 coyotes in Arizona in 1969, or a total of $150,760. Subtract the presumed savings of $42,211 in livestock, and the net cost is $108,549 in one representative year.[3]

However, even this is the erroneous cost accounting of unnatural history. Coyotes eat more rabbits and rodents than livestock, and such natural prey eats forage that could sustain livestock. To simplify the complex natural economy for illustrative purposes, 148 black-tailed jackrabbits annually consume the forage of one cow or five sheep. Rabbit meat averages 30 percent of the coyote diet. Assume, then, that five coyotes kill 148 jackrabbits per year, and the coyotes destroyed annually in Arizona cost taxpayers about $53,000 in range forage lost to cattle. Add this to $108,549, and coyote meat could cost Arizonans at least $161,549 annually.[4]

Of course, there is no reason to expect coyotes, intelligent carnivores, to refuse unguarded livestock, and the herdsman-guardian tradition is all but lost in the Borderlands. Instead of staying with our herd animals and using dogs for herding and protection—the reason we domesticated them in the first place—we let livestock roam untended on overstocked ranges lacking protective cover. And we dump unwanted city dogs in the countryside to become worse livestock killers than the native predators. Is it any wonder that ewes cannot defend lambs or that calves die of exposure and are eaten by scavenging coyotes, which are then blamed for their deaths?

Modern man so hates the large carnivores that he poisons, traps, and shoots all native predators, not just the offenders. "Varmints and woolly boogers are the devil's agents," a retired trapper told me one day. "That must be true," I thought to myself, "else why should we lose our sense of reason and remove inexperienced juvenile or potentially dumb coyotes in our predator-eradication programs. We're just

---

[3]G. A. Cole, "Notes on the Cost of Coyote Meat in Arizona," *J. Arizona Acad. Sci.* 6 (1970):2, 85. My arithmetic and dietary statistics differ slightly from Cole's.
[4]Ibid.

selecting for superior intelligence in the art of avoiding man." I believe the coyotes that survive man's traps and poison baits have the firsthand experience and avoidsmanship mentality necessary to harass man henceforth. Certainly *el coyote* is as abundant as ever and perhaps more widespread today than before.

Is it possible that those first coyotes on the fringes of bison and mammoth slaughters were especially crafty? Or are their descendants crafty because the early ones that got too close were killed, leaving only coyotes that wait until man sleeps? Has man always selected for intelligence in coyotes? Why haven't other large carnivores been so successful? Many, like the gray wolf, are larger, easier targets, because they range more widely, require wilderness-type terrain, and cannot subsist on watermelons, chilis, and cotton rats, as coyotes can. Probably the larger predators never were as generalized as the coyote. If so, this makes coyote genes easier to work with. Original generalization may be the coyote's original sin as far as man is concerned.

Of several personal experiences with wild coyotes, one especially stands out as indicative of high intelligence in the species. This concerns an animal I released from a trap. When I first approached, it growled and snapped, so I retreated and changed my behavior. Instead of being brusquely superior, the only creature able to save—actually the coyote had about gnawed its foot off and may have known perfectly well it would free itself—I became soft-spoken and slow, quiet and noncondescending in my second approach. Curiously, my own nervousness subsided together with the coyote's. The animal became meek and mild, its ears forward instead of back. It was gone on three legs the instant of release.

Two moonlit nights of yips and howls are with me still. I was the unwitting observer of family coyote hunts in the Texas shrub desert. Desert cottontails were the prey; three and five coyotes, the predators—both family groups. I saw no kill either time, but the widely spaced shrubs and the moon permitted me to see everything else. Yipping was communication, for when one coyote seemed to lose sight or scent of the quarry, it yipped, bringing another into the proximity of the chase. Once a rabbit and its pursuer ran within a few feet of me. I sat perfectly still, transfixed by my good fortune. Relays and the ambush learned by man were never more evident than in the behavior of those native predators.

One hundred years ago, naturalists discoursed on coyote cunning, and in 1905 Vernon Bailey stated succinctly what men already knew: "In spite of the enmity of man, in spite of traps, poison, gun, and dogs, the coyote over most of his old range fairly holds his own." Writing again in 1931, Bailey reinforced the appraisal: "After many years of persistent hunting . . . and of the constant warfare of stockmen and ranchers who never miss an opportunity to kill a coyote, the numbers in most localities are apparently as great today as they were in 1889 . . . ."[5] In full view of the evidence, then, man's blind intolerance leads him to continue to kill coyotes with the same old indiscriminant methods, constantly and consistently selecting for intelligence in this species.

After a century of wasted money and effort, I hope we finally will learn to use the coyote's intelligence to eliminate its threat of predation on livestock. I hope we will employ aversive conditioning.[6] With this technique meat is treated with a sublethal dose of poison like lithium chloride. Then it is like eating in the "wrong restaurant." The scavenging coyote becomes ill, vomits, and with only one or two experiences learns to refuse lamb or beef through olfactory cues peculiar to the meat and the associated experience of illness. Of course, livestock must be sacrificed to provide bait, but the loss of a few head is preferable to losing dozens. Too, we must resist the temptation to kill with a lethal dose of the poison, for an experienced coyote may teach its offspring to avoid the kind of meat that made it sick, but a dead coyote will only teach man about his intolerance.

The gray wolf has not fared so well as the coyote in its relations with the arch predator. Less nocturnal perhaps, certainly more gregarious in forming large packs and more wide-ranging, some three times larger than the coyote, this specialized predator of grazing animals is

[5] E. C. Coues and H. C. Yarrow, "Report upon the Collections of Mammals Made in Portions of Nevada, Utah, California, Colorado, New Mexico, and Arizona during the Years 1871, 1872, 1873, and 1874," in *Report upon Geographical and Geological Explorations and Surveys West of the One Hundredth Meridian*, comp. G. M. Wheeler, vol. 5, pp. 35–128 (Washington, D.C., 1875); V. Bailey, *Biological Survey of Texas*, N. Amer. Fauna 25 (1905), p. 176; idem, *Mammals of New Mexico*, N. Amer. Fauna 53 (1931), p. 312.

[6] C. R. Gustavson, J. Garcia, W. G. Hankins, and K. W. Rusiniak, "Coyote Predation Control by Aversive Conditioning," *Science* 184 (1974):581–583; C. R. Gustavson, D. J. Kelly, and M. Sweeny, "Prey-lithium Aversions. 1:Coyotes and Wolves," *Behav. Biol.* 17 (1976):61–72.

Unnatural history: overgrazing on dark brown part of the hillside, Clanton Canyon, Arizona, in March.

Natural history: lightning-caused grass and woodland fire at night, Mustang Mountains, Arizona, June.

Left: Unnatural history: tire tracks in succulent desert south of Wellton, Arizona, in April. *Right*: Natural history: monsoon thunderstorm, Chiricahua Mountains, Arizona, August.

Left: Unnatural history: mine tailings and polluted creek near Clifton, Arizona, in June. *Right*: Natural history: unpolluted Sonoita Creek, south of Patagonia, Arizona, in April.

Left: Unnatural history: cultural desert, Boundary Monument 1, El Paso, Texas, in June. *Right*: Natural history: natural shrub desert at sunset, near Boundary Monument 198, Sonora. Sand dunes are ripple-marked by wind.

both more destructive to cattle and an easier target. Gray wolves were eliminated from the United States Borderlands, except Arizona, by the 1940's. New Mexico is a case in point: widespread wolves in the late 1800's, perhaps 100 in the entire state in 1917, and no more than 45 the year after. Stragglers continue to show up, particularly in the New Mexico panhandle and the Big Bend of Texas, but they are hunted down relentlessly. It is no different in Mexico, where only about 50 remained in the late 1970's. Maybe the arch predator carries an extra weapon against *el lobo*, a special fear and hatred, the cultural inheritance of European ancestors who also knew the gray wolf.[7]

With wolves and coyotes about—large wild cats, too—even game animals are presumed unsafe. Game, of course, includes those birds and mammals that make good targets because they are large and numerous yet noncompetitive with man and tolerant of his unnatural landscapes. Though he understood the scientific and aesthetic value of all native animals, Vernon Bailey spoke of areas infested with wolves, keeping cougars under control, menaces to game, and similar things.[8] This was but a sign of the historic era of intolerance and extirpation that followed the prehistoric era of slaughter and extinction in the Borderlands.

There is evidence from Arizona that gray wolves have persisted, perhaps adapted to man, by becoming more secretive. Several are reported from the Huachuca and Catalina mountains in the 1940's and 1950's, including a 1942 den with six pups. Active dens were located in the Catalinas and Empire Mountains in 1970, and a small pack may operate in the Galiuro Mountains in the early 1970's.[9] Wolves could simply exist in severely reduced numbers and be overlooked, but I doubt it. The Galiuro pack seems not to vocalize or raid livestock, and I cannot obtain solid evidence of howls or raids along the fabled wolf run, the Canelo Hills. Yet I see what I think are wolf footprints in 1971.

[7] Bailey, *Mammals of New Mexico*, p. 307; J. F. Scudday, "Two Recent Records of Gray Wolves in West Texas," *J. Mammal*. 53 (1972):598. An exposition of the European cultural inheritance of fear and domination of nature is in R. Nash, *Wilderness and the American Mind* (New Haven: Yale Univ. Press, 1967).

[8] For example, Bailey, *Mammals of New Mexico*, pp. 217, 306, 311–312.

[9] D. F. Hoffmeister and W. W. Goodpaster, *The Mammals of the Huachuca Mountains, Southeastern Arizona*, Illinois Biol. Monogr. 24 (1954); K. I. Lange, "Mammals of the Santa Catalina Mountains, Arizona," *Amer. Midl. Natur*. 64 (1960):436–458; Raymond P. Davis, personal communication (1971).

Maybe it is just wishful thinking, but a few wolves may have learned that secrecy is one way to survive.

When aborigines switched from hunting giant bison to modern bison, the dire wolves and great cats of the last glaciopluvial were extinct. Perhaps man knew specialized feline predators of the giant grazing mammals, species like the giant lion, one of the last to disappear. Its terminal dates coincide with the wave of megafaunal extinction ten to twelve thousand years ago. Could overkill indirectly cause extinction of this species by eliminating its food supply? Why is the modern jaguar so much smaller and a general predator of vertebrates from fish to mammals? Is it adapted to coexistence with aboriginal man, the foremost predator of the largest mammals? Coexisting carnivores usually differ in body size and size of prey they select.[10]

The jaguar was never common in the Borderlands in historic time. I find only thirty specimen records between Boundary-survey days and 1905, no skins or skulls from New Mexico after that, and only one more from Texas in 1946. In Arizona, however, thirty-six jaguars have been reported killed since 1905, half of them before 1920, but one as recently as 1971. Thus, jaguars are increasingly scarce but persistent on the U.S. side of the Border. A similar situation exists in the Mexican Borderlands with no more than six specimen records in Tamaulipas, Sonora, and Baja California.[11]

I believe that jaguars are mere wanderers in and out of the last

[10] M. L. Rosenzweig, "Community Structure in Sympatric Carnivora," *J. Mammal.* 47 (1966):602–612.

[11] Jaguar records for the United States are from Bailey, *Biological Survey of Texas*; idem, *Mammals of New Mexico*; R. J. Hock, "Southwestern Exotic Felids," *Amer. Midl. Natur.* 53 (1955):324–328; K. I. Lange, "The Jaguar in Arizona," *Trans. Kansas Acad. Sci.* 63 (1960):96–101; and W. P. Taylor, "Recent Record of the Jaguar in Texas," *J. Mammal.* 28 (1947):66. For Mexico I use T. Alvarez, "The Recent Mammals of Tamaulipas, Mexico," *Univ. Kansas Publs. Mus. Nat. Hist.* 14 (1963):363–473; S. Anderson, *Mammals of Chihuahua: Taxonomy and Distribution*, Bull. Amer. Mus. Nat. Hist. 148 (1972); R. H. Baker, "Mammals of Coahuila," *Univ. Kansas Publs. Mus. Nat. Hist.* 9 (1956): 125–335; W. G. Burt, *Faunal Relationships and Geographic Distribution of Mammals in Sonora, Mexico*, Misc. Publ. Mus. Zool. Univ. Michigan 39 (1938); and A. S. Leopold, *Wildlife of Mexico: The Game Birds and Mammals* (Berkeley and Los Angeles: Univ. California Press, 1959). I cannot accept sightings and some recent records, since I have seen immature, spotted cougars called jaguars and also suspect that Mexican jaguars have been released in the United States for hunting purposes.

century of Borderlands history; I doubt their residency. Their rarity suggests this, as do a sex ratio heavily weighted toward males and an apparent lack of dens with cubs. Most Borderlands jaguars are not only males but old ones, presumably driven out of territories deep in Mexico and given to wandering. The few California and Baja California records substantiate long movements. One old male must have traveled over 500 miles from Sonora, across the Sonoran desert region, and nearly a quarter of the distance down the peninsula of Baja California. The vagrancy thesis is widespread among *ganaderos*, Mexican cattlemen, who quickly track and kill such individuals.

Jaguars suffer double jeopardy in Mexico. The demand for food by the exploding population means that livestock is at a premium. And when a stock killer's spotted hide can be sold in the fur market for a price that buys a dozen or more range cows, the hunting of *el tigre* becomes an even more valuable activity. Between 1968 and 1970 the average annual decline of Mexican jaguars was 36 percent, judging from skins received in the United States fur market.[12] Obviously, *mexicanos* hunt jaguars without thought of sustained yield.

By making some assumptions and using data on the jaguar's known and inferred life history, I can construct a simple model of its impending extirpation in Mexico. Thus, if there are a thousand animals in 1970 and no immigration, two-thirds are sexually mature, half females each averaging 1.8 cubs every 2.2 years, 3.0 years from birth to reproductive maturity, 25 percent annual natural mortality of cubs, 5 percent annual natural mortality of adults plus senility, and 36 percent annual mortality from hunting and habitat destruction, I predict A.D. 1991 as the year of the last jaguar. To achieve a stable population, unnatural mortality cannot exceed 17 percent.[13]

Cougars have always been more abundant than jaguars in the Bor-

---

[12] N. Myers, "The Spotted Cats and the Fur Trade," in *The World's Cats*, vol. 1, ed. R. L. Eaton, pp. 276–326 (Winston, Oreg.: World Wildl. Safari Publ., 1973). Throughout Latin America, 1968–1970, the annual overkill of jaguars averaged 23 percent.

[13] The estimate of 1,000 jaguars is from C. B. Koford, "Status Survey of Jaguar and Ocelot in Tropical America," in *World Wildlife Yearbook*, ed. P. Jackson, pp. 215–217 (Morgan, Switzerland: IUCN, 1973). Present population models employ matrix algebra (eigenvalue = 1 for stability): $0.3075y^2 = 1 - 0.95x$, where y = the survival rate of juveniles and x of adults. Of course the models are overly simplistic, because nothing is known of age, sex, and density-specific mortalities. See also R. S. Miller and D. B. Botkin, "Endangered Species: Models and Prediction," *Amer. Sci.* 62 (1974): 172–181.

derlands. No one disputes their residency. They too are rigorously persecuted but, unlike *el tigre*, furnished real varmint-killer satisfaction in the first half of this century. Between 1915 and 1941, for example, the annual Federal "control" kill averaged 14 in Texas, 36 in New Mexico, and 82 is Arizona. Today the situation is different, as annual control becomes annual overkill, despite the cat's status as game animal except in Texas, and rises to perhaps 100 cats a year in New Mexico alone. Is the cougar in trouble?

Around 2,300 cougars live in the four U.S. Border states, but I judge no more than a fifth of these inhabit the Borderlands proper, including Mexico.[14] Cougar life history is like jaguar life history, so I can model the 460 cougars using jaguar-style assumptions. If I apply the current estimate of human impact in New Mexico (29 percent), the highest I know of, cougars decline at a rate of 18 percent per year. The population stabilizes only if man-induced mortality drops to 17 percent annually—the jaguar lesson. Though declared a game animal, the cougar remains a varmint in the mind of the arch predator, who does not plan his cat hunting with cat population dynamics in mind.

Resident cougars range more widely than resident jaguars, occupying almost all wild landscapes with deer, from mountain peaks to desert basins. They are habitat generalists and food specialists, the opposite of jaguars, which is probably why the two coexist over a third of the Western Hemisphere. The ranging ability and broad environmental tolerances of cougars, plus their love of deer meat, a food cultivated by man, facilitates natural stocking of depleted cougar country. Similarly, immigrant jaguars could restock wild terrain but are not at home in high mountains, and females are not wanderers like the dispossessed males. Jaguars are provincial lowland animals like man, and this compounds their endangerment through competition for space as well as livestock.

The big cats must learn to be a bit quieter around man. Of four personal experiences I have had with them, half involved the cats' giving their presence away by vocalization, and the single jaguar incident

[14] Modern cougar numbers and mortality are from R. L. Eaton, "The Status, Management, and Conservation of the Cougar in the United States," in *The World's Cats*, vol. 1, pp. 61–86. Historical data are in Bailey, *Mammals of New Mexico*, p. 288; and S. P. Young, *The Puma, Mysterious American Cat*, pt. 1 (Washington, D.C.: Amer. Wildl. Inst., 1946), pp. 15–36.

caused its death. I heard this cat's coughing roar several times, but the tropical forest had given me malaria along with the jaguar, and I could not join *campesinos* in the ensuing hunt. I saw only the cat's carcass and gained only a sad memory of that particular tropical forest. Another time Nancy and I were camped at the Border near Quitobaquito Spring in Organ Pipe Cactus National Monument, southwest Arizona. Soon after dark a cougar surprised three feral burros at the spring, missed a kill, and gave us a minute's worth of bloodcurdling screams. Then the burros provided hours of hee-hawing, the Border Patrol several checks, and around that night's experience we got very little sleep.

To this day Nancy has not seen a cougar, though several have seen her, judging from fresh tracks and scat found later. Without dogs to expose it, a quiet cougar is seen only by chance. My own score is one good observation in twenty-six years. That was at a fresh deer kill, cached in upper Carr Canyon, Huachuca Mountains, Arizona, a place where cougars had been killed by sport hunters using dogs. Yet others had taken their place, because ribbons of evergreen woodland offer secluded travel connections between mountain islands in the region, and the montane fastness affords some refuge from the arch predator. That meeting was twenty years ago, and I often consider whether my chances of another restful scene, a cougar at her meal, decrease in direct proportion to the burgeoning human population in and around the Huachucas.

One carnivore travels alone in time and space, the last of the Pleistocene giants, the largest in North America. It fears no living thing. This is its undoing. Unless any large animal learns to avoid the arch predator, its future is uncertain. But it is difficult to be secretive when one weighs up to 500 pounds and lives in the open plains and woodlands—in short, when one is a grizzly bear. And it is difficult to avoid men who leave cows behind fences. In ten thousand years the wild dogs and cats learned to run and hide, but not the grizzly. Interspecific aggression, particularly with man, elicits flight except in *el oso plateado*.

The coyote is furtive by nature around larger predators, hence preadapted for avoiding man. The wild cats are secretive and solitary, hence provided with a modicum of advantage. But, except for the last hundred years of Borderlands history, an adult grizzly has had nothing

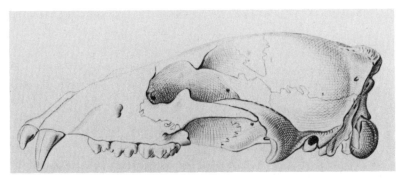

Grizzly Bear Skull (Emory)

to fear except a stronger grizzly. Not even aborigines preempted the grizzly's place in the ecological theater, so the great bear's genes are almost totally unfit in unnatural landscapes today. This species is biologically defenseless against our intolerance of native predators and can survive only if left strictly alone in a large, natural preserve. The Borderlands grizzly, a distinctively small subspecies, is the ultimate test of an era of knowledge and appreciation.

Boundary surveyors knew the grizzly well in the New Mexico panhandle between 1851 and 1855. Grizzlies must have been frequent if not abundant in the Sierra de San Luis and Peloncillo-Guadalupe Cordillera. A family group, presumably a sow with cubs, was killed by the surveyors in the Animas Valley or on an adjacent slope of the Sierra de San Luis in October, 1855. Grizzlies persisted in this area during the 1890's but were already rare. They remained more common elsewhere in the northern Sierra Madre Occidental; yet the species' Border range collapsed southward in the twentieth century, leaving about ten individuals in the isolated Sierra del Nido of Chihuahua until 1973 and perhaps a couple of dozen in the Sierran watershed of the Río Yaqui, Sonora. These last are the pitiful remnant of a once commanding species.

Grizzlies were abundant on the Mogollon Rim of western New Mexico and adjacent Arizona at the turn of the century but were reduced to an estimated forty-eight by 1917 in New Mexico and extirpated in both border states in the 1930's. The species' tragedy in California is especially painful, because Californians adopted the bear as the state's official emblem and then exterminated it by the mid-1920's.

Texans never had more than one documented grizzly, an old male, undoubtedly a vagrant, killed in the Davis Mountains in 1890. Sight records are lacking in Texas, and I question the status of grizzlies in adjacent Coahuila. I do not have evidence of a breeding population east of the Sierra del Nido in Mexico or the Rio Grande in southern New Mexico.[15]

The grizzly bear's large size, usually solitary behavior, and preference for open country should make family groups quite conspicuous in the eastern Borderlands. But there is no such evidence of permanent residency there or in the Chihuahuan and Sonoran desert regions generally. Unless I know of females with young or immatures without signs of captivity, I am disinclined to admit any species to any landscape except on a vagrancy charge. And to distinguish between residency and vagrancy is critical to the conservation of any large, mobile predator; for no preserve can contain a wandering grizzly bear, cougar, or jaguar capable of traveling several hundred miles.

Large preserves may harbor predators that raid surrounding ranches, as I first learned in the case of coyotes along the lower Rio Grande. Perhaps individual predators learn where easily caught stock lives and where it is safe to retire for a leisurely meal—behind refuge signs. Historically, in fact, grizzlies were said to roam out of the Sierra Madre in Chihuahua and Sonora to feed on cattle carcasses.[16] So before

[15] Grizzly bear records are from the state mammal works cited above, plus S. F. Baird, "Mammals of the Boundary," in W. H. Emory, *Report on the United States and Mexican Boundary Survey*, vol. 2, pt. 2, 34th Cong., 1st sess., 1859, House Exec. Doc. 135, pp. 24–29; E. L. Cockrum, *The Recent Mammals of Arizona* (Tucson: Univ. Arizona Press, 1960); J. S. Findley, A. H. Harris, D. E. Wilson, and C. Jones, *Mammals of New Mexico* (Albuquerque: Univ. New Mexico Press, 1975); E. A. Mearns, *Mammals of the Mexican Boundary of the United States*, U.S. Natl. Mus. Bull. 56 (1907); A. S. Leopold, "Grizzlies of the Sierra del Nido," *Pacif. Disc.* 20 (1967):30–32; and B. Villa-R., "Major Game Mammals and Their Habitats in the Chihuahuan Desert Region," in *Symposium on the Biological Resources of the Chihuahuan Desert Region, United States and Mexico*, ed. R. H. Wauer and D. H. Riskind, pp. 155–162, U.S.D.I., Natl. Park Serv. Trans. and Proc. Ser. 3 (1977). These references imply that the species was absent or a vagrant only in most Borderlands mountains. See also A. M. Gustafson, *John Spring's Arizona* (Tucson: Univ. Arizona Press, 1966), p. 302. The scarcity of fossil grizzlies in Texas and Coahuila (one or two records each) substantiates my hypothesis of vagrancy (see W. S. Dalquest, E. Roth, and F. Judd, "The Mammal Fauna of Schultze Cave, Edwards County, Texas," *Bull. Florida St. Mus.* 13 [1969]:205–276; W. W. Dalquest, "Mammals of North-central Texas," *Southwest. Natur.* 13 [1968]:13–21).

[16] Anderson, *Mammals of Chihuahua*, p. 378.

we can seriously consider saving the remnant grizzlies of Sonora, we must be prepared to pay the price of livestock killed by vagrants in a buffer zone of ranchland as large or larger than the preserve itself.

The last grizzlies are too few for experiments in aversive conditioning, too scarce to be sacrificed in any manner. Killing or displacing more than four culprit bears annually will extinguish the population quickly if, indeed, only two or three dozen remain. About this number were eliminated from the Sierra del Nido between the time of their rediscovery in the mid-1950's and 1973, when no more could be found. The overkill, estimated to be about 30 percent annually, occurred even though the grizzly became fully protected by law in 1959.

A simple model predicts the rate of overkill. My assumptions are: no change in available habitat, thirty-six bears to begin with, 64 percent adults, half females averaging 1.8 cubs every 3.2 years, 5.0 years from birth to reproductive maturity, 25 percent annual natural mortality of yearlings, and 5 percent annual natural mortality of adults plus senility.[17] The small grizzly population stabilizes with 9 percent annual unnatural mortality. Any greater impact equals overkill and eventual extinction. The remaining grizzlies in Sonora give man a chance to see if he can live with any other superpredator, and I hope to visit the upper Río Yaqui a decade or two hence to gauge our compatibility.

If I cannot find a grizzly in the 1980's, perhaps I will see a black bear in grizzly habitat, for removal of the dominant grizzly may release the black bear from forested mountains to roam more widely in the open country below. Today, however, the two bears furnish evidence that two closely related predators with similar food habits do not often coexist. Both omnivorous, they are spatially segregated, the black in closed-canopy forests, the grizzly in open-canopy woodlands. I can predict release of the black following extinction of the grizzly by analogy with expansion of the coyote after removal of gray wolves and timber in the Sierra Madre.[18] Man's seemingly simple landscape alterations can have such manifold consequences.

---

[17] Background data for the grizzly bear model are from G. F. Cole, *Management Involving Grizzly and Black Bears in Yellowstone National Park 1970–75*, U.S. Natl. Park Serv. Natur. Res. Rept. 9 (1976); and C. J. Martinka, "Population Characteristics of Grizzly Bears in Glacier National Park, Montana," *J. Mammal*. 55 (1974):21–29. The model is like that for large cats, except that $0.225y^4 = 1 - 0.95x$.

[18] Leopold, *Wildlife of Mexico*, p. 396.

Black bears may also provide a test of compatibility with man. They are large and solitary but secretive, unlike grizzlies. Among the modern array of large carnivores, *el oso negro* is least likely to become a stock or game killer by virtue of its behavior and food habits. The arch predator should have little quarrel with this species unless his image of another "devil's agent" evokes that old intolerance-extirpation syndrome. Presently, no more than a few dozen black bears live in the New Mexico–Arizona borderlands, usually in mountains above 7,000 feet. In Texas the species is gone; in Mexico it has been removed from large areas and is declining in others.

Without protection no large predator can survive, and this is nicely demonstrated by the black bear. Legal protection was not afforded in Texas until too late. The species was extirpated as a breeding population about 1960, although vagrants still come south from New Mexico along the Sacramento-Guadalupe upland corridor and could reestablish residency in Guadalupe Mountains National Park. I think that two or three ranch families are responsible for the Guadalupe overkill, which I estimate as twenty-four bears between 1945 and 1960. An annual fall hunt took ten black bears in 1900 and four in 1902 in the Davis Mountains. Though the effect of such organized activity is conjectural, the species disappeared from the Davis Mountains in 1940, two decades earlier than in the Guadalupes.[19]

Possibly black bears persist in the western Borderlands because there are more, higher mountains there and because of a cultural refutation of my hypothesis of competitive release. With removal of the grizzly, black bear populations should expand into bearless territory— into greater proximity with man—but they do not. Instead, I think they treat man as they would a grizzly bear—as a superior protagonist. I believe the arch predator is selecting for avoidsmanship in the black bear by continual persecution or by reinforcing such behavior inherited from ancestral black bears in the millenia of coexistence with and avoidance of grizzlies.

To view a fellow creature on the eve of its extinction is to realize the full destructive power of the arch predator—aboriginal or tech-

[19] Bailey, *Biological Survey of Texas*, p. 188. I am uncertain when black bears ceased to reproduce in the Guadalupe Mountains, Texas, but the last evidence I found was a small cub in June, 1960.

nological. Even now that he has learned better, it seems unlikely that constructive behavior will counter the millenia of indirect and direct attack on certain creatures. Once reduced to thirty to forty individuals, a large species with a slow reproductive rate may not acquire the genetic capacity to adjust to man's fast-changing landscapes. Inadequate time is as much a problem as the instability of space, and captive breeding programs cannot replace natural history in selecting fit individuals for survival in the wild.

In August, 1977, I watched at a requiem. Five California condors flew overhead on Mount Pinos, California—four adults and one youngster. They represented about an eighth of their declining species. Two decades earlier, these giant scavengers numbered perhaps sixty to seventy. Before that who really knows? They nested in the Chisos Mountains, Texas, only 1,500 to 3,000 years ago. Within historic time they graced Arizona skies, chiefly between 1865 and 1885, but as late as the 1920's.[20] Now the great game herds and unfenced ranges of their pluvial age have vanished, and the condors have retreated into southern California.

Could these thunderbirds have persisted through the nineteenth century because of man's uncontrolled livestock? As the largest birds of our continent, they are equipped to forage dead mammoths and bison, or their horse and beef replacements—large beasts of open spaces—not road-killed rabbits and snakes in the manner of their turkey vulture cousins. Indirectly, then, condors have suffered by the hand of primitive man. Directly, they are shot, poisoned, and simply frightened away from their nesting caves and ledges in what were remote mountains but have become every man's grab for grazing, lumbering, drilling, and hunting privileges.

I had an unsettled feeling, as I watched those splendid birds with their nine-foot wingspans, wheeling, effortlessly riding the midday singing winds. Golden eagles looked like pygmies beside them. A red-tailed hawk was a flea. Guns boomed, for this was hunting season. Would frustrated deer hunters potshot the birds? Some crippled and unfound deer would be left to the condors, no doubt, as the birds come

---

[20] A. Wetmore and H. Friedman, "The California Condor in Texas," *Condor* 35 (1933): 37–38; A. Phillips, J. Marshall, and G. Monson, *The Birds of Arizona* (Tucson: Univ. Arizona Press, 1964), p. 19. For recent status, see S. R. Wilbur, *The California Condor 1966–1976: A Look at Its Past and Future*, N. Amer. Fauna 72 (1978).

and go with the deer season on Mount Pinos.[21] Younger predators, left behind in the campground, were shooting smaller game. Wisely perhaps, Forest Service rangers were somewhere else. My dishpan held no water when I returned that night. It was full of holes.

[21] D. VanVuren, "California Condor Behavior near Mount Pinos, California," *Southwest. Natur.* 24 (1979): 190–191.

6. *The Landmark*

"The road was quite tortuous, winding among and over hills, in a direction nearly west, towards the bold head of the great Guadalupe Mountains, which had been before us some eight or ten days. This is a most remarkable landmark, rising as it does far above all other objects, and terminating abruptly about three thousand feet above the surrounding plain." Thus John Bartlett approached the Guadalupe Mountains, Texas, in 1850.[1] Now, over a century later, man has so compressed time and space that he first glimpses the Guadalupes only a few hours away. As I travel westward across the High Plains I cannot use the Guadalupe peaks to guide me. I move too fast. Still I search the horizon. I always thrill at the first, low purple line above creosote bush and try to imagine Bartlett's five-day journey from the Pecos River to the mountains.

Railroad advertisements used to feature El Capitan, the southern, slightly isolated peak in the Guadalupe line. And Texas always boasts of Guadalupe Peak, at 8,700 feet the highest in a state notably deficient in high mountains. I fully expected to see an Irish green landmark, as I first approached the Guadalupes in 1954, but I had failed to study the ad carefully. The Guadalupes are not forested except in deep canyons or protected mountaintop places. Instead, they are glaringly bare, especially after midsummer downpours, when the limestone crevices and ledges glisten in the sun. And they are startlingly deficient in one large mammal of the ledges, *borrego cimarrón*, the bighorn sheep, a species I can no longer find there.

> While sweeping the slopes with the glass one evening near our camp in one of the big canyons opening into the Guadalupe Mountains, I located

[1]J. R. Bartlett, *Personal Narrative of the Explorations and Incidents in Texas, New Mexico, California, Sonora, and Chihuahua, Connected with the United States and Mexican Boundary Commission during the Years 1850, '51, '52, and '53*, vol. 1 (New York: D. Appleton and Co., 1854), p. 117.

El Capitan, Guadalupe Mountains (Bartlett)

three sheep halfway up the face of the rocky slope 1,000 feet above me. To the unaided eye they were invisible among the ledges and broken rocks, whose colors they matched to perfection, but through the glass they were conspicuous as they moved about feeding and climbing over the rocks. There were an old ram, a young ram, and a ewe. It was too near dark to make the long roundabout climb necessary to reach them, so I returned to camp and early the following morning started my camp man up the slope to the spot, while I went back up the canyon to get beyond them if they should run up the ridge. As I swept the slopes with the glass I heard a shot up where the sheep had been the evening before and soon located the hunter, watched him shoot two of them, while three others which were above climbed the cliff and finally disappeared over the crest of the canyon wall.[2]

Vernon Bailey, who narrates this incident, is prophetic: "It is with some hesitation that I make public these facts as to the abundance, distribution, and habits of mountain sheep in western Texas, and only in the

[2] V. Bailey, *Biological Survey of Texas*, N. Amer. Fauna 25 (1905), p. 71. Bailey's published account does not implicate him in the shooting, but his unpublished field notes for August 31, 1902, say he instructed McClure Surber to collect the animals.

hope that full knowledge of the conditions and the importance of protective measures may result in the salvation instead of extermination of the species. It would not be difficult for a single persistent hunter to kill every mountain sheep in western Texas if unrestrained. Not only should the animals be protected by law, but the law should be made effective by an appreciation on the part of residents of the country of the importance of preserving for all time these splendid animals."[3] Edgar Mearns expresses the same belief: "The opinion is general among white settlers along the Mexican border that in that region the bighorn is doomed to extinction at an early period."[4]

At the time of Bailey's visit in the Guadalupes in 1902, bighorns probably numbered around 300. By 1928 Bailey estimated 100 head, by 1940 they were down to 25, and the last one was seen about 1950. Soon after Bailey's first visit a group of hunters herded a band of 20 against ledges and killed all but 2. Yet hunters cannot be blamed entirely. Nor can natural predators be held responsible, since bighorns thrived when cougars hurt the Guadalupe horse raisers and did not decline until after cougars were "controlled" by the growing livestock industry. Competition with domestic sheep and goats, plus transmission of disease from these animals must be implicated. William Davis and Walter Taylor graphed the number of domestic sheep against bighorns in each of the trans-Pecos, Texas, counties in the 1930's. Where domestics numbered 60,000, bighorns numbered less than 25; where 10,000 or less, bighorns reached their greatest concentrations.[5]

Bighorn sheep are wilderness animals, as were Nancy and I in that Guadalupe summer of 1960 when we looked for them in vain. We had been in McKittrick Canyon two weeks without seeing either the sheep or other men. Wallace Pratt had just donated five sections of land to the U.S. National Park Service, and we were studying its biotic diversity as background for a potential park. Then one afternoon our reverie

[3] Ibid., p. 75.

[4] E. A. Mearns, *Mammals of the Mexican Boundary of the United States*, U.S. Natl. Mus. Bull. 56 (1907), p. 238.

[5] V. Bailey, *Mammals of New Mexico*, N. Amer. Fauna 53 (1931), p. 19; W. B. Davis and W. P. Taylor, "The Bighorn Sheep of Texas," *J. Mammal.* 20 (1939):440–455. See also J. E. Gross, "History, Present, and Future Status of the Desert Bighorn Sheep (*Ovis canadensis mexicana*) in the Guadalupe Mountains of Southeastern New Mexico and Southwestern Texas," *Trans. Desert Bighorn Council* 4 (1960):66–71.

was broken by the sound of a vehicle. A jeep came chugging up the dry streambed. Three oil-company geologists got out and began surveying for a drilling site at the mouth of McKittrick. For us then, as for *el borrego* a decade earlier, the Guadalupe wilderness vanished forever.

My field studies on the landmark concerned the identification and dynamics of its natural communities. I placed 183 transects at random along twenty miles of its eastern front including six major canyons. Each transect was a line, up to 600 feet in length, divided into points 50 feet apart. Each point was subdivided into quarters by extending another measuring tape at right angles to the transect tape. Quarters became study plots in which I measured grasses, forbs, and woody plants of shrub and tree stature. The assay included vertebrates, too— mammals, birds, and reptiles. I wanted to discover the relative togetherness of plant and animal species for purposes of community delineation.[6]

Lizards give some interesting answers. When species occurrences are plotted against vegetation types, only the side-blotched lizard, Texas horned lizard, and little-striped whiptail reach maximum abundances in the shrub desert. Conversely, the round-tailed horned lizard, checkered whiptail, and greater earless lizard are most common in succulent desert. Species within each group are most frequently associated, so if I find a side-blotched lizard I can expect to turn around and find a Texas horned lizard under a creosote bush, not a round-tailed horned lizard under a lechuguilla agave. Clearly, the six lizards segregate into two groups that support the recognition of two different desert communities.

Because most lizards of the Guadalupes bask to elevate their body temperatures to normal activity levels, they require sunlight. And because shrubs are larger and trees are added with increasing elevation and moisture, the amount of sunlit space diminishes, and lizards become less numerous. So it isn't strange that local woodlands and the coniferous forest lack specific lizard indicators, although I do find that

[6] F. R. Gehlbach, "Biomes of the Guadalupe Escarpment: Vegetation, Lizards, and Human Impact," in *Biological Investigations in the Guadalupe Mountains National Park, Texas*, ed. H. H. Genoways and R. J. Baker, pp. 427–439, U.S.D.I., Natl. Park Serv. Trans. and Proc. Ser. 4 (1979).

Great Plains Skink (Emory)

the Chihuahua whiptail, Great Plains skink, and many-lined skink are reasonably good indicators of woodland in general.

The Great Plains skink, centered in deciduous woodland, is more dry-adapted than the many-lined, hence located more often at lower elevations and in sparser vegetation. Although both skinks are secretive, burrowing in leaf litter, the Great Plains species, averaging four inches in adult body length, is nearly twice the size of the many-lined. Perhaps it is twice as likely to be noticed by visitors to national parks. Is it twice as useful in natural history interpretation, therefore?

I think that large size, frequent association with other lizards, and spatial focus in a certain vegetation type are elements of lizard lifestyle important to man in learning landscape patterns. Size and daytime, above-ground activity contribute to such utility, for a species is then more conspicuous to us. If more than one species can be counted on in a certain desert or woodland, our recognition of that community is enhanced. And when communities are recognized by using both plants and animals, we begin to understand that they are integrated components of the living landscape.

The Great Plains skink turns out to be only moderately useful. It is large and indicative of deciduous woodland but secretive and lacks strong ties with other lizards. A utility value—a measure of its usefulness in identifying communities—can be obtained for this or other lizards by multiplying average adult size times a value for behavior—higher if more conspicuous—by number of species associations and halving this final product if the species' distribution is not centered in a certain vegetation type. This procedure ranks the Great Plains skink seventh among fourteen lizards. By contrast, the similarly large, checkered whiptail forages in full view and is closely associated with two other lizards in succulent desert. It ranks fifth.

Park visitors are not the only people confronted with community identity problems. Park managers must recognize the kinds and degrees of community change or secondary succession arising from human impact if nature is to be managed in keeping with their dictum, "unimpaired for future generations." The basic successional pattern of increasing variety of species and dominance by more species over time applies to both plants and lizards of the Guadalupes, but lizards seem less affected by man's disturbances. Unlike plants, no purely pioneering lizards precede others of the climax community. On a sewer-line construction scar in succulent desert, grasses lead the reestablishment of vegetation, while the checkered whiptail and greater earless lizard prevail throughout.

How much faunal change is apparent to either park visitor or manager? Can a quantitative measure of succession be used to indicate a visible return to climax conditions, following some interlude of unnatural history? I think so and have suggested a way to use the utility indices of all species in a community, comparing an appropriate climax model with the successional situation at hand. For lizards on the sewer-line scar, for example, I found that 74 percent of the presumed climax condition returned in the four years following construction.

Of all sites on the landmark, McKittrick Canyon must have the greatest biotic and geologic diversity. This major cleft in the eastern escarpment is 1,800 feet deep and supports a perennial stream that cements its course by depositing travertine, hence preserving surface flow, a magenta display of cardinal flowers in midsummer, and the orange wood lily at its southernmost station in North America. The watercourse is a puzzle, for there are no native fishes or turtles in it, although the rich Pecos River fauna is close at hand. Probably the stream never ran to the Pecos or even to nearby Delaware Creek. It is only about a million years old and should require at least another millennium to cut its way to an eastern rendezvous.

Above the stream at the canyon forks are opposing north- and south-facing slopes, living museums of contrast like the stream itself and what it might become. The north-facing slope supports evergreen woodland, dominated by gray oak and alligator juniper. The hotter, drier south-facing slope is covered by succulent desert and a desert-woodland continuum. Old streambeds or terraces left stranded above the downcutting creek also display a continuum. Below the forks the warm-dry-adapted gray oak replaces the cool-wet chinkapin oak, an eastern relict at its western edge of range. Red-berry juniper from the High Plains begins to mingle with one-seed juniper and alligator juniper. McKittrick is wider and its stream terrace sites receive longer periods of sunlight downstream.

The terrace woodland is mostly deciduous, painted by red bigtooth maples, yellow chinkapin oaks, and green Texas madrones with bright red berries in November. This species of madrone is my favorite plant. No other can match its white spike of fragrant April blossoms, its pinkish bark peeling to smooth white, its glossy evergreen leaves, and its picturesque countenance. McKittrick's madrones are the finest I know of in the Borderlands, but their future is in jeopardy. They are being girdled, eaten alive by an overly large mule deer herd. They are not reproducing from seed, either, although plenty of berries feed plenty of band-tailed pigeons in wet years. Are there not enough wet years?

The tree layer of the deciduous and evergreen woodlands shades a shrub layer composed largely of skunk-bush but with evergreen sumac, sacahuista, Mexican orange, and other species that add foliage diversity. A ground layer rich in grasses like bull muhly, pinyon rice grass, and side-oats grama contributes to the diversity of living space for animals. I have never discovered another canyon quite like McKittrick, where I record up to thirty-two nesting birds in fifteen-acre plots on the stream terraces and lower-slope woodlands—2.1 species per acre. In other big canyons of the western Borderlands, I find no more than 1.9 species per acre. Undoubtedly, resource heterogeneity afforded by the vegetation determines McKittrick's singular variety of birds.

My 1960–1969 bird study can be compared with George Newman's in the same area of McKittrick in 1972–1974.[7] We each averaged

[7]G. A. Newman, "Compositional Aspects of Breeding Avifaunas in Selected Woodlands of the Southern Guadalupe Mountains, Texas," in *Biological Investigations in the Guadalupe Mountains*, pp. 181–237. Species similarity is $2C/(A+B) \times 100$, where A and B are the number of breeding species in my plots and Newman's, respectively, and C is the number in common. Species diversity ($H' = -\Sigma p_i \times \log_2 p_i$) is calculated using

twenty-eight breeding species, but five I found nesting were not present in the 1970's, when four new species appeared. Of the forty-four species documented altogether, only twenty were present in each census year. Mean species similarity was but 67 percent, yet individual birds remained about equally abundant over the fourteen-year interval. My fifteen-acre plots averaged five adult birds per acre, and Newman's twenty- to twenty-four-acre sites averaged six. Species diversity values (H') of the easily counted, territorial males were 4.75 in the 1960's and 4.70 in the 1970's, so aside from the particular species present the woodland avifauna remained relatively stable structurally.

Species flux must be expected in this canyon, as droughts and flash floods rearrange the landscape in manifold ways. For instance, in 1960 a pair of mountain chickadees fledged four young and did not nest again in that decade. Hairy woodpeckers and yellow-billed cuckoos pulled the same disappearing act. Grace's warblers nested in 1960, skipped 1965, and returned in 1969. Gray vireos declined from four pairs to one or none, while solitary vireos increased from one to six pairs. Similarly, western and hepatic tanagers exchanged places. Equally interesting was the sudden arrival of elf owls in 1968, which had not previously been found this far north in Texas.[8]

The vireos and tanagers exemplify the interplay of species variety and abundance in the face of climatic change. Consider that the 1950's were drought years and the 1960's relatively wet, following floods in 1957 and a dramatic climatic change. Also, consider that, while similar in nesting and feeding habits, the solitary vireo and western tanager are more wet-adapted than their congeners, the gray vireo and hepatic tanager. Then the play is easy enough to reconstruct. The environmental shift from a dry decade to a wet one favored the increase of solitaries and westerns and their competitive replacement of grays and hepatics, resulting in species flux but less change in overall density and diversity of the woodland avifauna.

mean number of territorial males per species (p_i) from two- to three-hour censuses at dawn in June on as many consecutive days as required to find no new species and no increases in individuals per species on fifteen-acre plots.

[8]R. K. LaVal reported elf owls in McKittrick Canyon (*Bull. Texas Ornithol. Soc.* [1969]:24). I first found them there in June, 1969. Cf. J. C. Barlow and R. Johnson, "Current Status of the Elf Owl in the Southwestern United States," *Southwest. Natur.* 12 (1967):331–332,

As I muse upon the nature of community stability, a whip-poor-will shadow flits across the front porch of a stone house in my memory. I think of the wisdom of Wallace Pratt, donor of the land, who wants to keep McKittrick Canyon forever as it is. Will the National Park Service keep the trust? Can the public behave the way the Apaches did a scant century ago—visit, perhaps disturb, but not destroy? Already I hear of plans to bus visitors in and out of this canyon. Last summer the landmark produced a flood that washed the canyon road out, and I know that will happen again and again until the creek joins the Pecos River. "For-tu-nate, for-tu-nate," sings that shadow in my mind.

Whip-poor-wills are nocturnal, but most birds, like most men, are visual creatures that conduct most of their activities in the daylight. We relate well to birds, therefore, and bird-watching has become our most popular nonconsumptive use of native faunal resources. We even seem to sing and dress like birds. And we fly, but not like birds, since we are committed to flying farther, faster, and higher and must trade what landscapes tell us for purely unnatural navigation. Except for a few glider enthusiasts, men forego the quiet soaring of the golden eagle and create thunder that tears apart canyon walls, adding a new dimension to their erosional competence. One day, as another commercial jetliner booms by, Nancy and I decide to walk down to the canyon mouth, to substitute the ringing of the canyon wren for the noise of the plane.

We pass an old camping spot and watch an eastern cottontail rabbit chase an eastern tiger swallowtail butterfly, or so it seems. Bull muhly is profuse in the disturbed area, for the early-day campers kicked apart their fires, scattered their rocks, and changed locations. It is like the mescal roasting pits of Apaches rather than abandoned ranch sites studded with mesquite. And it is not denuded ground like the oil-well drilling site turned parking lot. That scar is the result of pure avarice; Wallace Pratt had told the oilmen those strata did not hide oil or gas, but they had mineral rights to be exercised before the Park Service closed down the place.

A dark shape a yard long, sitting on a juniper snag, stares me in the eye as we round the last bend out of the creekbed. It is probably the same fledgling eagle we saw here yesterday—still hungry and wanting another bite from a dried-up old cow at the fence. It is late

August, and I suppose the youngster is on his own for the first time. Probably he isn't very successful at catching live things and is attracted to the skin-and-bones carcass from last winter. What would happen to him if *el macho* appeared—rancher in pickup truck with guns in rear window?

Earlier in the summer a local high school student studied a golden eagle's nest in Walnut Canyon, twenty miles to the north, and found the parent birds bringing rock squirrels and rabbits to feed their nestlings. Only one fawn bone was recorded and no livestock. Golden eagles do kill occasional lambs and kid goats, but their destructive influence on livestock is minimal in the Borderlands. In fact, 79 percent of their food consists of rabbits, rodents, and squirrels, the major competitors with livestock for forage grasses.[9] Mainly eagles are scapegoats for those with the varmint-hater hang-up, because they scavenge at winter-killed beef and coyote leavings and are varmintlike—big and "mean-lookin'."

Snakes, too, are "low-down" and all the more interesting for it. The woodland leaf litter of McKittrick Canyon conceals a small serpent of particular concern.[10] This miniature predator is dull blue-gray to greenish above with a bright yellow belly sporting miscellaneous black spots. The yellow encircles the creature's neck, hence the name ringneck snake, although the ring is lacking in some individuals on the landmark. Pestered ringnecks hide their heads and coil their tails in a tight spiral, displaying the orange-red undersurface, presumably frightening predators by such behavior. Also, they seem to venomize their prey but never bite their human captors. Instead, they play possum when severely harassed.

The landscape assay of the Guadalupe Escarpment turned up adult ringnecks of two distinct size classes, some about a foot long on the average and others nearly two feet. This invited further study, because ringnecks in west Texas generally are intermediate between a

---

[9]Tom Broadbent's 1960 study in Walnut Canyon was personally communicated. See also E. G. Bolen, "Eagles and Sheep: A Viewpoint," *J. Range Mgmt.* 28 (1975): 11–17; and R. R. Olendorff, "The Food Habits of North American Golden Eagles," *Amer. Midl. Natur.* 95 (1976):231–236.

[10]F. R. Gehlbach, "Evolutionary Relations of Southwestern Ringneck Snakes (*Diadophis punctatus*)," *Herpetologica* 30 (1974):140–148.

large Borderlands form and a much smaller type found in central Texas and eastward. Are all ringnecks from New York to California a single species except those in the Guadalupes? I must test reproductive isolation, the ultimate criterion. Since local ringnecks are snake eaters, the larger form might eat the smaller if it is a different species but might mate with or at least avoid eating a ringneck of the same species. I could test for readiness to eat or mate by placing a snake of a third kind together with a male and female ringneck.

My hypotheses predicted different results with ringnecks from the Guadalupes, compared with those from almost anywhere else, and I got them. Most pairs attempted copulation, including control pairs of the smaller form from within and without the Guadalupe area. This was a check on adult size and mating season. One large female from the Pajarito Mountains, Arizona, mated with a small male from central Texas and laid six fertile eggs. Furthermore, all potential prey snakes save ringnecks became actual prey. But while the large and small Guadalupe ringnecks did not consume one another, neither did they copulate or attempt to, so I suspect a selective disadvantage for smallness genes in large ringnecks and vice versa. I must do more explaining.

Suppose that a prehistoric ringneck population in moist forests was split by the evolution of arid, midcontinental grasslands and Borderlands deserts. And suppose small size was ancestral and retained by eastern ringnecks because the eastern environment remained ancestrally moist and forested. Then small ringnecks stranded in increasingly arid woodlands of the Boundary region might evolve large size, since this would facilitate predation on the larger reptilian prey that would become more available than earthworms and small salamanders, the prey of eastern ringnecks. Too, large size would enhance water conservation in the arid Borderlands, because as animals become larger their body volume—water-storage reservoir—increases faster than their skin surface area.

But the evolutionary play goes on. A glaciopluvial period brings cooler, wetter climates to the Border country, and forests begin to grow there. Small ringnecks follow the habitat expansion westward and interbreed with large ringnecks in west Texas. Then the forests break up, as climates become warm-dry once again. This leaves intermediate ringnecks in west Texas, large ones farther west, and the small form in central Texas and the East. More importantly, I postulate that

only large ringnecks inhabited the landmark during the last interpluvial period, a time before the mountains reached their present
height and so remained quite arid.

Last scene—a cool-wet climate and its forests return, as the last
great continental ice sheet expands north of the Borderlands. Ringneck genes begin to flow from east to west, and small ringnecks arrive
on the higher, wetter Guadalupe Escarpment. But the small form has
been isolated from the large one long enough to be avoided as a mate,
though not so long as to be considered food. Moreover, small ringnecks
have a selective advantage in moist deciduous woodlands like those of
McKittrick Canyon, whereas large ringnecks are more fit in the drier
evergreen woodland of surrounding slopes. The habitat separation,
though not complete, fosters reproductive isolation.

Maple-leaf litter that hides small ringneck snakes may represent
concurrent history, since the leaves are intermediate between bigtooth
and sugar maple types, although closer to the eastern sugar maple. I
postulate an ancestral maple population, split by midcontinental dryness, evolved into the western bigtooth and eastern sugar maples, and
reconnected across Texas by the westward marching sugar maple during the last glaciopluvial spell. Then, because the interbred populations became isolated in canyons and on mountain islands with the
return of warm-dry conditions, gene flow was restricted once more,
essentially as it is in the current ringneck situation.

This scenario is not finished, I discover, as I stand before a favorite
alligator juniper at the canyon forks. I have watched this tree, four feet
through and thirty feet tall, gradually fail to replenish its scalelike
leaves over the years. Others died in the 1950's drought and, despite
the wetter 1960's, the death march continues. Woodlands are segregating toward canyon bottoms and mountain peaks, and woodland animals
must go with their woodland livelihood. Sugar-maple influence and
small ringneck snakes may disappear one day, if my hypotheses about
the warm-dry adaptations of bigtooth maples and large ringnecks are
correct.

I climb a steep trail up the eastern escarpment to reach the Bowl,
a special valley near the head of South McKittrick Canyon. It is slightly
over 2,000 feet up from the east, and the spatial isolation helps save
the Bowl's coniferous forest. There have been fires and some cutting,
but 80-foot Douglas firs and southwestern white and ponderosa pines

still dominate the landscape. Gambel's oak and quaking aspen grow in naturally disturbed areas, brushy ponderosas on man-impacted sites. At 7,600 feet, the Bowl has a Rocky Mountain atmosphere.[11]

Perhaps it is the "quick-three-beers" of the olive-sided flycatcher that reminds me of the Rockies. Certainly it reminds me of what I wish I'd packed for a respite after the strenuous climb. Maybe it is the pygmy nuthatches tooting around me. Or is it brown creepers, orange-crowned warblers, gray-headed juncos, and hermit thrushes that, like the flycatcher, nest no farther south in these eastern Borderlands? Also, there are nesting American robins, pine siskins, and even red crossbills in some years, plus the saw-whet owl found for the first time in 1973.

Flammulated owls apparently were nesting in the Bowl when Thomas Burleigh and George Lowery collected thirty-three species there in 1938–1939.[12] I did not find them but recorded the first spotted owls in Texas among the thirty-three breeding birds I saw in 1965 and 1969. George Newman noted flammulateds again in 1972–1974 and found thirty-two nesting species, a mean density of five birds per acre and mean species diversity of 4.34 in his twenty-four-acre study plot. Compared with the more diverse, higher density woodland avifauna of McKittrick Canyon, these values suggest that coniferous forest resources are in short supply. Yet they are distinctive resources—the cool-wet climate included—and contribute to a distinctive avifauna.

Except for similar relict patches in the Davis (Limpia) and Chisos mountains southward in Texas, and the Sierra del Carmen in Coahuila, coniferous forest simply does not exist along the Border east of the Continental Divide. Regional climates are too hot and dry, and the mountains too low. Have the seas between mountain islands prevented most Rocky Mountain birds from reaching the more southern ranges in postpluvial time? Are those forests filled with Mexican—Sierra Madrean—replacements? Fortunately, thorough studies in the Chisos and Sierra del Carmen help to answer these questions, but the high Davis Mountains need more attention.

[11] On floral aspects of the Rocky Mountains atmosphere, see M. C. Johnston, "The Guadalupe Mountains—A Chink in the Mosaic of the Chihuahuan Desert?" in *Biological Investigations in the Guadalupe Mountains*, pp. 45–49.

[12] T. D. Burleigh and G. H. Lowery, Jr., "Birds of the Guadalupe Mountain Region of Western Texas," *Occ. Papers Mus. Zool. Louisiana St. Univ.* 8 (1940):85–151.

Among birds breeding above 7,000 feet, I find that 46 percent of those in the Guadalupes' coniferous forest also nest in the Chisos, but only 24 percent of the Guadalupes' and 28 percent of the Chisos' avifaunas nest in the Sierra del Carmen.[13] Other montane birds in common show an opposite trend (29, 54, and 62 percent similarities, respectively), suggesting that replacements from the Sierra Madre do indeed appear. Besides the five species that reach southern breeding limits in the Bowl, I know of six that do so in the Davis or Chisos mountains, but the eleven Rocky Mountain dropouts are replaced by only four Sierra Madrean arrivals in the Chisos and two more in the del Carmens.

Steller's jays give way to Mexican jays; orange-crowned, yellow-rumped, and Grace's warblers, to painted redstarts and Colima warblers in the Chisos plus olive warblers in the del Carmens. Furthermore, gray-headed juncos are replaced by yellow-eyed juncos in the del Carmens. Is competitive replacement a factor confounding the hypothesis of forest discontinuity and distance? Possibly, but the mountain chickadee, hermit thrush, brown creeper, American robin, olive-sided flycatcher, and western tanager are not so closely matched in the Chisos and del Carmen mountains, and the Hutton's vireo does not fully qualify for substitution until the warbling vireo drops out in the del Carmens.

Perhaps the strangest phenomenon of all is what I call the hop, skip, and jump type of breeding distribution.[14] It is illustrated by house wrens' being in the Guadalupes and del Carmens, but not in the Davis or Chisos, or pygmy nuthatches in the Guadalupe, Davis, and del Carmen ranges but not in the Chisos, or northern pygmy owls in the del

[13] Species lists for the $2C/(A+B) \times 100$ index (see n. 7, this chapter) are from G. A. Newman, "Compositional Aspects of Breeding Avifaunas," pp. 181–237; A. H. Miller, "The Avifauna of the Sierra del Carmen of Coahuila, Mexico," *Condor* 57 (1955): 154–178; and R. H. Wauer, "Ecological Distribution of Birds of the Chisos Mountains, Texas," *Southwest. Natur.* 16 (1971): 1–29. A similar, recent study is by R. H. Wauer and J. D. Ligon, "Distributional Relations of Breeding Avifauna of Four Southwestern Mountain Ranges," in *Symposium on the Biological Resources of the Chihuahuan Desert Region, United States and Mexico*, ed. R. H. Wauer and D. H. Riskind, U.S.D.I., pp. 567–578, Natl. Park Serv. Trans. and Proc. Ser. 3 (1977).

[14] "Hop, skip, and jump" is also known in trees of the Guadalupe, Davis, Chisos, and del Carmen mountains and is described by P. V. Wells, "Late Pleistocene Vegetation and Degree of Pluvial Climatic Change in the Chihuahuan Desert," *Science* 153 (1966): 970–975.

Carmens, not elsewhere in the region, but reappearing in the Sacramento Mountains, New Mexico, immediately north of the Guadalupes. Either hop, skip, and jump is a historical accident—the species just missed a brief, pluvial, forest connection between mountain islands—or it is still another example of wet-adapted species nesting in wet years and not dry ones. Maybe it is both, depending on the sedentary versus migratory nature of particular species, the nuthatch and pygmy owl compared with the house wren, for example.

There are other relict vertebrates in the Bowl. The Mexican vole and short-horned lizard tempt my curiosity, because their small, isolated populations seem to be interdependent here, although they represent Pleistocene pluvial dispersals from opposite directions. Voles range northward from the Mesa Central, the great tableland of Mexico between the Sierra Madres, while the horned lizards range southward from high grasslands and woodlands of the Rocky Mountain uplift. The five-inch, snuff-brown voles inhabit grassy openings in the Bowl and West Dog Canyon. They make inch-wide runways among the bunchgrass clumps and share their highway system with various lizards and western harvest mice.

Short-horned lizards are fellow travelers in the mini-sea of grass. Rock and black-tailed rattlesnakes also follow these paths of least resistance and greatest olfactory allure. One sunny June morning I attempted to trace a runway system in a plot that, 100 by 100 feet, proved too large an undertaking. My inability to draw a vole road map was discouraging, and my nerves were jangled by the traffic at nearly every turn. First I flushed a black-chinned sparrow from a nest with four eggs, then a half-grown horned lizard, some vole or other mouse, and finally a foot-long rock rattler. Then I quit. Unwittingly I placed my hand within a few inches of the snake before meeting its gaze. And wittingly I withdrew—pronto.

Around 8,000 years ago Mexican voles lived with yellow-bellied marmots, bushy-tailed woodrats, and long-tailed voles, plus now-extinct shrub oxen, mountain deer, and camels, on the landmark. The fossils of all are found in Burnet Cave.[15] Because the marmot, woodrat,

---

[15] C. B. Schultz and E. B. Howard, "The Fauna of Burnet Cave, Guadalupe Mountains, New Mexico," *Proc. Acad. Nat. Sci. Philadelphia* 87 (1935):273–289; and K. F.

and long-tailed vole live in coniferous forest and mountain grassland far to the north today, I assume they became extinct locally when the Guadalupes began to dry out and wet communities began to shrink after the last Pleistocene pluvial period. It was cooler and wetter in the Guadalupes during this pluvial. Salt Flat, a playa just west of the range, dates from this time. Such physical evidence and the mammalian fossils suggest more forest and meadow on the landmark in pluvial time.

The extinct shrub ox and its large, plant-eating associates are not present among Dry Cave fossils deposited 14,000 years ago, but the Mexican vole is there with the marmot, woodrat, long-tailed vole, and such small grassland rodents as the sagebrush and prairie· voles.[16] These last two no longer live in the Guadalupes either; their fossils suggest that sagebrush-studded grasslands were present then as in central Wyoming today. Bones of the short-horned lizard are scattered among the fossil mammals and support the grassland hypothesis. Several different communities must have been present in that ancient Guadalupe landscape, as they are in similarly diverse landscapes today.

The last Pleistocene ice sheet and cool-wet climate were in full retreat northward at the time the cave fossils were deposited. Wet meadows became dry grasslands, perhaps first of the plains type and then desert grassland. Forests retreated upslope and were replaced by woodlands. Plants and animals of the forest were cut off from their relatives in nearby ranges like the Davis and Chisos mountains and the Sierra del Carmen. It must have been like a decaying west Texas cowtown with scions leaving for the big city, never to return, and whole families locally dying out in a few generations.

I can estimate the speed of natural community extinction by looking further at prehistoric evidence, for example short-horned lizard fossils in Pratt Cave, McKittrick Canyon.[17] The species is not in McKit-

---

Murray, "Pleistocene Climate and the Fauna of Burnet Cave, New Mexico," *Ecology* 38 (1957):129–132.

[16] A. H. Harris, "The Dry Cave Mammalian Fauna and Late Pluvial Conditions in Southeastern New Mexico," *Texas J. Sci.* 22 (1970):3–27. See also R. A. Smartt, "The Ecology of Late Pleistocene and Recent Microtus from South-central and Southwestern New Mexico," *Southwest. Natur.* 22 (1977):1–19.

[17] F. R. Gehlbach and J. A. Holman, "Paleoecology of Amphibians and Reptiles from Pratt Cave, Guadalupe Mountains National Park, Texas," *Southwest. Natur.* 19

trick today. Dry-adapted western box turtles in the same deposit, contrasted with bones of the wet-adapted eastern box turtle in Burnet Cave at an earlier time, indicate the shift to drier conditions. This change eventually put the horned lizard a thousand feet higher on the landmark. If I consider coniferous forest and mountain grassland at Burnet Cave 4,600 feet in elevation and 8,000 years ago, mountain grassland at Pratt Cave 1,000 feet higher and 6,000 years later, and neither community lower than 7,600 feet today, the upslope retreat of cool-wet forest and grassland is a few inches to perhaps a foot per year—a mere fraction of man's cowtown syndrome.

(1974):191–198. A radiocarbon date since this publication indicates that the fossils are no older than 3,000 years (see E. L. Lundelius, Jr., "Post-Pleistocene Mammals from Pratt Cave and Their Environmental Significance," in *Biological Investigations in the Guadalupe Mountains*, pp. 239–258).

7. Oñate's Legacies

JUAN OÑATE, colonizer of New Mexico, brought seven thousand head of livestock along El Camino Real from Chihuahua through El Paso del Norte to Santa Fe in 1598. This may have been the start of desertification in the Borderlands. Yet by 1846, when William Emory rode south from Santa Fe along the Rio Grande, black grama grass grew lush on well-drained hills bordering the river, and tobosa occupied the swales. Emory and John Bartlett noted that these uplands were rich grazing country, and the river valley was densely timbered with cottonwoods and mesquite. Both may have traveled along the Camino Real by following its lines of mesquites planted by Spanish cattle two centuries earlier.[1]

As Edgar Mearns explored the Boundary in the 1890's, riparian woodlands of the river near El Paso were lined with Rio Grande cottonwoods and seepwillow, while adjacent bottomland was grown to mesquite and tornillo.[2] Most of the valley was natural as far south as Fort Hancock, but orchards, gardens, and fields of grain and alfalfa were present near Belen. This particular section had been thickly settled earlier, as William Emory noted in 1851, but El Paso–Juárez now swallows Belen and the remaining pastoral landscape. The fingers of creeping urbanism grasp San Elizario and become unnatural pathways for the northward dispersal of culturally induced invaders like the great-tailed grackle.

The changing landscape of the Rio Grande Valley between El Paso and San Antonio, New Mexico, is the subject of historical sleuthing by

[1] J. L. Gardner provides a historical summary plus photos of the Camino Real (figure 7) and shrub desert that used to be grassland (figure 2) in his "Vegetation of the Creosotebush Area of the Rio Grande Valley in New Mexico," *Ecol. Monogr.* 21 (1951): 379–403.

[2] E. A. Mearns, *Mammals of the Mexican Boundary of the United States,* U.S. Natl. Mus. Bull. 56 (1907), pp. 77–79; W. H. Emory, *Report on the United States and Mexican Boundary Survey,* vol. 1, 34th Cong., 1st sess., 1857, U.S. House Exec. Doc. 135, pp. 90–91.

Original Monument 1, near El Paso del Norte (Emory)

John York and William Dick-Peddie.[3] Was this region desert grassland
before human impact, as suggested by Emory's observations? Is the
present shrub desert here to stay, a culturally induced climax? For answers, territorial survey records were searched. Surveyors of the last
half of the nineteenth century evaluated land for dry farming versus
ranching, so they, too, paid attention to indicator species. Except for
using cedar and greasewood as names for juniper and creosote bush,
they employed Spanish terms—*largoncillo* ("white-thorn acacia"), for
example—as there was no applicable English before the Boundary survey volumes became widely used in decades following the Civil War.

Rapid and extensive demise of grassland is the general outcome of
Anglo settlement. Grass cover predominated in 1853 but began to dis-
appear by the 1880's in concert with the postwar and railroad era of
Anglo ranching. Between 1882 and 1884 alone, sixty thousand cattle
were added to the existing nine thousand in Socorro County, New
Mexico. The Jornada Valley was 90 percent grass when it all started,

[3]J. C. York and W. A. Dick-Peddie, "Vegetation Changes in Southern New Mexico
during the Past Hundred Years," in *Arid Lands in Perspective*, ed. W. G. McGinnies and
B. J. Goldman, pp. 157–166 (Tucson: Univ. Arizona Press, 1969). See also L. C. Buf-
fington and C. H. Herbel, "Vegetational Changes on a Semidesert Grassland Range from
1858 to 1963," *Ecol. Monogr.* 35 (1965): 139–164.

but by 1963 it was less than 25 percent grass. Mesquite and creosote bush had taken over. The grass removal–soil erosion–shrub invasion syndrome—desertification—is recurrent in the unnatural history of the Borderlands.

Aridity can be implicated but not blamed entirely for the desertification since no trend toward undue dryness is evident before the 1890's. Nor is unnatural fire prevention an important factor in the making of shrub deserts, because the original, natural landscape did not encourage widespread fire. It was and is too rocky. Fire certainly fosters grassland, as I observe today in Chihuahua, where natural fires burning uncontrolled eliminate woody shrubs, not perennial grasses. But these natural fires usually burn out on rocky ridges, lacking the dry-grass fuel to carry them, and cease with hard rain or wind shifts that cause back-burning. Moreover, such natural fires usually start with lightning, hence are too irregular in time and space to be of primary importance in grassland preservation.[4]

Instead, I agree with York and Dick-Peddie that overgrazing transformed desert grassland into shrub desert in the Rio Grande Valley of southern New Mexico. Most of the valley is permanent desert now. Even if native grasses are reintroduced, desert grassland will not regrow widely, because most original surface soils are long gone down arroyos or blown into dunes covered by mesquite. Today's landscape supports at most one cow per hundred acres, except in the intensively farmed valley bottom with its hundred alfalfa-fed Holsteins per acre of dairy feedlot. And when the upland ranchers can't make a living, roads are bulldozed over the skeletons of their ranges, further increasing erosion, as ranching turns into ranchette development.[5]

The shift from natural to cultural succession beckons Easterners,

[4] Fire ranks ahead of climatic change, overgrazing, plant competition, and rodent transport of seeds in maintaining desert grassland, according to R. R. Humphrey, "The Desert Grassland: A History of Vegetational Change and an Analysis of Causes," *Bot. Rev.* 24 (1958):1–62. That overgrazing is a more important factor is supported by J. R. Hastings and R. M. Turner, *The Changing Mile* (Tucson: Univ. Arizona Press, 1965), pp. 40–41 (see chapter 13 of the present volume), although fire may be comparatively more important in plains grassland (see J. H. Bock, C. E. Bock, and J. R. McKnight, "A Study of the Effects of Grassland Fires at the Research Ranch in Southeastern Arizona," *J. Arizona Acad. Sci.* 11 (1976):49–57; and chapter 2 of the present volume.

[5] For an appraisal of ranchette development see C. E. Campbell, "The Economic Impact of Rural Subdividing in the Arid Southwest: Development or Destruction," *J. Arizona Acad. Sci.* 9 (1974):25–28.

to whom the shrub desert offers cleaner air—downwind of El Paso– Juárez—and a startling contrast in color and simplicity. These Border- lands are brown most of the year, something very difficult for forest and bluegrass people to get used to. Creosote bush alone or with tar- bush or white-thorn acacia covers a range otherwise marked only by the gridlike network of ranchette roads and incongruous street signs of the Sun City. Blooming annuals, deposited by summer rains, do pro- vide vegetational diversity plus patchwork quilts of color. And the fo- liage profile diversifies slightly along arroyos, with added mesquite, lit- tleleaf sumac, Apache plume, or desert willow.

It is not just the brown landscape newcomers must adjust to. The heat too presents a real challenge. "How do you stand it?" a transposed bird-watcher queries. "Very well, for I ask how the birds stand it and discover how those few breeding species are able to tolerate summer temperatures above 100 degrees." One strategy, the siesta approach, is to retreat to shady spots and be inactive at midday. Even when feeding nestlings, for example, cactus wrens are about half as mobile at midday as at sunrise. And for cooling, desert birds may hold their wings away from their bodies, transferring heat from their thinly feathered sides to the desert air. Others pant or rapidly flutter the throat, facilitating evaporative cooling from the moist surface of the respiratory tract. This can be 25 percent more effective in the desert-adapted road- runner than in a more water-dependent, dooryard bird like the Inca dove.[6]

Lack of water, too, is a desert feature that birds must reckon with. They have an advantage over mammals since they conserve more water in their nitrogen excretion. In ridding themselves of toxic nitro- genous wastes, both birds and reptiles excrete uric acid as small, yel- lowish or white pellets. These semisolid packets contain much less water than the amount in mammalian urine and may be three thou- sand times more concentrated than blood. Despite the efficient waste packaging, desert birds lose up to 2.4 times more water through flutter cooling and uncontrolled evaporation than they produce metabolically,

---

[6] Desert bird physiology is reviewed by W. R. Dawson and J. W. Hudson, "Birds," in *Comparative Physiology of Thermoregulation*, ed. G. C. Whittow, pp. 223–310 (New York: Academic Press, 1970); and W. R. Dawson and G. W. Bartholomew, "Temperature Regulation and Water Economy of Desert Birds," in *Desert Biology*, vol. 1, ed. G. W. Brown, Jr., pp. 357–394 (New York: Academic Press, 1968).

Narrowleaf sotol in succulent desert, April; darker green is cooler-wetter, north-facing slope, where shrub density is greatest.

Left: Saguaro cactus bloom, April. *Right*: Saguaro nursery group beneath foothill paloverde.

Orange wood lily, May.

Blue flax, August.

Cardinal flower, June.

Left: Madrean ladies tresses, July. *Right*: Barrel cactus, August.

Left: Mexican gold poppies, August. *Middle*: Texas madrone berries, November. *Right*: Bigtooth maple leaves, November.

so they must obtain water from insect and plant foods. But they typically drink only half as much free water as nondesert birds.

Moreover, it pays to be large in deserts, since the reduced ratio of surface area to volume of any large organism cuts down its water loss. White-winged, mourning, and Inca doves, which all appear in deserts, illustrate this nicely; they weigh an average of 140, 105, and 42 grams respectively. The white-wing loses only 4.0 percent of its body weight per day when deprived of water at sixty-eight to seventy-five degrees, while the mourning dove loses 4.8 percent, and the Inca dove 6.1 percent. In fact, the ten best indicators among shrub-desert birds average 1.4 times the weight of their ten lowland riparian counterparts—55 versus 38 grams.[7] But streamside birds have surface water and abundant shade to counter any tendency to lose water for cooling purposes.

Shrub-desert birds are a select few, indeed. Only three to thirteen species breed in this community on undissected sites, and eleven to sixteen species in tracts of the same size with arroyos and their added vegetative structure. Breeding-species diversity is 1.77 to 3.43 compared with 3.52 to 4.39 in lowland riparian sites. Only the black-throated sparrow typically uses creosote bush for nesting, so in areas dominated by this plant other birds must crowd into the remaining, relatively scarce shrubs. Nesting density is strongly correlated with the density of shrubs other than creosote bush. In southern Arizona, for example, at least half the breeding birds use jumping cholla.

Best indicators among shrub-desert breeding birds anywhere in the Borderlands are the black-throated sparrow, verdin, mourning dove, cactus wren, black-tailed gnatcatcher, house finch, and crissal thrasher, in first-to-last rank order. Seven species is the average on diverse, twenty- to fifty-acre sites. If three more species are added, they

[7]The indicator evaluation of lowland riparian birds is given in chapter 10. The following references furnished data for the present shrub desert list, based on my computation of the ten highest products of mean density times frequency: K. L. Dixon, "Ecological and Distributional Relations of Desert Shrub Birds of Western Texas," *Condor* 61 (1959):397–409; K. E. Franzreb, "Breeding Bird Densities, Species Composition, and Bird Species Diversity of the Algodones Dunes," *Western Birds* 9 (1978):9–20; M. M. Hensley, "Ecological Relations of the Breeding Bird Population of the Desert Biome in Arizona," *Ecol. Monogr.* 24 (1954):185–207; R. J. Raitt and R. L. Maze, "Densities and Species Composition of Breeding Birds of a Creosotebush Community in Southern New Mexico," *Condor* 70 (1968):193–205; C. S. Tomoff, "Avian Species Diversity in Desert Scrub," *Ecology* 55 (1974):396–402. Data on densities, richness, and diversity (calculated as $H'\log_2$ of breeding males) were obtained here also.

are most likely to be the ash-throated flycatcher, mockingbird, and scaled quail. Then, however, density of the avifauna increases by an average factor of five. Density is an exponential function of added species, and species arrive with environmental diversity. The frustrated birder from the East might do some planting and furnish water at his suburban ranchette.

Interspecific territoriality explains why species variety and overall density increase at different rates. Birds, like most creatures, are territorial. They set up boundaries around resources, defended largely by song. Desert birds typically defend suites of resources, presumably because food, vertical space, and shelter are relatively rare. This fosters severe interspecific as well as intraspecific competition, since the variety of desert-adapted species is small, increasing the likelihood of similar demands on resources. In less stressful environments like suburbia, most birds defend specific items only and share a greater proportion of the total resource spectrum.[8]

I find evidence for the compacting power of interspecific territoriality at Organ Pipe Cactus National Monument, Arizona. There Max Hensley censused a hundred-acre plot of flat, shrub desert in which the individuals of nine birds defended twenty-five territories averaging 16.3 acres. An adjacent plot of 70.0 acres, dissected by a major arroyo, housed twelve species in forty territories averaging 8.8 acres. Moreover, individuals of the eight species nesting in both plots had territories 3.0 to 28.0 acres smaller in the arroyo-sliced plot.[9] I believe the 1.5-fold increase in species and 1.6-fold in territories added proportionately greater interspecific rivalry and caused the 1.9-fold reduction in territory size.

Alternatively, territories in the smaller plot may have been smaller because local resources were more plentiful. Although Hensley suggested this, I find no confirmatory evidence in his data on vegetative richness. In fact, there were two more plant species and 0.1 additional plants per acre in the larger plot. Instead, territories might be smaller in diverse, arroyo-sliced landscapes because vegetative resources and birds are clumped, in contrast to the widely spaced shrubs and nesting

[8] J. T. Emlen, "An Urban Bird Community in Tucson, Arizona: Derivation, Structure, Regulation," *Condor* 76 (1974): 184–197.

[9] M. M. Hensley, "Ecological Relations." Plant data are reduced from his table 3 and bird data from his table 15 on areas 1 versus 3.

birds of the flat desert. Certainly both plants and birds line up along arroyos in proximity to the ephemeral water supply.

One special adaptation for subdividing deserts into territories is song mimicry by mockingbirds. Mimicking mockers do have an intra-specific advantage. The fancier their repertoires the larger their territories and the better their chances of securing mates.[10] Particularly in desert communities mockingbirds should benefit by commanding more territory, and they could do this by deterring other birds through song mimicry at the same time as increasing their own fitness through added mates. Indeed, I would broaden the song mimicry–expanded resources idea to suggest that among mockers and thrashers in general, song mimicry evolved in communities of simple structure in response to scarce resources.

Indicator birds of today's shrub desert must have been absent or confined to gravelly foothill areas originally, while species associated with black grama and tobosa held sway. Unfortunately, most Rio Grande grasslands were destroyed before man learned their value, so I must extrapolate from experience in the plains grassland between Marfa and Valentine, Texas. Here the most frequently encountered breeding species are western meadowlark, horned lark, and Cassin's sparrow, with the brown-headed cowbird added close to ranch edifices and the white-necked raven or Swainson's hawk where yuccas are present.

Brown-headed cowbirds were scarce in this relict grassland and others of the region prior to the 1890's.[11] Certainly they increased with ranching, since they accept Herefords to follow in lieu of bison, feeding on insects kicked up or seeds dislodged by the hoofed grazers. They thrive on grain in the feed necessary for cattle on overgrazed ranges and benefit from a ranch's proliferating stock tanks and home

---

[10] R. D. Howard, "The Influence of Sexual Selection and Interspecific Competition on Mockingibrd Song (*Mimus polyglotos*)," *Evolution* 28 (1974):428–438, eschews the interspecific competition hypothesis, but see J. R. Krebs, "The Significance of Song Repertoires: The Beau Geste Hypothesis," *Anim. Behav.* 25 (1977):475–478.

[11] A. R. Phillips, "The Instability of the Distribution of Land Birds in the Southwest," in *Collected Papers in Honor of Lyndon Lane Hargrave*, ed. A. H. Schroeder, Papers Archaeol. Soc. New Mexico 1 (1968), pp. 129–162. H. W. Phillips and W. A. Thornton, "The Summer Resident Birds of the Sierra Vieja Range in Southwestern Texas," *Texas J. Sci.* 1 (1949):101–131, do not list cowbirds in the region.

plantings. The tanks provide water and invite green vegetation, which invites a variety of nesting birds, while home plantings and windbreaks invite nesting birds directly. More trees beget more host nests, which beget more cowbirds.

Consider a hypothetical sequence: seasonal, migratory bison are replaced by resident cattle after the Civil War. Brown-headed cowbirds increase. Cattle are fenced as the era of market drives ends with the opening of the Southern Pacific Railroad and cowboys become settled ranchers with houses and stock tanks. Cowbirds increase to the point of scientific notice. Ranges deteriorate with overgrazing, and the era of feedlots and feeding begins. Brown-headed cowbirds fairly swarm. Finally—and this is no mere hypothesis—bronzed cowbirds invade the Borderlands, arriving first in southern Arizona in 1909, then in southwestern New Mexico in 1947, and in the Big Bend of Texas in 1969.[12] Oñate's livestock legacy works in subtle ways.

Settled cowboys, often city residents now, have had profound influences on other birds, like the Inca dove. This dooryard species, *tortolita*, for centuries adapting to life around Mexico's pueblos, was not seen on the First Boundary Survey. It appeared at Laredo, Texas, in 1866.[13] Six years later it nested at Tubac, Arizona, and spread northward in that state at about five miles per year. In New Mexico there were stragglers in the 1920's but no nesters until the 1940's in the Rio Grande Valley. Then, however, northward dispersal averaged six miles a year, a rate like that in Texas. Today this charming bird has ventured far north of the Borderlands but always remains in close association with humanity.

The proliferation of gardens and hummingbird feeders at ranches and towns is credited with the eastward movement of Anna's hummingbirds. The same may be suggested for the northward spread of violet-crowned and berylline hummers in Arizona.[14] In 1976, for the first time in the United States, a berylline tried to nest near a feeder in the Chiricahua Mountains, and in 1978 another fledged two young

[12] A. R. Phillips, "Instability of the Distribution of Land Birds," pp. 129–162. On Texas arrival of the bronzed cowbird see R. H. Wauer, "Bronzed Cowbird Extends Range into Texas Big Bend Country," *Wilson Bull.* 85 (1973):343–344.

[13] A. R. Phillips, "Instability of the Distribution of Land Birds," p. 138.

[14] D. A. Zimmerman, "Range Expansion of Anna's Hummingbird," *Amer. Birds* 72 (1973):827–835. See also A. R. Phillips, "Instability of the Distribution of Land Birds."

near feeders in Ramsey Canyon of the Huachuca Mountains. Ranch and urban plantings may also have aided northward range expansions of the hooded oriole and cardinal in this century. Will the simultaneous spread of bronzed and brown-headed cowbirds countervail?

Great-tailed grackles must have followed expanding irrigation agriculture first and suburbia second in their northward push. This conspicuous front-lawn and freeway performer of courtship displays was found in abundance only at Matamoros, Tamaulipas, during the First Boundary Survey. It was a rare visitor at San Elizario on the Rio Grande in 1849 but presently is an abundant nester from there to Albuquerque, New Mexico.[15] By 1913 great-tailed grackles reached Las Cruces and by 1938 Albuquerque, thus moving at the rate of seven to eight miles per year when they really got going. We are great benefactors of these blackbirds, for we furnish city conifer plantings for nests and roosts plus grain crops for food.

But we certainly are malefactors of avian diversity when we build cities in the middle of desert seas. John Emlen compared the resident bird life of an urban tract in Tucson, Arizona, with that of a nearby shrub desert and found fourteen urban versus twenty-one rural species. His species-diversity value in Tucson was but 79 percent of that in the shrub desert, despite increased urban habitat diversity, because a few superabundant species commanded the largely cultural resources. Two-thirds of the urban birds were edificial—influenced by man's edifices—species like the native Inca dove and exotic house sparrow and starling. The only other sizeable component, 30 percent, included broadly adapted species such as the mourning dove, mockingbird, and cardinal.[16]

Tucson's bird density was twenty-six times greater than that of the natural landscape, suggesting to me that man's gifts of food, water, and shelter exceed those of nature. Yet there is a catch to urban munificence, since it is accomplished at the cost of natural communities. For

---

[15] G. A. McCall, "Some Remarks on Habits, etc., of Birds Met with in Western Texas between San Antonio and the Rio Grande, and in New Mexico: With Descriptions of Several Species Believed To Have Been Hitherto Undescribed," *Proc. Acad. Nat. Sci. Philadelphia* 5 (1851):213–224; A. R. Phillips, "The Great-tailed Grackles of the Southwest," *Condor* 52 (1950):78–81; and J. P. Hubbard, *Checklist of the Birds of New Mexico,* New Mexico Ornithol. Soc. Publ. 3 (1970).

[16] Emlen, "Urban Bird Community."

every drop of birdbath water or foot of green lawn or garden, Tucson's groundwater supply declines, because this city annually consumes ten times the amount of water that it gets from precipitation.[17] And for each cultivated sunflower or millet seed furnished an urban cardinal, native seed makers make fewer seeds for rural cardinals, because their growing space is traded for domestic vegetation.

The urban diversion of groundwater is duplicated in the countryside, for example on the eastern flank of the Rio Grande north of El Paso—el Valle Jornada del Muerto, "the valley of the journey of death." Historically this was a waterless but lush desert grassland in which many a refugee from Oñate's colonies, escaping the Indian uprising of 1680, died of thirst. "The whole extent, as far as vision reached ahead, was a level plain, covered thickly with the most luxurious grass, and filled with beautiful wild flowers. Hundreds and hundreds of thousands of acres, containing the greatest abundance of the finest grass in the world, and the richest soil are here lying vacant and looked upon by the traveler with dread, because of its want of water." So exclaimed Edward Beale in 1858.[18]

Today the Jornada is better watered because its skin has been pierced by wells and stock tanks, so the valley exhibits some peculiar natural history. I think, for example, of the tiger salamander, a ten-inch, yellow-and-black blotched amphibian that cohabits pocket gopher and ground squirrel burrows during the Jornada dry season. Originally this beast must have depended on temporary, monsoon rain pools to complete its life cycle. Now, however, standing surface water in stock-tank form is available for longer periods and in places where it may never have accumulated naturally.

In the traditional amphibian mode, the tiger salamander lays its eggs in water once or twice annually. These hatch in nine days at summer water temperatures averaging seventy-seven degrees Fahrenheit, and the larvae, locally known as mudpuppies or waterdogs, grow about a millimeter a day in that thermal regime. Salamander larvae are quite unlike the tadpoles of frogs and toads, since they possess four spindly

[17]A. W. Wilson, "Tucson: A Problem in Uses of Water," in *Aridity and Man*, ed. C. Hodge and P. C. Duisberg, pp. 483–489, Amer. Assoc. Advanc. Sci. Publ. 74 (1963).
    [18]Beale, quoted in H. J. Dittmer, "Vegetation of the Southwest: Past and Present," *Texas J. Sci.* 3 (1951):350–355.

Tiger Salamander (Emory)

legs at the outset and bushy external gills throughout larval life. Transformation into the terrestrial burrow dweller involves loss of gills and fins and the growth of more robust legs and a thicker, more imperme-able skin—all triggered by a drying pond.[19]

But some Jornada ponds persist, and so do their waterdogs. This strategic alternative to transformation is interesting, because the creatures then become sexually mature and reproduce as larviform individuals, omitting the terrestrial stage entirely. What keeps them in persistent ponds? What makes them leave is easily observed by looking at the mud-cracked bottom of Taylor Well when it is dry. Apparently the tiger salamander has the best of its two worlds, for it has parlayed its traditional life cycle into single or multiple uses of resources, depending on the most advantageous situation under the prevailing climate.

Perhaps the major reason for the single-use strategy—reproducing larvae in a relatively permanent pond—is the pond's considerable productivity compared with that of the mammal burrow environment. Surely the buffered thermal regimes of ponds and burrows and the water supplies of each relative to the demands of larvae and adults, respectively, cannot be determining factors. But ponds do furnish more food for larval growth than burrows provide for adult growth,

[19] R. G. Webb and W. L. Roueche, "Life History Aspects of the Tiger Salamander (*Ambystoma tigrinum mavortium*) in the Chihuahuan Desert," *Gt. Basin Nat.* 31 (1971): 193–212. See also R. G. Webb, "Survival Adaptation of Tiger Salamanders (*Ambystoma tigrinum*) in the Chihuahuan Desert," in *Physiological Systems in Semiarid Environ-ments*, ed. C. C. Hoff and M. L. Riedese, pp. 143–146 (Albuquerque: Univ. New Mex-ico Press, 1969); and W. J. Hamilton, Jr., "Summer Habitat of the Yellow-barred Tiger Salamander," *Copeia* (1946):51.

judging from comparative growth rates of each form. And the faster, larger growth of larvae permits access to a wider range of food types and better escape from predators and competitors. Size is power in natural communities.[20]

Nonetheless, opposing selective forces are at work on a tiger salamander's larval stage, since only ephemeral ponds lack fish predators and are favorable for larvae. When such a pond persists during a series of wet years, tendencies to transform are selected against by the comparatively inhospitable terrestrial environment. Transformed individuals may desiccate moving overland to a chance encounter with a mammal burrow and may die. During several dry years, however, any tendency to remain larval is disadvantageous, as larvae cannot crawl, burrow, or resist desiccation as well as transformed individuals. Then the species must switch to its multiple-use strategy and may not even reproduce annually if the drought is prolonged.

In 1966 Taylor Well held water for over a year, and some of its tiger salamanders remained larval while others transformed. This peculiar circumstance suggests that unnatural history can upset the species' natural adaptive strategy. The arid Jornada Valley, normally with ephemeral playa ponds, should be a stage setting for the multiple-use strategy in the last few thousand years of postpluvial evolutionary play. However, by building a more permanent pond from a natural depression, man the stagehand changes things too quickly. He re-creates a pluvial climatic phenomenon and thereby selects for the single-use strategy against genetic pressure to transform. No wonder the Jornada's tiger salamanders lead a Jekyll-and-Hyde existence.

East of the Jornada Valley and over the Franklin–Organ–San Andres Cordillera lies a black and white chessboard, the Tularosa Valley. This ecological theater of black lava beds juxtaposed with white sand dunes and its company of black and white actors contribute as much to my delight and instruction in the evolutionary play as any place in the Borderlands. I return time and again just to sit on an isolated sand

---

[20] Somewhat different reasons for the maintenance of a larval stage are given by H. M. Wilbur and J. P. Collins, "Ecological Aspects of Amphibian Metamorphosis," *Science* 182 (1973): 1305–14; and W. G. Sprules, "The Adaptive Significance of Paedogenesis in North American Species of *Ambystoma* (Amphibia: Caudata): A Hypothesis," *Canadian J. Zool.* 52 (1974): 393–400.

dune and watch and think, shaded perhaps by an umbrella, or to wander about at night with my black and white teachers of evolutionary theory. Fortunately I can continue to learn, because part of the theater is protected purposely in White Sands National Monument and part inadvertently in the U.S. Air Force's ballistic missile range.

Mouse and lizard costuming appropriate to background coloration is critical in the *malpaís* and *médanos*, the lava beds and sand dunes, because predators choose or are more likely to see visually distinctive prey.[21] If a mouse is to live in the chessboard theater, it must do several things. It must run from shrub to shrub at night, preferably, but most mice do this anyway in shrub deserts. However, the hide-and-go-seek food and shelter strategy is difficult when shrubs are yards apart, as they often are in this desert. To minimize its chances of being gobbled up, a mouse can evolve visual anonymity—color like the rock or sand environment. But what if the creature is white like the sand and runs onto black lava next door? Then its chances of being selected against by being eaten increase compared with its stay-at-home siblings, since it is so conspicuous against the wrong backdrop.

Thus, any genetic tendency to produce white offspring that stay in the white neighborhood is selectively advantageous, and over evolutionary time genes for pale pelage increase in a mouse population on white sand, relative to genes for the original brownish coat color. Eventually the whole population may consist of light-colored individuals, as demonstrated by Apache pocket mice on the Tularosa sands. This logic obtains also in the black neighborhood of the lava, where dark-colored races of mice, woodrats, and rock squirrels have evolved.

Concealingly colored rodent populations on the white sands can be "diluted" genetically through interbreeding with individuals from darker populations in adjacent habitats. Of the eight small species on the sands—those smaller than a jackrabbit, hence with limited mobility—five are found in bordering communities.[22] None of these is cryptically colored on the sands, presumably because dark color genes flow

---

[21] D. W. Kaufman, "Concealing Coloration: How Is the Effectiveness of Selection Related to Conspicuousness?" *Amer. Midl. Natur.* 93 (1975):245–247; H. C. Mueller, "Hawks Select Odd Prey," *Science* 188 (1975):953–954.

[22] W. F. Blair, *Ecological Distribution of Mammals in the Tularosa Basin, New Mexico*, Contrib. Lab. Vert. Biol. Univ. Michigan 20 (1943). See also the classic study of S. B. Benson, "Concealing Coloration among Some Desert Rodents of the Southwestern

into their white-sands populations. The southern plains woodrat on the sands is but slightly paler than in adjacent communities. The Apache pocket mouse, the palest of all, occurs nowhere else in the region. No larger mammals of the sands, such as the black-tailed jackrabbit or the kit fox, have evolved local color races, for they transmit genes freely from Texas to California.

Since time is a requisite in selecting against or removing dark color genes from species that colonize the sands, it is probable that the whiter the local population, the longer it has occupied the environment. Apache pocket mice, for example, probably have occupied the dunes the longest, while southern plains woodrats may be in the process of colonizing the sands from adjacent communities. These woodrats are common in mesquite-dominated portions of the Tularosa Valley and comparatively rare on the *médanos*. If the colonization is historic in time frame, perhaps the master stagehand is involved.

Are sand dunes marginal environments for southern plains woodrats? Can this species be forced into the *médanos* through competition with the white-throated woodrat? Is the white-throat moving out of its lava-bed and foothill habitats, displacing the southern plains species, because man has rearranged the landscape? Perhaps so. Vernon Bailey found the white-throat restricted to rocky uplands and the southern plains woodrat throughout the valley lowlands in the first decade of the twentieth century. Now, however, the white-throat is in the Jornada Valley, and the southern plains woodrat is confined to overgrazed and naturally disturbed sites such as arroyos, floodplains, and shifting sands.[23]

Running about sand dunes or lava beds at night is one thing, but running by day is quite another. Watch a family of stagehands with barefoot children let out at noon at White Sands National Monument for a graphic demonstration of why daytime activity among white-sands animals is limited to early morning and late afternoon. Midday ground-surface temperatures typically reach 115 degrees Fahrenheit

United States," *Univ. California Publ. Zool.* 40 (1933):1–70; and K. S. Norris and C. H. Lowe, "An Analysis of Background Color-matching in Amphibians and Reptiles," *Ecology* 45 (1964):565–580.

[23]V. Bailey, *Mammals of New Mexico*, N. Amer. Fauna 53 (1931), pp. 173–175; M. W. Wright, "Analysis of Habitats of Two Woodrats in Southern New Mexico," *J. Mammal.* 54 (1973):529–535.

on the reflective gypsum sands and approach 150 degrees on the more absorptive adobe and lava soils.

Yet some creatures are exclusively diurnal. There are ground squirrels in both habitats, many of the characteristic shrub-desert birds, and several species of reptiles. The lives of three white-sands lizards make an especially instructive character study, as they intersect through the controlling force of daytime heat but are different enough to allow coexistence with little or no competition. For them, as for all desert reptiles, the critical problem is to avoid temperature extremes while using heat. All are ectothermic—dependent on environmental temperatures to maintain their metabolism at activity levels. So they thermoregulate behaviorally, alternately seeking sun and shade, posturing, panting, continually adjusting their body temperatures.

Just after the summer dawn, soil-surface temperatures rise to about 84 degrees on the sands, and a few eastern fence and lesser earless lizards become active. They flatten against the ground, oriented toward the oblique rays of the sun. Their body temperatures are 89 to 95 degrees now but will rise rapidly, reaching normal activity temperatures of 96 to 100 degrees. Around 10 A.M. I see more fence and earless lizards than at any other time of day. Now little-striped whiptails get up. They are late risers, since they require 100-degree body temperatures for optimum activity. Because soil temperatures peak between noon and 2 P.M. and have risen 5 to 10 degrees beyond the tolerance limits of all lizards, I note a dramatic decline in activity just before noon. The lizards repair to burrows. Around 3 to 4 P.M., as environmental temperatures fall, fence and earless lizards reappear briefly, but little-striped whiptails have called it a day.

Eastern fence lizards remain no more than ten feet from desert shrubs, which they use for escape, shade, and late afternoon heating pads. James Dixon, who postulated the heating-pad phenomenon, recorded late afternoon soil temperatures in the open sands at eighty-three degrees, while beneath the shrubs the soil was ninety-five degrees.[24] Apparently, fence lizards maintain their body temperatures at activity levels late in the day by staying where it remains hottest longest. And the sand beneath the shrubs is the hottest, because the in-

---

[24] J. R. Dixon, *Aspects of the Biology of the Lizards of the White Sands, New Mexico*, Los Angeles Co. Mus. Contrib. Sci. 129 (1967).

sulative quality of vegetative cover slows the radiation of heat into space. In contrast to fence lizards, lesser earless lizards move more freely in the open sands. Their maximum body temperatures are a few degrees higher than those of fence lizards, reflecting their particular life-style away from shrub cover.

Little-striped whiptails also frequent open sand dunes, where they forage in jerky spurts and eat insect larvae that they dig from beneath leaf litter around the bases of shrubs. Fence and earless lizards eat different insect foods, rarely dig for them, and move without the jerkiness characteristic of all whiptails. Different food habits, body temperatures, and uses of vegetation versus open ground indicate that the three *lagartijas* play three distinctive roles in the chessboard ecologic theater. More than anything, they instruct me that most organisms evolve ways of reducing or eliminating competition, obviating resource scarcity, while man does just the opposite. Is this the essence of unnatural history?

Ten thousand years ago and more the white gypsum sands of the Tularosa Valley lined the basin of Lake Otero. When the lake became extinct in postpluvial time, its sands blew about the valley and formed the dunes that now support white lizards and mice. Yet that ancient lake remains a landscape influence in another, more direct way, for it leaves a living reminder, a small blue pupfish in Malpais Spring and Salt Creek. Inadvertently guarded in the U.S. Air Force's ballistic missile range, the white sands pupfish remained isolated from landscape inventories until 1975.[25] I wish other relict pupfishes were equally well off, since all are or were live evidence of wetter prehistoric and historic days. But the others are not so well protected.

Once there were many pupfish springs in the Borderlands. Historically, at least four supported endemic species of aggressive, one- to two-inch pupfish—active, apparently playful, hence puppylike creatures, which appear most joyful when it is hottest. A spring run in a desert sea is the key to understanding pupfish natural and unnatural history. The various species are especially well adapted to high salt concentrations and summer water temperatures that reach 105 de-

---

[25] R. R. Miller and A. A. Echelle, "*Cyprinodon tularosa*: A New Cyprinodontid Fish from the Tularosa Basin, New Mexico," *Southwest. Natur.* 19 (1975):365–377.

grees Fahrenheit in the shallows of their headwater rivulets. No other fish can tolerate such stress.

The pupfish ecologic role is beautifully adjusted to various thermal stage settings. Not only can most species tolerate hot water, but their tolerance levels and choices of water temperature vary with the season and time of day. Critical thermal maxima and minima are those water temperatures in which a pupfish dies or loses its ability to orient and so to escape an unfavorable environmental condition. Such temperatures are lower in the morning than afternoon, and winter values are lower than summer ones, suggesting acclimation in harmony with the days and seasons.

Yet thermal adjustments are even more finely tuned. For instance, the Comanche Springs pupfish prefers seventy- to seventy-seven-degree water on a late summer afternoon, whereas its cohabitant, the Pecos mosquitofish, chooses seventy-nine- to eighty-six-degree water. If tested alone, however, the pupfish chooses the higher thermal regime, suggesting that the thermal segregation reduces competition, as it does among lizards. Equally interesting is the fact that the Leon Springs pupfish begins to spawn at about seventy-two degrees. As the water temperature rises, this species lays its eggs with increasing frequency up to around eighty-six degrees, but at that point spawning drops off as rapidly as it rose in the first place.[26]

In glaciopluvial time several intermontane basins besides the Tularosa contained large lakes, interconnected on occasion and then isolated by drought. Pupfish genes must have spread about the expanded lake landscape, perhaps along hot, saline lakeshores and via streams, because the living species of Malpais Spring, the Pecos River, and as far east as Leon Creek in Texas are closely related. But the great lakes dried away forever several millenia ago, leaving remnant pupfish populations isolated in springs and their outflows, the only permanent surface water. Locally distinctive traits evolved when the spring stages could no longer exchange pupfish actors, and species were left to be discovered and then endangered by the arch predator.

Nothing is more frustrating than to try to tell a pupfish story, for

[26] F. R. Gehlbach, C. Bryan, and H. W. Reno, "Thermal Ecological Features of *Cyprinodon elegans*, and *Gambusia nobilis*, Endangered Texas Fishes," *Texas J. Sci.* 30 (1978):99–101; S. E. Kennedy, "Life History of the Leon Springs Pupfish, *Cyprinodon bovinus*," *Copeia* (1977):93–103.

just as soon as a species' situation seems stable man turns to new and better ways of indirect overkill. Now, for example, introduction of bait fish that hybridize with native pupfish seems to supplement the planting of predators and competitors and overpumping of groundwater as major tools of destruction. A terrestrial animal might hide on a remote mountain, but a two-inch spring fish cannot escape. Its water supply is too small, too well known, and too valuable in arid land. In fact, the Comanche Springs and Leon Springs pupfishes were discovered in 1851 by Boundary surveyors seeking water.

I know a tale of two springs. It begins at Fort Stockton, Texas, home of the distinctive Comanche Springs pupfish between the year of its discovery and 1952, when it was last seen there. Heavy pumping of the aquifer that fed Comanche Springs caused a 61 percent decline in water flow during that century, and the springs dried up completely in 1961. Irrigation agriculture was the principal beneficiary. Fortunately the pupfish also occurred in Phantom Cave and San Solomon Springs plus Toyah Creek some sixty miles to the west. So in 1955 I saw my first Comanche Springs pupfish through a face mask in the pool of San Solomon Spring and enjoyed living evidence of the last ice age instead of pickled proof in a museum jar.[27]

By 1970, though, I could not find the species in the swimming pool at San Solomon. I learned that the water level was periodically lowered and chlorine added for the safety of visitors. San Solomon Spring and its immediate outflow are in Balmorhea State Park, Texas. Moreover, the flow at San Solomon had dropped 37 percent in the present century, Phantom Cave Spring had declined an alarming 85 percent, and all the remaining pupfish—some few thousand adults— lived in concrete irrigation canals by 1970. Overpumping of the spring aquifers continues. At current rates of decline, the Comanche Springs pupfish cannot survive another century. Irrigation agriculture will see to that. Or will it?

Perhaps a small but steady flow of water can be engineered. Why

---

[27] A. A. Echelle, "A Multivariate Analysis of Variation in an Endangered Fish, *Cyprinodon elegans*: With an Assessment of Population Status," *Texas J. Sci.* 26 (1975): 529–538. See also R. R. Miller, "Man and the Changing Fish Fauna of the American Southwest," *Papers Michigan Acad. Sci., Arts, Letters* 46 (1961):365–404. My analysis of spring flow is from data in G. Brune, *Major and Historical Springs of Texas*, Texas Water Devel. Bd. Rept. 189 (1975), pp. 48, 62.

not build a stream-style refuge in the state park, screen it from the predaceous green sunfish and catfish dumped into park waters, and manage it expressly for Comanche Springs pupfishes and the similarly threatened Pecos mosquitofish? Surely even a recreational park can have an educational function, and the Comanche Springs pupfish has a singular story to tell—of vanishing lakes, adaptation to hot, shallow water, and inability to survive naturally with man.

Indeed, such a refuge stream was completed in 1975. But pupfish thrive only in the downstream half, while sunfish patrol the upper end, secreted and cooled in underground pipes, because the artificial habitat remains unmanaged. Pecos mosquitofish are absent. Somehow man must learn that unnatural landscapes are not self-sustaining. To build a refuge is the first and easiest step in conserving nonconsumable resources. The hard part, the commitment to sustenance—management—is too often unrecognized or ignored. Building may be a good deed forgotten. Preservation through management is genuine stewardship.

Now comes the new danger of extinction via hybridization with an introduced relative. The variegated pupfish is dumped into Balmorhea Lake below the state park. Probably it comes as fish bait. By 1968 its genes begin to swamp those of the Comanche Springs pupfish, where the spring water from San Solomon and Phantom Cave flows into the lake via an irrigation canal.[28] A hybrid population commands that habitat, but the alien genes cannot ascend the concrete canal because of a drop-off at the canal-lake junction. Suppose, though, that someone fishes in the lake, uses variegated pupfish bait, and then visits the state park. The park waters, particularly the unattended pupfish refuge, certainly are an inviting place to dump leftover bait, aren't they?

Can stewardship evolve rapidly enough to save the Comanche Springs pupfish? I wonder, apprehensively, as I recount events in the second chapter of my tale. They concern the sister spring, Leon, and its own endemic pupfish at Fort Stockton. After its original discovery in 1851, the Leon Springs pupfish was not seen again until 1965. It was considered extinct, and for good reason, during the century that the

---

[28] M. M. Stevenson and T. M. Buchanan, "An Analysis of Hybridization between the Cyprinodont Fishes *Cyprinodon variegatus* and *C. elegans*," *Copeia* (1973):682–692.

Comanche Springs pupfish was extirpated from its home spring only eight miles away. Leon Springs was dammed about 1910, game fish and carp were stocked, the water was poisoned to eliminate carp in the 1940's, and the flow declined to zero during the period of landscape tinkering.[29]

Apparently no one looked in Leon Creek or Diamond-Y Spring and its own rivulet a few miles downstream. Perhaps this is because the flow sometimes ceases near highways, as during the 1950's drought, and traveling naturalists have the unfortunate tendency to stop only at highway stream crossings. Too often we are in too big a hurry. Furthermore, the Leon Creek drainage is an imposing oil and gas field. I spent nearly a day in August, 1972, securing permission from entangling rancher–oil industry alliances before venturing forth in the desert of pipeline scars, and I recall thinking that if the Leon Springs pupfish really lived it must be in extreme jeopardy.

My mental travail seemed unfounded, as I saw a supposedly extinct fish several thousand strong, living throughout three miles of desert stream and isolated potholes. The Leon Springs pupfish was alive and well in both Leon and Diamond-Y creeks. Of special interest was the species' abundance in shallow pools dammed by oil and gas lines. I could not believe my eyes. A year later Stephen Kennedy figured that summer populations reached 1,800 and 2,700 in two such unnatural environments compared with 180 and 260 in two natural habitats. However, the following winter population counts revealed drastic declines in the artificial habitat, while slight increases were observed in the natural stream. My uneasiness returned.

Oil spills could account for the population crash, although insufficient food and extreme temperature flux in the artificial habitats may be involved. Kennedy later confirmed the destructive influence of oil. Of four serious spills he saw near Diamond-Y Spring in 1973–1975, three reached its outflow and two killed pupfish. The landowners, the U.S. Soil Conservation Service, and naturalists had designed and built a diversion dike around Diamond-Y in 1974, but it protected only the headspring. And spills continued despite the fact that oil company representatives were present at our planning sessions and sympathetic to

[29] Kennedy, "Leon Springs Pupfish"; Miller, "Man and Changing Fish Fauna," pp. 381–382.

the cause. The long-lost Leon Springs pupfish might be lost again, this time for good.

Meanwhile, the familiar threat of extinction through hybridization appeared. Variegated pupfish were dumped into Leon Creek in 1974, and the endemic species, like its Comanche Springs counterpart, had no reproductive isolating mechanisms against the invader. I believe the pools dammed by pipelines favored the hybridization process, acting as reservoirs for propagation, since within the same year a hybrid swarm extended throughout the lower half of the creek. Regardless of the reason, the amalgamation was astoundingly swift. Something would have to be done quickly to save the historically and genetically significant Leon Springs pupfish.

Naturalists opted for arch-predator status. They removed pure Leon Springs pupfishes for planting in abandoned Federal fish hatchery pools at Dexter, New Mexico, alongside pools with Comanche Springs pupfish, Pecos mosquitofish, and other threatened species. And they poisoned the lower creek's hybrid swarm with rotenone in February, 1976, killing untold thousands of fish but saving specimens for laboratory studies.[30] After time to allow the creek to cleanse itself of the biodegradable poison, pure Leon Springs pupfish from upstream were seeded in the devastated lower half. But a recheck in November revealed that genes from the variegated invader remained, although pure aliens could not be found.

Is the saving of a small, instructive pupfish a sound investment in unnatural history? Surely it is a measure of man's concern for his benign associates in the actors' guild of life. Furthermore, it gauges man's ability to perfect his landscape engineering to include natural diversity in his future. From the practical standpoint, the arch predator is foolish if he will not try to save genes that tolerate hot, salty water. Think of a future when all Borderlands streams are dammed and all the reservoirs thermally polluted because of man's overwhelming energy requirements.

[30] In 1972 Pecos mosquitofish seemed threatened by hybridization with common mosquitofish in Leon Creek but experienced little or no contamination at Phantom Cave Spring and Blue Spring in New Mexico (see C. Hubbs, T. Lucier, E. Marsh, G. P. Garrett, R. J. Edwards, and E. Milstead, "Results of an Eradication Program on the Ecological Relationships of Fishes in Leon Creek, Texas," *Southwest. Natur.* 23 (1978):487–496.

8. Wrong Way West

BECAUSE of an error on a map, the 1851 U.S.–Mexican Boundary ran the wrong way in the western Borderlands—west from the Rio Grande Valley at Dona Ana, then north to the Gila River, and down the Gila to its junction with the Colorado River at Yuma, Arizona.[1] This mistake led to John Bartlett's replacement by William Emory as head of the U.S. Boundary Commission, the Gadsden Purchase, and the present International Border whose natural and unnatural history I recount. It also led to discoveries on the upper Gila watershed. As I shiver under snowflake stars near the headwaters of the Gila's west fork, I marvel again at both Bartlett and Emory, generalists in the tradition of Thomas Jefferson. Very little natural history escaped their attention.

Here at the Gila's head it is thirty-eight degrees. How can bats feed this June evening? Yet I hear them above me and recall that Clyde Jones found the majority of the bats he studied in southwestern New Mexico above 7,000 feet in these coniferous forests.[2] Sixteen of the nineteen species he captured in mist nets were taken at air temperatures below sixty-eight degrees Fahrenheit. Eleven species flew at temperatures below fifty degrees, and the silver-haired and hoary bats flew during freezing weather. These findings could be a bit misleading, though. Since Jones's nets were stretched over water, perhaps he caught bats that were only thirsty, not foraging more generally. Any-

[1] On the human drama of the First Boundary Survey, see O. B. Faulk, *Too Far North . . . Too Far South* (Los Angeles: Westernlore Press, 1967); and R. V. Hine, *Bartlett's West: Drawing the Mexican Boundary* (New Haven: Yale Univ. Press, 1968). See also J. R. Bartlett's own *Personal Narrative of the Explorations and Incidents in Texas, New Mexico, California, Sonora, and Chihuahua, Connected with the United States and Mexican Boundary Commission during the Years 1850, '51, '52, and '53*, 2 vols. (New York: D. Appleton and Co., 1854).

[2] C. Jones, "Ecological Distribution and Activity Periods of Bats of the Mogollon Mountains Area of New Mexico and Adjacent Arizona," *Tulane Studies in Zool.* 12 (1965):93–100.

way, I am intrigued that species like the long-eared myotis, whose body is but two inches long, live almost exclusively in these forests where temperatures are so low.

Small mammals like bats, compared with large ones like bears, have proportionately more skin-surface area relative to their body volume. Also, the more and larger the appendages, the more skin area. With their skin-covered, finger bone–supported wings, bats have quite a bit more surface area than birds, whose wings are mostly feathers. So bats lose a lot of heat in flight, whereas they conserve heat during daytime rest with their heat radiators folded.[3] Tonight a small bat's life strategy must be to determine whether flying will net enough insects to transform into the energy to fly twenty-four hours hence, or whether resting with folded wings—even folded ears in some species—is the proper energy management. If the cold continues, bats can conserve body energy by lowering heat output, becoming inactive or torpid, or they may simply migrate southward.

With so many species in these forests, I wonder how bats avoid competition for the insects they chase? One answer is tolerance of different temperatures, so some species fly earlier when it is warmer and some fly later at cooler temperatures. Predators in the same community often segregate by being active at different times. But Jones's study does not show any time-temperature correlation, because he netted at water holes. Some bats, like some humans, drink before dining, while others may be hungry enough to eat first and drink later. Nevertheless, insectivorous bats feed at different heights and on different sizes of prey according to their own body size. In partitioning resources, habitat dimensions are more important than food types, which are more important than temporal divisions among animals in general.[4]

Hummingbirds are the smallest feathered users of the aerial space

[3] R. E. Henshaw, "Thermoregulation in Bats," in *About Bats: A Chiropteran Biology Symposium*, ed. B. H. Slaughter and D. W. Walton, pp. 188–232 (Dallas: S. Methodist Univ. Press, 1970). See also F. Bourliere, "Mammals, Small and Large: The Ecological Implications of Size," in *Small Mammals: Their Productivity and Population Dynamics*, ed. B. Golley, K. Petrusewicz, L. Ryszkowski, pp. 1–8 (London: Cambridge Univ. Press, 1975).

[4] T. W. Schoener, "Resource Partitioning in Ecological Communities," *Science* 185 (1974):24–39.

in coniferous forest, and they face the same heat conservation problem as bats. Consider the Anna's hummer, studied in California by Oliver Pearson.[5] Like others of its nectar-feeding brethren, the Anna's has evolved the strategy of becoming torpid at night to conserve energy. This bird does not merely sleep when it turns aerial space over to bats at night. Rather its high daytime heat production drops precipitously to a new low level. Such torpidity saves three times the energy saved by sleeping. Pearson calculated that Anna's hummers spend about half their daily energy intake perching, a third feeding, and much smaller amounts defending territories and catching insects. He figured that the nectar of 1,022 fuchsia blossoms is required to supply the daily energy demands of one Anna's hummingbird.

Male hummers can afford to go torpid, since they leave family affairs entirely to the females. But what about a female hummingbird that must incubate its eggs during this cold mountain night? Surely it must produce more heat than torpidity allows, or its eggs will not develop. Female hummers have evolved continuous nest construction and proper placement plus vigorous evening feeding to obtain energy sufficient for nocturnal incubation. Those of us with hummingbird feeders know our clients are most active in the evening and still fly at dusk. If I watch the flurry of evening activity closely during the nesting season, I see a majority of females in the last wave of arrivals. Watchers of Anna's hummingbird nests have found that females are away twice as long in the evening as in the morning, presumably feeding.[6]

Here in the Mogollon Mountains and elsewhere broad-tailed hummingbirds place their nests beneath sheltering branches or leaf clumps and continue to weave spider webbing around moss, lichens, and bark fragments, enlarging their nests daily during incubation and brooding of young. At one nest, measured before dawn, broad-tail eggs were ninety-two degrees Fahrenheit, the incubating female's back was fifty-four degrees, the air immediately above her thirty-eight degrees, and the open sky above the leafy canopy below freezing. Like broad-tails, blue-throated hummingbirds continue to add to their nests while

[5]O. P. Pearson, "The Daily Energy Requirements of a Wild Anna's Hummingbird," Condor 56 (1954):317–322.

[6]W. K. Smith, S. W. Roberts, and P. C. Miller, "Calculating the Nocturnal Energy Expenditure of an Incubating Anna's Hummingbird," Condor 76 (1974):176–183.

Broad-tailed Pair (*upper*) and Black-chinned Hummingbirds (Emory)

raising two or three broods per summer per nest up to four summers in a row. Herbert Brandt records one blue-throat nest used for ten consecutive years in the Huachuca Mountains.[7] Blue-throat "mountains" may reach three inches in diameter and five inches in height. I am im-

[7] W. A. Calder, "Microhabitat Selection during Nesting of Hummingbirds in the Rocky Mountains," *Ecology* 54 (1973): 127–134; H. Brandt, *Arizona and Its Bird Life* (Cleveland: Bird Res. Foundtn., 1951), p. 657. Carroll and Joan Peabody of Ramsey Canyon, Huachuca Mountains, record nine consecutive years of two broods each in a blue-

pressed by the insulating potential of such structures, which, to my thinking, resemble mummy-type sleeping bags.

Several miles to the east and in similar coniferous forest on the east fork of the Gila River is Wall Lake, a man-made fishing hole for hatchery-reared, non-native rainbow trout. Here too are species summarily killed by fishermen, because they eat rainbows: the Sonoran mud turtle and narrow-headed, black-necked, and western garter snakes. Yet these semiaquatic reptiles have lived in the east fork with the native Gila trout for millenia. Once I did find a twenty-four-inch western garter snake eating a four-inch hatchery rainbow, and Eugene Fleharty, who studied the three garter snakes at Wall Lake, noted exotic green sunfish and rainbows in the stomachs of the western and narrow-headed species.[8] If there is trouble, it is because man produced a slow, warm-water pond where a fast, cold-water stream should be.

Fleharty's study demonstrates how closely related predators in the same community divide up space and food in a manner that reduces competition. The narrow-headed garter snake is best adapted to streams and feeds exclusively on fish. Its habitat features shady conditions and consequently low environmental and body temperatures. This species spends more time in the water than the other two. As a specialized feeder, the narrow-head lives among the eight remaining native fishes of the upper Gila River, a predator nicely adjusted to its prey.

While Wall Lake has been detrimental to native fishes and probably to the narrow-headed garter snake, it seems to benefit the black-necked and western species. These two maintain higher body temperatures by basking and are usually found under sunny skies rather than in the shade. Possibly they compete for basking space, but the black-neck feeds exclusively on frogs and tadpoles, whereas the western is catholic in food habits and much more terrestrial. I have watched this species eat insects, mice, lizards, and earthworms, besides trout. By creating a sunlit pond, I believe man inadvertently promotes black-necked and western garter snakes.

throated hummingbird's nest located apparently where the nest collected by Herbert Brandt was found three decades earlier.

[8] E. D. Fleharty, "Comparative Ecology of *Thamnophis elegans, T. cyrtopsis,* and *T. rufipunctatus* in New Mexico," *Southwest. Natur.* 12 (1967):207–230.

What will we do next? Well, we might fill Wall Lake up with beer cans, a proposition I overhear one hot afternoon as a comradely eastern fence lizard and I drape a ponderosa pine log in the campground. Children are busily hacking up the campsite's trees. I watch, mentally reviewing my first aid, as they chop live pines cross grain instead of using a saw on dead timber. Later, tubing downstream, I am turned away by a noisy group chucking rocks at a beaver lodge, preparing an assault on the Gila Wilderness Area. I apologize to the spirit of Aldo Leopold, creator of this reserve, and drift on with the current into less hectic surroundings.

Among major waterways in these western Borderlands, the upper Gila River may be least culturally altered. Eight of the nine native fishes found by William Koster in the 1940's are still here in 1972, and they include the endangered loach minnow, spikedace, and Gila trout.[9] Roundtail chubs and coarse-scaled and Gila mountain suckers also remain, but the Gila topminnow is gone. This one- to two-inch species, known only from the Frisco Hot Springs area, was eliminated when the common mosquitofish was introduced and possibly ate it up.

The longfin dace is abundant in the upper Gila and invades upstream as silt replaces gravel, pools are filled, and water temperatures ameliorate. It seems to be displacing the speckled dace, found as low as 4,500 feet in the 1940's but only above 6,000 feet now. Elsewhere, on and below the Mogollon Rim, a similar tale is told. Of seventeen sites once inhabited by both dace in Arizona, five no longer support either species, and the remaining twelve support longfin dace alone.[10] Thus, among native fishes of the Gila River, the longfin dace seems well suited to withstanding man. I must look at its use of stream resources sometime.

There were six introduced fishes in the upper Gila in 1940 and fifteen by the 1960's. One, the rainbow trout, doubtlessly helped to place the native Gila trout on the endangered-species list by polluting its genes through hybridization. This bit of unnatural history reminds

[9] H. F. LaBounty and W. L. Minckley, "Native Fishes of the Upper Gila River System, New Mexico," in *Symposium on Rare and Endangered Wildlife of the Southwestern United States*, pp. 134–146 (Santa Fe: N.M. Dept. Game and Fish, 1972). Roundtail chubs have been rediscovered here since this report of their demise.

[10] Figure 8 in J. E. Deacon and W. L. Minckley, "Desert Fishes," in *Desert Biology*, vol. 2, ed. G. W. Brown, Jr., pp. 385–488 (New York: Academic Press, 1974).

me of the pupfishes in Texas, where there was no resistance to re-productively compatible, introduced species because there had been no natural requirement for it. And Wall Lake, locally suitable for exotic and hybrid trout, is like the pipeline pools in Leon Creek, Texas—a reservoir of extinction by means of hybridization.

Eastward is the Mimbres River Valley, described by John Bartlett in April, 1851, as the first greenery he had seen since leaving central Texas. It was a mile wide somewhere between Santa Rita and Deming, New Mexico, but the river proper was ten to twenty feet wide. Six weeks later and fifteen miles south, Bartlett noted that the Mimbres was dry.[11] Today it remains dry except at its headwaters, so it is difficult to visualize a live drainage into Laguna de Guzmán, Chihuahua, much less one that gave up the first and nearly the last Chihuahua chub in 1851. When rediscovered in the upper Mimbres 124 years later, only a few dozen Chihuahua chubs remained in the United States.

It is almost axiomatic that if native fishes survive in the Border-lands, they do so in springs and headwater creeks that are permanent and unpenetrated by the genes of introduced species. Large fishes can-not reach or reproduce in shallow headwater flows, hence we lose such natives as the two- to six-foot Colorado River squawfish and the one- to three-foot humpback sucker. Fortunately, large exotic predators like the black basses of the upper Gila cannot reach the headwaters either. Survival is most probable for small species—fishes or terrestrial ani-mals, it makes no difference. The evolutionary trend toward large size in all vertebrates became a distinct disadvantage once man appeared.

Will we wind up being the biggest animals left on earth? Even if not, we certainly will build some big monuments to unnatural history. The copper smelter stacks at Hurley, New Mexico, remind me of that, as I emerge with the Gila River from the Mogollon Plateau. It is im-possible to get lost between El Paso and Ajo, Arizona, because of the many visual and olfactory landmarks associated with copper mining and smelting. My entry into Clifton, Arizona, just north of the entry of

[11] Bartlett, *Personal Narrative*, vol. 1, p. 221. Note also W. H. Emory, *Notes of a Military Reconnaissance from Fort Leavenworth in Missouri to San Diego in California, Including Parts of the Arkansas, Del Norte, and Gila Rivers* (New York: H. Long and Brother, 1848), pp. 96–97, which mentions trout (= Chihuahua chubs?) in the Rio Mimbres.

Santa Rita del Cobre (Bartlett)

the San Francisco River into the Gila, can only be described as a step back into history. I found conditions in June, 1971, essentially as Vernon Bailey described them in June, 1907: "a big, noisy, booming, banging, slamming, mining town. . . . The mine hills . . . are enormous and fill the canyon with a horrid din and vile sulphurous odors and pour down floods of thick, grey poisonous mud into the river."[12]

Hurley, New Mexico, is next door to Santa Rita del Cobre, the Spanish copper mining town that was headquarters of Bartlett's Boundary survey in 1851. Nearby is Fort Bayard, headquarters of naturalists on various U.S. Army explorations in the nineteenth century. Before traveling downriver along Bartlett's wrongly chosen Boundary, I had recalled a bit of scientific sleuthing associated with Fort Bayard—some historical-biological research not unlike my search for the rough-footed mud turtles of Texas. This particular investigation by John Hubbard

---

[12] Unpublished field notes of Vernon Bailey, 1902, on file in U.S. Fish and Wildlife Service Laboratory, Natl. Mus. Nat. Hist., Washington, D.C. On biotic repercussions of pollution associated with copper mining and smelting, see C. W. Wood, Jr., and T. N. Nash III, "Copper Smelter Effluent Effects on Sonoran Desert Vegetation," *Ecology* 57 (1976): 1311–16.

focused on April 23, 1876, when Frank Stephens had collected certain eggs near Fort Bayard. For a century they were New Mexico's only tangible claim to the gray hawk.[13]

Gray hawks nest in the U.S. Borderlands mainly in south-central Arizona, along Sonoita Creek, the San Pedro River and the Santa Cruz River between Tucson and Nogales. Early egg dates here are clustered in the second and third weeks of May, although Frank Stephens once found eggs on May 2. Here also, the gray hawk is a deciduous woodland species, nesting in cottonwoods and sycamores below 4,500 feet. But Fort Bayard is at 6,000 feet, and April 23 is a week earlier than any other confirmed date in the United States. The date is about right for the Cooper's hawk. John Hubbard had the identity of the Fort Bayard eggs checked by an expert on raptorial birds, but I think things "smelled like rotten eggs" to him.

It would be a simple matter to get the historic eggs and compare them with modern gray and Cooper's hawk eggs except that of the original four only one remains. Nevertheless, measurements and descriptions are available on all four, and Hubbard ruled out all possible species except the gray and Cooper's. Egg color is identical in both, and measurements can be used only after regional differences in size are accounted for. Upon final comparisons the problematic eggs from Fort Bayard are the same size as Cooper's hawk eggs from New Mexico or Arizona and significantly smaller than the eggs of Arizona gray hawks. Frank Stephens erred.

Another collector of hawk eggs did not err, fortunately, and his brief episode illustrates the vicissitudes of investigating natural history on the nineteenth-century frontier. Modern students of raptors, equipped with metal helmets and climbing irons or ladders, emanating from vehicles driven near nest tree or cliff, would do well to know this story. It seems that when Charles Bendire was stationed at Fort Lowell near Tucson, Arizona, in 1872, he located a zone-tailed hawk's nest forty feet up in a cottonwood. Upon climbing to obtain an egg, undescribed at that time, the intrepid Major Bendire noticed a band of Apaches watching him. So he carefully put the two-inch egg in his mouth,

[13]J. P. Hubbard, "The Status of the Gray Hawk in New Mexico," *Auk* 91 (1974): 163–166. For another view see D. A. Zimmerman, "On the Status of *Buteo nitidus* in New Mexico," *Auk* 93 (1976): 650–655.

climbed down, and rode his horse five miles to the safety of his camp. There the slightly incubated egg was extracted from his aching jaws.[14]

The zone-tailed hawk nests in the Gila River Valley and, like the gray hawk, is a tropical species that ranges somewhat north of the Borderlands. Despite their black-and-white-banded tails, zone-tails and even common black hawks very closely resemble vultures in flight style and profile. The zone-tail seems to mimic the turkey vulture, while the black hawk mimics the black vulture. When the zone-tail flies with vultures, as it often does, it is said to dive suddenly on unsuspecting prey, using the vultures as cover. Presumably small birds, mammals, and reptiles, familiar with the eating habits of vultures, do not hide when they and the zone-tail approach. This phenomenon is called aggressive mimicry.[15]

I have watched zone-tailed hawks in many Border places, particularly along the Devils River in Texas. Several times they flew with turkey vultures and even black vultures, but never did I see them forage from such flocks. Twice zone-tails were attacked by nesting red-tailed hawks and Cooper's hawks when flying alone, yet I never saw this when they flew with vultures over the same aeries. Perhaps in addition to using vulture flocks for aggressive mimicry, zone-tails use them for protective mimicry, concealment against the attacks of territorial birds that do not concern themselves with nonpredaceous vultures. Also it seems likely that these hawks and vultures simply aggregate in local thermal winds that facilitate dispersal in the search for food.

John Hubbard finds nine raptors nesting in the Gila River Valley, New Mexico, seven of which use the deciduous woodland.[16] Almost half the breeding birds of this valley are dependent on riparian hab-

---

[14] F. M. Bailey, *Birds of the Santa Rita Mountains in Southern Arizona*, Pacific Coast Avifauna 15 (1923). A somewhat different story is in H. Brandt, *Arizona Bird Life*, p. 112, perhaps because of confusion on identity of the eggs. See C. Bendire, *Life Histories of North American Birds with Special Reference to Their Breeding Habits and Eggs*, U.S. Natl. Mus. Spec. Bull. 1 (1892), pp. 231–233.

[15] E. O. Willis, "Is the Zone-tailed Hawk a Mimic of the Turkey Vulture?" *Condor* 65 (1963):313–317. An early reference to black hawk–black vulture mimicry is by A. H. Clark, quoted in J. B. May, *The Hawks of North America* (New York: Natl. Audubon Soc., 1935), p. 72.

[16] J. P. Hubbard, *The Summer Birds of the Gila Valley, New Mexico*, Nemouria 2 (1971). See also R. D. Porter and C. M. White, "Status of Some Rare and Lesser Known Hawks in Western United States," in *World Conference on Birds of Prey*, ed. R. D. Chancellor, pp. 39–57 (Hampshire, England: Internatl. Council Bird Preserv., 1977).

itats. This fraction includes the endangered Mexican duck, the only New Mexico population of the Abert's towhee, the northward-penetrating cardinal and hooded oriole, and such common riparian indicators as the brown-crested flycatcher, yellow and Lucy's warblers, yellow-billed cuckoo, western wood pewee, and blue grosbeak. Since four reservoirs are proposed for the Gila River between the mouth of Mogollon Creek and the Arizona border, can we assume that extirpations will exceed additions to the breeding avifauna in the future?

So far only two birds are gone from the original Gila River fauna. The turkey, *el guajolote,* had been gunned down by 1910 and was reintroduced thereafter—an expensive bird—while the American bittern disappeared with the once-extensive marshes at Mangas Springs about the same time the turkey did. Eight native species have invaded the Gila Valley, however. First to arrive were the cardinal and Gila woodpecker about 1908, then the Lucy's warbler, Inca dove, and common black hawk in the 1920's, the common crow, great-tailed grackle, bronzed cowbird, and indigo bunting in the 1960's, and finally the gray hawk in 1975. I cannot forget Old World imports, either—the house sparrow that arrived about the turn of the century, the starling of the 1960's, and the purposely introduced ring-necked pheasant.

Our landscape tinkering favors many of the arrivals, but the effects may be indirect. In the Gila Valley I suspect that more dead cottonwoods, killed by more water diverted away for more irrigation, and hence drilled by more woodpeckers, provide more nesting cavities for starlings. Then too, the irrigated fields favor more western meadowlarks, and I agree with John Hubbard's supposition that shrubs spread by overgrazing attract thrashers, brown towhees, and black-throated sparrows at the expense of grassland birds like horned larks and eastern meadowlarks. Certainly more buildings invite more Say's phoebes, barn swallows, and house finches, while road culverts house more cliff and barn swallows plus black phoebes. Edificial effects influence these species directly.

From dispersal records of the Inca dove, bronzed cowbird, and great-tailed grackle in the U.S. Borderlands, I discover that their northward spread averages six miles per year and is positively correlated with average size of the species.[17] True, larger birds are poten-

---

[17] Northward dispersal rates of 4.5–8.5 ($\bar{x} = 5.9 \pm 0.5$) miles per year correlate ($r = 0.80$, $P<0.02$, 6 $d.f.$) with mean weights of the Inca dove (47 g.), bronzed cowbird

tially more vagile, hence preadapted for the invasion, but I think I see the continuing evolution of large size. It is well known that a species may evolve its largest size at its northern, coldest limits of range. This promotes heat conservation. In addition, perhaps ongoing evolution of large size is a selective requisite for successful penetration of the U.S. interior by invaders that are culturally induced away from their warmer bases in Mexico.

Rapid evolution is known in house sparrows, so why not expect it in native Americans?[18] Indeed, great-tailed grackles from central Texas in the 1970's have significantly longer legs and bills and are heavier than those of the 1950's.[19] Over the past two decades alone, they have gained an average of four millimeters of appendage length and five grams of body weight, so they have apparently evolved larger size at average rates of two-tenths of a millimeter and three-tenths of a gram each year. Since 1849, when they nested no farther northeast than the Texas-Tamaulipas border, great-tails have invaded the heart of Texas and beyond at an average speed of 8.5 miles per year.

Urbanites have surely subsidized the new evolutionary role of the great-tailed grackle, as I noted earlier in New Mexico's Rio Grande Valley. But have they paid close attention to the entire cast of the new play they have financed in ecological theaters of cultural design? Who, for instance, has walked city streets recording bird identities and numbers to relate to the increasing diversity of urban vegetation over time?

(54 g.), and great-tailed grackle (159 g.). Dispersal was calculated from data in various references (see nn. 11–15, ch. 7, and n. 19 below).

[18] J. B. Calhoun, "The Role of Temperature and Natural Selection in Relation to the Variations in the Size of the English Sparrow in the United States," *Amer. Natur.* 81 (1947):203–228; R. F. Johnston and R. K. Selander, "House Sparrows: Rapid Evolution of Races in North America," *Science* 144 (1964):548–550.

[19] Wintering great-tailed grackles from Waco (1978, $N = 116$; 1974, $N = 79$) were compared with those from Austin, 1956, taken by R. K. Selander ("Age Determination and Molt in the Boat-tailed Grackle," *Condor* 60 [1958]:255–276). Unweighted mean wing, tail, exposed culmen, tarsus, and weight (corrected for crop contents at Waco) measures were tested with two-way analysis of variance (ANOVA) comparing years versus sex and age class (juvenile or adult). Significant ($F = 13$–520, $P<0.05$, 2 $d.f.$) interyear differences, showing a progressive size increase in bill, tarsus, and weight, were subjected to Student-Newman-Keuls tests, which revealed significant distinctions in seven of the nine mean comparisons. Speed of northward movement is the mean of five values, based on presumed dispersal from one city to the next one north (year first seen nesting) between Austin and Denton (H. C. Oberholser, *The Bird Life of Texas*, vol. 2, ed. E. B. Kincaid, Jr. [Austin: Univ. Texas Press, 1974], pp. 834–835).

Most of us observe cultural succession generally, but who watches the parade of birds on our city stages to learn whether an urban avifauna develops according to man's rules or nature's? Of course some birds can't stand cityscapes, just as some people can't, but perhaps an urban bird community diversifies and so becomes more interesting as a city ages.

I think of Tucson, Arizona, where the diversity of resident birds in a sixty-five-year-old suburb was but 79 percent of the natural shrub desert value. And I know of Claremont, California, where twenty-five-year-old suburbs have this same fraction of the avifaunal diversity characteristic of nearby chaparral communities.[20] Concurrently, seventy-year-old suburbs at Claremont contain 86 percent of natural diversity, one-year-old suburbs only 51 percent, so I suspect that cultural succession is much like natural succession in restoring the most complex community structure the local environment will support.

Birds are tied so closely to planted vegetation in Claremont that their increased diversity over time corresponds significantly to the parallel change in vegetative diversity. Further, I am struck by an equally strong concurrence between increased bird species diversity and decreased density of invader and edificial birds—the exotic rock dove, spotted dove, starling, and house sparrow, plus such natives as the mockingbird and house finch. In fact, the house sparrow and house finch independently account for most of this effect. Although declining in number as the city ages, they remain the two most abundant hence influential species in the successional sequence.

It is clear that bird species are few and the densities of some like the house sparrow and finch very high soon after suburban settlement. Then avifaunal diversity rises quickly with the coincident rise in plant species diversity. Other kinds of birds arrive, and abundances of the

---

[20] Calculations are based on data in tables 1 and 2 of D. A. Guthrie's "Suburban Bird Populations in Southern California," *Amer. Midl. Natur.* 92 (1974): 461–466. Others categories are omitted. Pearson correlation coefficients of bird species diversity (H') with plant species diversity (H') and total density of invader and edificial species equal 0.73 and -0.77, respectively ($P<0.01$, 11 $d.f.$). In a multiple stepwise regression (MSR) of bird species diversity on each species' density, r^2 additions of the house finch and house sparrow are 0.59 and 0.10 ($F = 17, 14, P<0.05, 11\ d.f.$). See also R. K. Lancaster and W. E. Rees, "Bird Communities and the Structure of Urban Habitats," *Canadian J. Zool.* 57 (1979): 2358–68.

species become more similar, as populations of edificial birds decline. Finally, bird species diversity continues to rise, but the rate of change slows down. It is not clear whether urban avifaunal diversity ever matches that of the natural community the city erased, although I find it reassuring that cultural succession follows the ground rules of natural succession.

9. The Landscape Maze

IF you are a grassland or desert dweller and run, fly, burrow, or are blown against the Sierra Madre Occidental, you have a transportation problem. The montane woodlands and forests are inhospitable and unsupportive, comparatively cool and wet. Either you stay where you are, in the Chihuahuan or Sonoran regional lowlands, or you traverse the low passes and mountain canyons. River routes may be open if you can swim or tolerate a wooded highway. Thus some species from each desert region penetrate through the upland barriers while others never make it. Genes, whether in two- and four-legged packages or as seeds and spores, flow through or are filtered out in the landscape maze of the New Mexico panhandle and adjacent Arizona, Sonora, and Chihuahua.

Pioneering man is no different, because he is a grassland animal. Concerned with crossing the sierras on his trip from Santa Rita, New Mexico, to Arizpe, Sonora, John Bartlett chose a passage through Guadalupe Canyon, 150 miles south of his Gila River Boundary. This route was also followed by William Emory in marking the Gadsden Purchase Border with its original stone monuments and by Edgar Mearns, whose Cloverdale and Hall's Ranch campsites I have studied. Lowland quadrupeds besides man have made the transmontane passage, though not always via Guadalupe Canyon, and even some fish have crossed over the Sierra Madre Occidental. Who they are and how and why they did it intrigues me greatly.

Most large mammals move through the sierras unimpeded and so have not evolved Chihuahuan versus Sonoran regional distinctions. Of seventeen species jackrabbit size or larger in both regional lowlands, only the black-tailed jackrabbit and kit fox have distinct geographic races or subspecies in each.[1] However, the white-sided jackrabbit of

---

[1] Geographic assessment of terrestrial vertebrates is based largely on range maps in E. R. Hall and K. R. Kelson, *The Mammals of North America*, 2 vols. (New York: Ronald

Near Mouth of Guadalupe Canyon (Emory)

Chihuahuan grasslands and the antelope jack, its Sonoran counterpart, suggest that populations of a common ancestor were isolated in each desert region long ago by a rising Sierra Madre and that this barrier to interbreeding caused the evolutionary divergence of these distinctive species.

By contrast with the large mammals, small ones and reptiles and amphibians have been roadblocked more often. They furnish additional examples of regional evolution at the species level. For instance, in the Chihuahuan region live the hispid cotton rat and Coahuilan fringe-toed lizard; in the Sonoran region, their specific relatives, the Arizona cotton rat and Sonoran fringe-toed lizard. Also, there are many cases of geographic differentiation at the subspecies level—incipient speciation, perhaps, if the present trickle of genes from one region to the other is ever shut off. Incidence of subspecies evolution ranges from 44 percent of all reptiles and amphibians in both Chihuahuan and Sonoran lowlands to 80 percent of the small mammals in these two areas.

For any vertebrate, gene flow is a matter of size-related mobility and avenues suitable for dispersal. Large mammals like javelinas can travel several miles a day through such structurally diverse communities as shrub desert and evergreen woodland. When snow covers the

Press, 1959); and R. C. Stebbins, *A Field Guide to Western Reptiles and Amphibians* (Boston: Houghton Mifflin Co., 1966).

ground in Guadalupe Canyon, javelinas move out completely, to return only as their foraging areas thaw. Their genetic features, unrestrained by the landscape maze, flow between Sonoran and Chihuahuan desert regions almost overnight. Conversely, desert pocket mice are but one five-hundredth the size of javelinas and scarcely venture out of half-acre home ranges in a lifetime. If a desert pocket mouse arrives in a grassy canyon bottom, it is there to stay until a population increase pushes individuals up-canyon in increments of half an acre per lifetime. Regional differences evolve readily when gene flow is such a trickle.

One ten-inch creature, the western whiptail lizard, is an exemplary actor in the mazelike ecological theater. An eastern subspecies, the marbled whiptail, is the race typical of the Chihuahuan desert region, living in shrub desert dominated by creosote bush or mesquite. The southern whiptail is its Sonoran desert regional counterpart. Both subspecies typify desert basins and avoid prime grassland, woodland, or forest. Neither occurs above about 4,500 feet, although both may reach such heights if shrub desert is present, as it is on some south- and west-facing mountain slopes.

In the landscape maze, shrub deserts of the Chihuahuan and Sonoran lowlands approach each other along the north-south–trending Peloncillo-Guadalupe Cordillera. Here, marbled and southern whiptails are juxtaposed but prevented from extensive contact by the uplands. However, each subspecies penetrates Steins and Granite passes from its own side of the mountains. North of the mountains the Mogollon Rim blocks these whiptails, although the Sonoran race has come eastward along the Gila River. South of the cordillera, grasslands and the Sierra Madre are barriers to dispersal. Only Steins and Granite passes, 4,000 to 4,500 feet high, are low enough to permit trans-sierran movement.

The southern whiptail seems to have used the two highways more effectively; it meets and interbreeds with the marbled whiptail on the eastern side of the passes, imparting its black chin and chest to its pink-chinned, pink-chested relative.[2] But both whiptails are rather uncommon in the passes and lowlands on either side. Richard Zweifel,

---

[2] R. G. Zweifel, "Analysis of Hybridization between Two Subspecies of the Desert Whiptail Lizard, *Cnemidophorus tigris*," *Copeia* (1962):749–766.

who made the study, found about one-third the number of individuals he had expected from field studies elsewhere. Small populations can promote interbreeding. The smaller two populations are, the greater the likelihood that an individual from one will meet and mate with an individual from the other, and the smaller of the two populations can be overwhelmed by the larger.

Of course, genetic similarity also promotes interbreeding, because organisms like the two whiptails must be close enough to recognize each other as potential mates. Marbled and southern whiptails must have shared a common ancestor, possibly during the warm-dry interpluvial period that preceded the last cool-wet pluvial. Maybe they interbred continuously across the landscape maze at that time. Then they were separated in shrub deserts to either side of the Peloncillo-Guadalupes as a pluvial climate returned with Wisconsin glaciation farther north. This separation could permit the black and pink colorations and other regionally distinctive features to evolve. Environments gradually dried out following retreat of the glaciers and associated pluvial conditions, and the two whiptails must have moved toward each other as their stage settings changed, finally meeting in Steins and Granite passes.

Is it possible that the present interbreeding is indirectly the work of modern man, hence only about a hundred years old? The Animas and San Simon valleys, respectively east and west of the Peloncillo-Guadalupe range, are plains and desert grassland for the most part. But both valleys have suffered from overgrazing, especially along their edges, where soils are shallow and grass is naturally limited. The two whiptails live primarily along the edges of these valleys today, and Zweifel suggests that where the two subspecies are now in contact they may have been separated by grassland until the era of overgrazing.

Grassland in the San Simon Valley is more arid than that in the Animas Valley and hence a better highway for whiptail dispersal. This, I believe, is why the southern whiptail traveled east to meet the marbled whiptail. This Sonoran regional form simply found a more favorable avenue for dispersal, one with more shrub desert, and made the journey first, while the marbled whiptail was slowed down in the Animas Valley.

Several other Sonoran beasts penetrate eastward through low passes or along drainageways. While some contact and interbreed with

Chihuahuan cousins, as the southern whiptail does, a few have no close relatives on the Chihuahuan side. Among reptiles in the latter group are the Gila monster and the Arizona coral snake. By their current ranges in the maze they demonstrate that Sonoran desert influence extends but slightly into southwestern New Mexico and then largely in the Gila River Valley.[3]

Chihuahuan regional character is more pronounced in southeastern Arizona, where desert and grassland invaders from the east live without Sonoran relatives. The hispid pocket and plains harvest mice are mammalian examples. And the western box turtle, western hognose snake, and desert grassland whiptail have made equal incursions. Of the seven small mammals and twenty-three reptiles and amphibians that thread the maze from east or west and lack close relatives on their invasion fronts, 73 percent come from the Chihuahuan side. Half of these have made the 150-mile trip to the grassland–desert basin transition near the Baboquivari Mountains, Arizona.

The roster of invaders from the east includes mostly grassland species because small Chihuahuan creatures are mostly grassland dwellers. For example, if the mammals are listed by occurrence in desert, grassland, woodland, and forest, a significant majority of the small species inhabit grasslands, whereas the other community types have no more or fewer species than would be expected from dividing the total equally among them.[4] I think the small Chihuahuan invaders find more opportunity for dispersal through the maze than their Sonoran counterparts because the region has more grassland than desert. Large mammals, however, are more evenly distributed, perhaps because they are more mobile.

Besides furnishing a valley pathway for terrestrial vertebrates, the

[3]C. H. Lowe, Jr., "The Eastern Limit of the Sonoran Desert in the United States with Additions to the Known Herpetofauna of New Mexico," *Ecology* 36 (1955):343–345. Also note figures 13–16 in J. S. Findley, "Biogeography of Southwestern Boreal and Desert Mammals," in *Contributions in Mammalogy—A Volume Honoring E. Raymond Hall,* ed. J. Knox Jones, Jr., pp. 113–128, Univ. Kansas Mus. Nat. Hist. Misc. Publ. 51 (1969); and pp. 127–130 in D. J. Morafka, *A Biogeographical Analysis of the Chihuahuan Desert through Its Herpetofauna* (The Hague: Dr. W. Junk Publ., 1977).

[4]$\chi^2 = 4.6$, $P<0.05$ for small mammals in grassland; $\chi^2 = 0$–3.4, $P>0.05$ for the other community types, small and large species analyzed separately. Data are reduced from table 1 in J. S. Findley and W. Caire, "The Status of Mammals in the Northern Region of the Chihuahuan Desert," in *Symposium on the Biological Resources of the*

Gila River is a potential aquatic route for fishes. These creatures can move from one river system to another as streams cut headward toward each other, lowering divides and eventually intersecting. This takes geologic time, of course, and the relatively young Sierran and Rocky Mountains highlands—some 70 million years old—will require considerably more weathering before there are widespread stream captures across divides. Meanwhile, the Gila River is a center of evolution, rather than a fish highway, for it harbors seven endemic species—fishes found nowhere else. The neighboring Rio Grande lacks endemics, but the Colorado River houses five and the Río Yaqui one.[5]

At least six fishes have crossed the landscape maze, usually from the Atlantic to the Pacific drainage through stream connections across the Sierra Madre Occidental. These six, the Rio Grande sucker, Río Conchos chub, Casas Grandes and ornate shiners, Mexican stoneroller, and Yaqui catfish, inhabit headwater tributaries and occur in the Rio Grande system in Chihuahua and the Río Yaqui in Sonora. The Rio Grande sucker's distribution suggests how a fish might travel over the Continental Divide, since it lives in the Río Casas Grandes on the Atlantic slope and the Río Gavilán, only three miles away, on the Pacific slope.[6] The Casas Grandes and Gavilán must have been connected at some comparatively recent time, and minor uplifts of the Sierra Madre plus recent aridity must have separated these drainages.

Whereas the incidence of regional evolution among terrestrial vertebrates that cross the mountains is at least 44 percent, such differentiation among the fishes is a mere 14 percent. Only the Casas Grandes shiner is subspecifically different in the Río Yaqui compared with its population in the Río Casas Grandes. This interests me, since it indicates that Pacific-slope populations of most transdivide fishes have had little time to evolve. But man is determined to change the

Chihuahuan Desert Region, United States and Mexico, ed. R. H. Wauer and D. H. Riskind, pp. 127–139, U.S.D.I., Natl. Park Serv. Trans. and Proc. Ser. 3 (1977).

[5]R. R. Miller, "Origin and Affinities of the Freshwater Fish Fauna of Western North America," in *Zoogeography*, ed. C. L. Hubbs, pp. 187–222, Amer. Assoc. Advanc. Sci. Publ. 51 (1958). See also S. E. Meek, *The Freshwater Fishes of Mexico North of the Isthmus of Tehuantepec*, Field Columbian Mus. Publ. Zool. Ser. 5 (1904).

[6]G. R. Smith, *Distribution and Evolution of the North American Catostomid Fishes of the Subgenus* Pantosteus, *Genus* Catostomus, Misc. Publ. Mus. Zool. Univ. Michigan 129 (1966).

natural evolutionary design, for he has introduced Casas Grandes shiners at Phoenix, Arizona.[7]

And man has so altered the Río Gavilán that its clear-water fishes are threatened. In 1937 Aldo Leopold was struck with the pristine coherence of this watershed compared with the Gila River, New Mexico, though he never got the chance to make a comparative study. By 1948 it was too late. Intending to start a detailed investigation in that year, Starker Leopold found graded logging roads, herds of livestock, and the Gavilán flood-scoured and turbulent with sawdust. Then in 1955 Joe Marshall photographed logged and overgrazed forests, plowed mountain grasslands, and brush invasion resulting from fire protection. Starker Leopold's epitaph—"Adiós Gavilán"—is appropriate indeed.[8]

From the historic copper mines at Santa Rita, New Mexico, John Bartlett's party traveled for three days in May, 1851, toward the landscape maze, across country "barren and uninteresting in the extreme." Through the Playas Valley they went, in a region of "sterile plains . . . unbroken wastes, barren, wild, and worthless."[9] Was this Bartlett's way of contrasting the desert grassland with the evergreen woodland he had just left? Or did the dry season's browns and vanished waters have their typical effect on the Easterner? In August, 1908, Vernon Bailey journeyed through the Playas Valley, then overstocked with cattle and nearly devoid of grass.[10] Even the second monsoon month did not erase man's mistreatment of the landscape.

My own impression in August, 1972, is different: "A great wildlife

[7] W. L. Minckley, *Fishes of Arizona* (Phoenix: Arizona Game and Fish Dept., 1973), p. 139.

[8] S. L. Flader, *Thinking Like a Mountain* (Columbia: Univ. Missouri Press, 1974), pp. 153–156; J. T. Marshall, Jr., *Birds of Pine-Oak Woodland in Southern Arizona and Adjacent Mexico*, Pacific Coast Avifauna 32 (1957): figs. 13–16, 23.

[9] J. R. Bartlett, *Personal Narrative of the Explorations and Incidents in Texas, New Mexico, California, Sonora, and Chihuahua, Connected with the United States and Mexican Boundary Commission during the Years 1850, '51, '52, and '53*, vol. 1 (New York: D. Appleton and Co., 1854), p. 247. Since Bartlett noted the contrast between the sterility and barrenness of the Playas Valley and the luxuriant grass of the Animas Valley in May, 1851, the present contrast between their respective desert grassland and plains grassland can be considered natural.

[10] From V. Bailey's unpublished field notes in the U.S. Fish and Wildlife Service Laboratory, Natl. Mus. Nat. Hist., Washington, D.C.

day. Golden eagle on a fence post just west of the end of pavement, two kit foxes sunning by their den in an abandoned kangaroo rat mound, and five pronghorn antelope just north of Antelope Wells." I am especially glad to see the pronghorns in an appropriately named spot, a place where Edgar Mearns found them frequently in 1892–1893. Mearns remarked that *el berrendo* was already a rare animal in the 1890's, although his observations suggest it remained abundant in this part of the Borderlands. Eighty antelope were killed for food by the Second Boundary Survey in this region during May–July, 1892. By the 1950's, due to overhunting, pronghorns in northwestern Chihuahua were limited to stragglers from New Mexico and one small herd.[11]

Yet *berrendos* persisted in the New Mexico panhandle, where in 1908 Bailey figured there were around 400 individuals.[12] Based on my counts in the 1971–1972 winter dry and summer rainy seasons, I estimate no more than 25 animals along this Border. The herd of 5 north of Antelope Wells is of average size; they are grazing by the big playa, which is full for the first time in five years. They eat green forbs grown by four inches of rain since June. For a while, anyway, the balance between desert grassland and shrub desert is tipped in favor of the grassland and *berrendos*. "Overgrazing temporarily discontinued," I think, as I head for San Luis Pass. "If John Bartlett had seen this country in August, would his feelings have been any different?"

I cross Whitewater Creek with its stand of Arizona sycamores and look again in vain for those Mexican birds of the Río Yaqui drainage which have threaded their way north among the sycamore linings of the canyons of Sonora and Chihuahua. Richard Johnston reported a similar attempt in 1957.[13] No thick-billed kingbirds here—only lark buntings, early grassland migrants to remind me that fall is in the air. Surely Mexican birds will follow the sycamores through the maze to this point. Or is Whitewater too dry too often? A white-sided jackrabbit hops from its form beneath my feet. I stop. It is August, 1893, and

[11] E. A. Mearns, *Mammals of the Mexican Boundary of the United States*, U.S. Natl. Mus. Bull. 56 (1907), p. 226; B. Villa-R., "Observaciones acerca de la ultima manada de berrendos (*Antilocapra americana mexicana*) en el Estado de Chihuahua, Mexico," *An. Inst. Biol.* (*Mexico*) 26 (1955):229–236.

[12] V. Bailey, *Mammals of New Mexico*, N. Amer. Fauna 53 (1931):28.

[13] R. F. Johnston and J. W. Hardy, "The Ridgway Whip-poor-will and Its Associated Avifauna in Southeastern New Mexico," *Condor* 61 (1959):206–209.

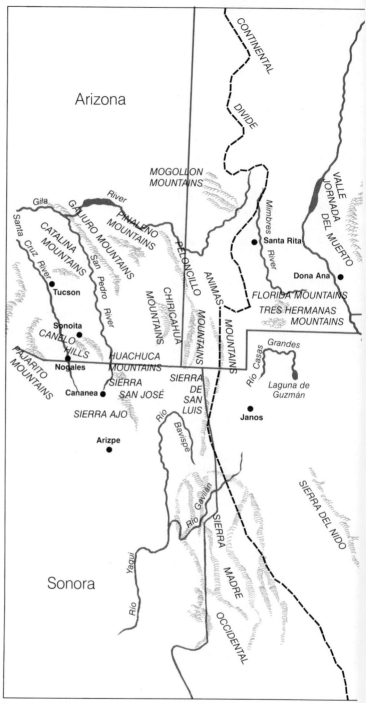

MAP 2. Middle Section of U.S.–Mexican Boundary

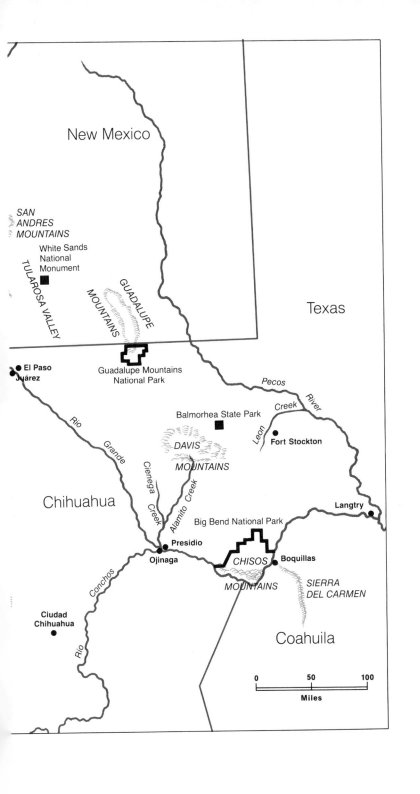

New Mexico

Texas

SAN
ANDRES
MOUNTAINS

White Sands
National
Monument

TULAROSA VALLEY

GUADALUPE
MOUNTAINS

Guadalupe Mountains
National Park

El Paso
Juárez

Pecos

Creek

River

Rio

Grande

Balmorhea State Park

DAVIS

MOUNTAINS

Leon

Fort Stockton

Chihuahua

Cienega

Creek

Alamito Creek

Langtry

Big Bend National Park

Presidio

Ojinaga

CHISOS

Boquillas

MOUNTAINS

SIERRA
DEL CARMEN

Conchos

Ciudad
Chihuahua

Rio

Coahuila

0	50	100

Miles

Edgar Mearns is in my place. He has discovered the first white-sided jack. The region abounds with antelope and black-tailed prairie dogs.

Mearns observed immense colonies of prairie dogs in southwestern New Mexico and adjacent Arizona, west to the San Pedro River: "Here the 'dogs' fairly reveled and overran the country." Finding the species particularly abundant in the New Mexico panhandle, he remarked that Dog Spring owed its name to these local inhabitants. As late as 1908, Vernon Bailey found many *perritos* in the Playas and Animas valleys—an estimated 10 per acre, giving 6,400,000 in the county, or 1,000 square miles of dog towns.[14] Publicly, Bailey blamed prairie dogs for denuding vegetation in parts of the Animas Valley missed by rainfall, but his unpublished field notes suggest that the presence of too many cattle deserved equal blame. Was this personal view suppressed by the varmint-hating establishment of those days? The black-tailed prairie dog was eliminated from these U.S. Borderlands in the first half of the twentieth century.

The reality of no prairie dogs and few antelope intrudes upon my reverie. I start westward over San Luis Pass. John Bartlett encountered a grizzly bear here in August, 1851. For me there is no such excitement. But the descent into the Animas Valley restores my soul, for the fine condition of its plains grassland brings back the winter of 1893, when native hay was cut here, baled, and sold to the Boundary surveyors.[15] Despite the great drought of 1890–1893, whose effects were intensified by overstocked ranges, the Animas grassland recovered or perhaps never deteriorated to the extent implied by Vernon Bailey. Certainly, Bartlett mentioned its luxuriant grass and prairie dogs in May, 1851. I see antelope again—two here, three there—pitiful, but reminders nonetheless.

On the western edge of the Animas Valley, the flank of the Peloncillo-Guadalupe Cordillera, the living landscape reminds me of the eastern Borderlands, specifically of the Davis Mountains, Texas. Evergreen woodland in both places is dominated by Emory and gray or Arizona white oaks plus alligator juniper. As Mearns drew it, this wood-

[14] Mearns, *Mammals of the Mexican Boundary*, p. 342; V. Bailey, *Mammals of New Mexico*, p. 124.

[15] U.S. Boundary Commission, *Report of the Boundary Commission upon the Survey and Remarking of the Boundary between the United States and Mexico West of the Rio Grande, 1891–1896*, pt. 2, 55th Cong., 2nd sess., 1898, Senate Doc. 247, p. 186.

land grows down the mountainsides and into the grassland in the form of tree ribbons along draws.[16] I camp in such a tree ribbon in the defunct town of Cloverdale. Mearns camped here in July, 1892. Three-quarters of the shade is provided by oaks, many larger than a foot in diameter. One Emory oak is 2.5 feet through at the standard survey height of 4.5 feet above ground.

Birds about this campsite also demonstrate that community patterns are similar across space and time. Elf owls, acorn woodpeckers, Cassin's kingbirds, western wood pewees, Hutton's vireos, white-breasted nuthatches, black-headed grosbeaks, and rufous-sided towhees are shared with the Texas-Coahuila woodlands. They range across the Mexican Plateau, but in patchy fashion, isolated in montane woodlands that may have spread as tree-ribbon dispersal routes through the valleys in pluvial time.[17] I meet a whiskered owl, two brown-backed woodpeckers, and some bridled titmice today and recognize the influence of the Sierra Madre Occidental. These woodland birds have traveled from one mountain island to another, too, perhaps via tree ribbons, but only in a northward direction.

Isolated sierras here are parts of a north-south island chain, an archipelago that permits some species to pass but blocks others. Sierra Madrean birds generally do not penetrate the Mogollon Plateau, north of the Borderlands, even though habitats there are suitable. The whiskered owl and brown-backed woodpecker do not penetrate it, for instance, while the bridled titmouse, an exception, does. Of twenty-eight Madrean birds only 29 percent nest in the White Mountains, Arizona, on the Plateau.[18] Similarly, the Rocky Mountains avifauna comes south through the Mogollon highlands and is filtered out in the series of isolated ranges farther south. Among thirty-seven such species, only 43 percent breed in the island chain. For example, the red-breasted nuthatch makes it to the Chiricahua Mountains, the western tanager a

[16] Mearns, *Mammals of the Mexican Boundary*, p. 92.

[17] The theory of trans-Plateau dispersal of woodland vertebrates in pluvial time is discussed in P. S. Martin, *A Biogeography of Reptiles and Amphibians in the Gómez Farías Region, Tamaulipas, Mexico*, Misc. Publ. Mus. Zool. Univ. Michigan 101 (1958), pp. 90–93.

[18] Synthesis of data from table 9 in J. T. Marshall, Jr., *Birds of Pine-oak Woodland*. See also J. P. Hubbard, "Summer Birds of the Forests of the Mogollon Mountains, New Mexico," *Condor* 67 (1965):404–415; and D. M. Niles, *Observations on the Summer Birds of the Animas Mountains, New Mexico*, New Mexico Ornithol. Soc. Publ. 2 (1966).

bit farther south to the Huachuca and Animas mountains, and the black-throated gray warbler still farther to the Ajo, Cananea, and San Luis mountains in Sonora.

The north-south, woodland-forest pattern includes small, terrestrial castaways on the mountain islands. These earthbound creatures are not susceptible to being blown about like birds and bats or wandering like the large quadrupeds. So if I find the recently discovered Arizona shrew or ridge-nosed rattlesnake in the Animas Mountains, I know it didn't get there by chance or contemporary dispersal. But if I find a white-eared hummingbird or buff-breasted flycatcher without evidence of breeding, I might guess that it is a freak occurrence or seasonal migration. Gene flow is discontinuous in at least thirty species of small, terrestrial mammals, reptiles, and amphibians in the mountain islands, because few if any wooded pathways run completely across desert and grassland barriers these days.

Sixty percent of the small mammals have evolved different subspecies north and south of the landscape maze, the result of isolation in the Rocky Mountains and Sierra Madre, respectively, or in one or more of the mountain islands. Examples include the Abert's squirrel, a Rockies derivative with disjunct races in the northern Sierra Madre, and the Apache squirrel from the Sierra with isolated subspecies in the Chiricahua Mountains and Sierra de San Luis. Thirty percent of the reptiles and amphibians have subspeciated in like manner, including the short-horned lizard and mountain kingsnake from the north and the plateau treefrog and Arizona alligator lizard from the south.[19]

Whether subspecifically distinct or not, certain island isolates exhibit reduced variation that could jeopardize their future if their habitat changed under the influence of man or nature. Apache squirrels of the Chiricahuas are less variable in body size than those of the northern Sierra Madre Occidental, for example, as are black-eared mice.[20] In general, small mice show less reproductive potential and habitat

[19]Calculated from range maps in Hall and Kelson, *Mammals*; and Stebbins, *Field Guide*.

[20]For the squirrels, mean skin and skull coefficients of variation are 0.35 and 0.18 compared with 0.36 and 0.27 (my calculations on populations A versus B–F in M. R. Lee and D. F. Hoffmeister, "Status of Certain Fox Squirrels in Mexico and Arizona," *Proc. Biol. Soc. Washington* 76 [1963]:181–190). Equivalent values for the mice are 0.38 and 0.25 compared with 0.58 and 0.30 (my data on population six described in J. H.

versatility at such marginal sites. The diminished variation means fewer deviant types that might be fit—might survive—in new environmental circumstances. Presumably, external features of body proportion, reproduction, and hence habitation are tied to genetic diversity, which declines with reduced island area, population size, and wider barriers to gene flow.[21]

Large woodland and forest mammals move more freely among the mountain islands, just as their desert and grassland counterparts move through the straits between islands. Sierran species like the coatimundi and jaguar go all the way north to the Grand Canyon, Arizona, although there is no evidence of breeding north of the Mogollon Rim. Rocky Mountains species like the river otter and black bear range southward into the Sierra Madre. Black bears reside in a few mountain islands but have wandered so little in postpluvial time that their Chihuahuan-Sonoran populations are subspecifically distinct. The otter has not lived in these border sierras recently, and its Mexican relative may be a distinct species. All other montane mammals jackrabbit size or larger are so mobile and tolerant of all natural communities that discontinuous woodlands and forests have little effect on their gene flow.

Mobile and tolerant mammal that I am—buffered by cultural accoutrements—I continue westward from Cloverdale, over 5,000-foot Guadalupe Pass into Guadalupe Canyon. My destination is Edgar Mearns's campsite in Sonora, under towering Arizona sycamores, near Boundary Monument 73. Sycamore groves, interspersed with equally huge Fremont cottonwoods along the lower two miles of the canyon, furnish the best shade. Riparian woodland is discontinuous. The canyon hillsides are sunbaked evergreen woodland, mostly scattered redberry junipers, but fine habitat for a few buff-collared nightjars, or

Bowers, "Genetic Compatibility of *Peromyscus maniculatus* and *Peromyscus melanotis* as Indicated by Breeding Studies and Morphometrics," *J. Mammal.* 55 [1974]:720–737; and computations from tables 12 and 13 in S. A. Anderson, *Mammals of Chihuahua,* Bull. Amer. Mus. Nat. Hist. 148 [1972]).

[21] D. S. Glazier, "Ecological Shifts and Evolution in Geographically Restricted Species of North American *Peromyscus* (Mice)," *J. Biogeogr.* 7 (1980):63–83; M. Soule and S. Y. Yang, "Genetic Variation in Side-blotched Lizards on Islands in the Gulf of California," *Evolution* 27 (1973):593–600; K. W. Corbin, "Genetic Diversity in Avian Populations," in *Endangered Birds: Management Techniques for Preserving Threatened Species,* ed. S. A. Temple, pp. 219–302 (Madison: Univ. Wisconsin Press, 1977).

cookacheeas, that nest only here in the vicinity of the Border. This northernmost population was discovered as recently as 1958. [22]

The most impressive natural feature of this east-west passage is not the cookacheeas, craggy setting, or old-age sycamores and cotton-woods, but the monsoon floods. In September, 1971, the stream ran at least twenty feet deep in the lower two miles of the canyon and washed the Mormon Battalion Monument a quarter-mile downstream along with other half-ton boulders. Logs a foot through and twenty to thirty feet long were deposited in surviving sycamores, cottonwoods, and walnuts, most of which are larger than a foot in diameter. The living stream was filled with gravel. No wonder native fish are lacking here. Was it always thus?

By 1890 there were 1,800 cattle in the canyon and on adjacent slopes. During the severe drought of 1890–1893, they must have eaten Guadalupe down to rock. [23] Although the herd was reduced to 400 in the next several decades, cattle and drought together can be blamed for the sunbaked aspect of Guadalupe's slopes. Grass is sparse in early summer before the monsoon. The soil is heavily compacted— what soil there is. When the rains come in July through September, water runs off the slopes instead of percolating through them, and a two-inch downpour causes major flooding.

I move camp a couple of miles up-canyon to an isolated sycamore grove in New Mexico, below open slopes threatened by a juniper in-vasion. I hear cookacheeas. Could Richard Johnston and John Hardy be mistaken when they imply that this bird is natural in Guadalupe Canyon? If the species was present before the era of overgrazing, why would Edgar Mearns and Frank Holzner have failed to find it? Mearns camped here July 6–8, Holzner, July 28–29, 1892. July is the bird's peak calling season, based on my experience here and near Ures, Sonora, where almost every tenth fence post holds a territorial male in cut-over tropical deciduous forest. The species' explosive coo-coo-coo-kachea is unmistakable. Why not attribute a cookacheea invasion to de-terioration of the canyon's vegetation due to drought and overgrazing,

[22] Johnston and Hardy, "Ridgway Whip-poor-will," pp. 206–209.
[23] L. G. Johnson, resident in Guadalupe Canyon, supplied information on the 1971 flood, size of cattle herds, and overgrazing hypothesis in May, 1971, and August, 1972. My own preflood and postflood observations contribute to the account.

Cassin's Kingbird (Emory)

since the species prefers open, arid woodland with trees of short stature?

If overgrazing helped to bring the cookacheea northward, to expand its breeding range, that is a plus among so many minuses. My theorizing beneath the sycamores is disturbed by the shriek of a Mexican jay in the clutches of a male Cooper's hawk—caught within fifty feet of me. The commotion doesn't seem to disturb Cassin's kingbirds close by, although Dale Zimmerman saw Cassin's, western, and thick-billed kingbirds jointly chasing Cooper's hawks right here.[24] I start! Those Cassin's kingbirds—their dusk and dawn chorus might sound like cookacheas to the uninitiated. Could Mearns and Holzner have mistaken nightjars for kingbirds? Anyway, I would like to think that overgrazing exchanged the cookacheea for the aplomado falcon or masked bobwhite instead of merely subtracting from my Borderlands heritage as it always seems to do.

Kingbirds and their flycatcher relatives hold center stage among local actors. Eleven species impress me by the way they divide up living space. Vermilion flycatchers occupy open, flood-scoured areas and fence lines, but Say's phoebes replace them at other man-made structures. Black phoebes stay among rocks along the stream, largely segregated from the Say's. I suspect there was a different situation originally, since both phoebes are streamside cranny nesters in the absence of man. Ash-throated, dusky-capped, and brown-crested flycatchers comprise a second, congeneric coterie. The ash-throated uses oaks and junipers on hillsides and terraces for nesting holes and foraging, seldom venturing among canyon-bottom cottonwoods commanded by the brown-crested, while the dusky-capped is thinly distributed throughout. Western wood pewees share the riparian timber but do not nest in holes, and they use velvet ashes and Arizona black walnuts as often as cottonwoods. And the tiny northern beardless tyrannulet nests in streamside shrub thickets.

The trio of kingbirds is most intriguing, because no overt habitat separation is evident. The thick-bill uses sycamore space as elsewhere on its northern invasion front but shares these trees and others with Cassin's and western kingbirds, particularly the Cassin's, in the open,

[24] D. A. Zimmerman, "Thick-billed Kingbird Nesting in New Mexico," *Auk* 77 (1960):92–94.

Walnut beetle.

Harlequin grasshopper.

Left: Malachite butterfly (hanging). *Right*: California sister butterfly.

Left: Colorado hairstreak butterfly. *Right*: Tripletail swallowtail butterfly.

Fledgling canyon wrens.

Yellow-eyed junco.

Acorn woodpecker.

Blue-throated hummingbird.

Elegant trogons; juvenile *left*, adult male *right*.

Green jay (banded).

Chachalaca.

Screech owl.

Juvenile Cooper's hawk (sunning).

discontinuous stands. Zimmerman found the two nesting only seventy-five feet apart. Western kingbirds are scarce, so I am less certain of their proclivities. This species and the Cassin's are interspecifically territorial over nest sites, much less so in foraging space.[25] Like Zimmerman I have not seen such aggression between Cassin's and thick-billed kingbirds.

Is interspecific competition reduced among the three kingbird look-alikes, as it is among the convergent great kiskadee, social, and boat-billed flycatchers I have watched in Tamaulipas? Did the invading thick-bill slip in easily among its congeners when first found in 1958? Martin Cody suggests that convergence in plumage facilitates spacing through interspecific territorial rivalry in a given structural habitat.[26] Thus an invading thick-bill might obtain space that would otherwise go to a resident Cassin's or western kingbird. If Cody is right, invaders should be seen first among residents they most closely resemble, and, indeed, the tropical kingbird is another look-alike found in this manner. Allan Phillips discovered it nesting with Cassin's and western kingbirds at Tucson, Arizona, in 1938.[27]

But convergent coloration alone cannot ensure the success of an invading thick-billed or tropical kingbird, because the newcomer may compete for food with a more abundant Cassin's or western kingbird population. Somehow the insect prey of coexisting kingbirds is parceled out, for thick-bills and tropicals seem to be spreading in southern Arizona. Comparisons of bill size and shape suggest how, based on the premise that species with different bills can eat different insects in the same place, while species with similar bills must catch similar insects in different places.

Dividing the product of the three dimensions of one species' bill by the comparable products of the other three kingbirds gives instructive ratios. All save the Cassin's versus western are 1.9 or larger, so the

[25] H. M. Ohlendorf, "Competitive Relationships among Kingbirds (*Tyrannus*) in Trans-Pecos, Texas," *Wilson Bull*. 86 (1974):357–373.

[26] M. L. Cody, "Convergent Characteristics in Sympatric Populations: A Possible Relation to Interspecific Territoriality," *Condor* 71 (1969):222–239. See also M. Moynihan, "Social Mimicry: Character Convergence versus Character Displacement," *Evolution* 22 (1968):315–331.

[27] A. R. Phillips, "Two New Breeding Birds for the United States," *Auk* 57 (1940): 117–118.

bigger-billed invaders could indeed coexist with each other and either the Cassin's or western kingbird but not both. The Cassin's-to-western ratio is 1.2, indicating similar food habits, as corroborated by a study in trans-Pecos Texas.[28] Thus, the Cassin's kingbird is an upland species, the western kingbird a lowland species, and the two exhibit vertical displacement along canyon-stream gradients.

Clanton Canyon is another passage from east to west through the Peloncillo-Guadalupe range. Compared with Guadalupe Canyon, it is an easy transect from plains grassland in the Animas Valley, New Mexico, up through evergreen woodland and then down into the more arid desert grassland of the San Bernardino Valley, Arizona. I find no hint that nineteenth-century naturalists traversed Clanton, but lots of evidence that twentieth-century biologists study there. Red flagging tape with numbers and a stock-proof exclosure are obvious signs. Turned rocks, as if a thousand coatis had passed by, and a lost live mammal trap with a brush mouse skeleton in it are more subtle reminders.

The variety of breeding birds is impressive. I record twenty-eight species in a half-mile transect along the canyon floor. There are five flycatchers—ash-throated, dusky-capped, and greater pewees, western wood pewee, and Cassin's kingbird—a record for species packing, exceeding even the eleven flycatchers in two miles of Guadalupe Canyon. Also, bridled and plain titmice nest together here. Elsewhere I can confirm this coexistence only at Cloverdale and in Cave Creek Canyon of the Chiricahua Mountains, Arizona, at the same 5,300- to 5,400-foot contour.

My March, 1971, and August, 1972, photos of the campground at 5,300 feet reveal essentially the same evergreen woodland as in Joe Marshall's April, 1955, picture. I see only a slight decrease in shrub foliage density. I can almost duplicate Marshall's bird record, too, except for the addition of a pair of whiskered owls and the absence of screech owls; hence I calculate an 84 percent species similarity between his list and mine.[29]

[28] Ohlendorf, "Competitive Relationships among Kingbirds." Using data from table 3 in H. A. Hespenheide, "Competition and the Genus *Tyrannus*," *Wilson Bull.* 76 (1964): 265–281, I computed the necessary ratios in addition to those already presented.
   [29] Percent similarity is $2C/A + B \times 100$, where A and B are number of species from table 3 in Marshall, *Birds of Pine-oak Woodland*, and my data, respectively, and C is the

If the woodland avifauna of Clanton Canyon has not changed appreciably in sixteen years, perhaps other, similar avifaunas of the region have not changed either. To test this hypothesis I chose three additional study sites in canyons and at elevations censused by Marshall sixteen to twenty-three years earlier. Unfortunately, though, Marshall did not adopt a quantitative definition of pine-oak woodland, as he called the natural community he studied, so I am not certain my transects are within the pine-oak framework. Nevertheless, I shall be intrepid and offer quantitative data on trees and breeding birds in what I think is pine-oak woodland, based on information in Marshall's pioneering study.

To begin with, I consider a particular tree a pine-oak indicator if it is conspicuous in a convincing majority (70 percent) of the twenty mountain ranges Marshall investigated.[30] Silverleaf oak, Arizona madrone, Arizona white oak, Chihuahua pine, and Apache pine qualify, and I find at least three of these species along each of my transects in Clanton Canyon, at Wet Spring in the Pinaleno (Graham) Mountains, and Turkey and Cave Creek canyons of the Chiricahuas. However, these trees make up only 25 to 76 percent of the vegetative structure. The rest includes a deciduous fraction contributed by Arizona sycamore, Arizona walnut, velvet ash, chokecherry, and similar trees, plus a small percentage of evergreenness afforded by alligator juniper, Arizona cypress, and other conifers. Could my transects represent an evergreen-deciduous continuum near the upper limits of riparian woodland?

Next I consider birds as indicators by multiplying mean density per mile times number of sierras for each species found by Marshall. The rationale, as with the trees or indicator lizards in the Guadalupe Mountains, Texas, is that indicators should be abundant, conspicuous, and widespread in a particular community if one is to recognize that community. Beginning with the best indicator, the bird with the largest product of mean density times frequency, and working down the list, the top ten birds are rufous-sided towhee, Bewick's wren, bridled titmouse, painted redstart, dusky-capped flycatcher, hepatic tanager,

number of species in common. For another sighting, see J. D. Ligon and G. L. Brenowitz, "First Record of the Whiskered Owl in New Mexico," *Condor* 78 (1976): 112.

[30] Based on table 1 in Marshall, *Birds of Pine-oak Woodland*.

western wood pewee, whip-poor-will, Hutton's vireo, and acorn wood-pecker. But most of these are also common and wide-ranging outside the pine-oak community.

Finally, analysis of my own data on mean density times frequency from two or three breeding seasons in 1971–1974 reveals that my top ten birds are the same as Marshall's, although their rank-order differs. If species exclusivity won't identify pine-oak woodland, persistence of indicators will. When my data are compared with Marshall's on all birds, species similarity indices range from 77 percent for Wet Spring through 80 and 83 percent in the Chiricahuas to 84 percent in Clanton. I conclude that my censuses represent the same community Marshall sampled and that it is an evergreen-deciduous continuum.[31]

Now I discover that the woodland avifauna of McKittrick Canyon, Texas, has been twice as dynamic by comparison. To gauge this I divide percentage dissimilarity (the converse of percentage similarity) by the number of years between my censuses and Marshall's in Clanton and between my earliest data and George Newman's in McKittrick. I obtain average turnover rates of 4.1 and 8.6, respectively. The twofold difference in Texas might be blamed on the greater drought there in the 1950's. Precipitation deficiency in the McKittrick area was nearly double that of Clanton Canyon between 1950 and 1956.[32]

The stability of a fauna seems to depend on persistence of its indicator species through major environmental upsets like drought or flooding. Besides birds, fishes in the Devils River and rodents in the subtropical woodland of Texas show such stability. Indicators are usually community dominants because of their high densities and frequencies. When such important species persist, leading roles change relatively little in the evolutionary play, and the community theater survives as the principal stage setting. If indicator birds are replaced by close competitors, as in the McKittrick avifauna, only scenes change in the play. Stage settings remain, with number of species, species di-

[31] The concept of pine-oak woodland as a continuum is stated by Marshall, *Birds of Pine-oak Woodland*, pp. 5, 64; and C. H. Lowe, Jr., "Biotic Communities in the Sub-Mogollon Region of the Inland Southwest," *J. Arizona Acad. Sci.* 2 (1961):40–49.

[32] The regional drought comparison is made from plate 1 in H. E. Thomas, *The Meteorologic Phenomenon of Drought in the Southwest*, U.S. Geol. Surv. Prof. Paper 372-A (1962).

versity, and densities still characteristic of a particular community, albeit in wetter or drier condition.

My Borderlands studies commenced about the time Joe Marshall's concluded, and I am grateful for sage advice from Albert and Anna Wright at that time: "In quest of the new, take the old with you." Without Marshall's volume in the field, and specifically his Clanton Canyon photo, I might not have noted the persistence of canyon-bottom woodlands. Marshall's method of finding owls also teaches me a measure of change, since my imitation of the whiskered owl's telegraphic toot brings it by for vocal verification but I fail to whistle up a screech owl. Over the campfire the owl talks with us—a splendid evening conversation.

10. *Mountain Islands*

CHIRICAHUAS, Huachucas, Santa Ritas—to naturalists these are the best known of all mountain islands in the western Borderlands. There are many other isolated, wooded ranges afloat between the thirtieth and thirty-third parallels, west of the Rio Grande and east of the Baboquivari and Pinitos ranges in Arizona and Sonora. Two dozen at least hold sizable acreages of evergreen woodland and lesser amounts of coniferous forest, but the Chiricahuas are the largest and the Huachucas and the Santa Ritas the most historic. I marvel every time I return to southeastern Arizona and enter Cave Creek Canyon, the eastern portal of lichen- and mineral-painted rocks. Lately, though, it has become difficult to find unmarked lizards or unshadowed birds here, and I prefer less trampled places.

From Granite Pass in the Peloncillo Mountains travelers bound for the eastern portal and its elegant trogons drop into the San Simon Valley and pass remnants of a cienega that John Bartlett called El Sauz in 1851. In 1947 Herbert Brandt commented on the self-draining of this marsh, through erosion of its stream channel, and warned of its demise.[1] Today the cienega is almost dead. San Simon Creek ceased to flow in 1952. A steep-banked pond, dug to save Mexican ducks, is about all that remains of permanent water with riparian vegetation. But Mexican ducks don't like such ponds, so the number of nesting pairs I count declines from a half-dozen to no more than two in the decade before the 1977 release of hand-reared birds.

Instead of the Granite Pass approach I prefer Clanton Canyon's entry through the Peloncillos into the San Bernardino Valley, Arizona, U.S. headwaters of the great Río Yaqui of Sonora. I have crossed this drainage at several points between cienega-fragment stock ponds on

[1] H. Brandt, *Arizona and Its Birdlife* (Cleveland: Bird Res. Foundtn., 1951), pp. 358–359. See also W. C. Barnes, "Herds in San Simon Valley," *Amer. Forests* 42 (1936): 456–457.

San Simon Cienega and Chiricahua Mountains (Bartlett)

the historic San Bernardino Ranch and cypress-lined channels near Ciudad Obregón, Sonora. It is a major Pacific-slope route of dispersal for aquatic and riparian species, including the distinctive Yaqui chub and Yaqui sucker and regional races of the longfin dace, Casas Grandes shiner, Gila topminnow, song sparrow, and, of course, the Mexican duck.

In Bartlett's May of 1851 the Río de San Bernardino ran past the ruins of an abandoned rancho. A century later the river is dry, although an 1892 photo shows the headsprings still alive and the run guarded by an extensive tule cienega. Edgar Mearns got malaria here in 1892. Now the only permanent water is stock-ponded at the resurrected ranch of John Slaughter. Only topminnows remained there in 1971. The last shiners were seen in 1970, and the Yaqui sucker disappeared when cattle trampled Black Wash dry in 1969. Yaqui chubs and longfin dace persist in Leslie Creek of the Swisshelm Mountains.[2]

[2] U.S. Boundary Commission, *Report of the Boundary Commission upon the Sur-*

Brandt's bird pond, the largest of the Slaughter Ranch stock ponds of 1948 survives, replete with exotic fishes, along with its pair or two of nesting Mexican ducks. A few more ducks still nest in the Animas Valley and the San Pedro River system, even along Babocomari and O'Donnell creeks, where I saw a pair almost every day in the summer of 1976. This vanishing bird numbers less than a thousand in the Borderlands, thinly dispersed among ponds and marshes between trans-Pecos, Texas, and the San Pedro drainage.

But the Mexican duck is really a southern race of the mallard, and Borderlands birds are quite intermediate between pure Mexicans from south of Durango and the more familiar Yankee greenhead. Even the first U.S. specimen, taken by Edgar Mearns near El Paso in 1893, was an intergrade. Can it be that the intermediate population is a feathered analogue of the Gila trout or Leon Springs pupfish? Does it feature amalgamation aided and abetted by man? Along the Rio Grande north of El Paso this population has become 26 percent more mallardlike since 1920.[3] Consider the declining water tables, disappearing riparian woodlands, and restricted breeding marshes of the Mexican form compared with the increase in steep-sided stock ponds and reservoirs more acceptable to the mallard form.

Canyons are the logical approaches to mountain islands, the best pathways, just as rivers are lowland routes that provide easy water transport and a ready supply of that most vital resource. West of El Paso and the Rio Grande, Boundary surveyors were forced to cut across divides as they forged an unnatural border. I certainly would rather walk up canyons and along ridges than beat the brush cross-country. If I minimize barrier crossings, I reduce my disturbance of the landscape, frighten fewer animals, and save energy for discoveries.

The more I look the more I discover that canyons, creeks, and rivers are focal points for other creatures, too, not only because of water and easy dispersal, but because resources are most diverse along

---

vey and Remarking of the Boundary between the United States and Mexico West of the Rio Grande, 1891–1896, pt. 2, 55th Cong., 2nd sess., 1898, Senate Doc. 247, p. 11; F. M. McNatt, "Reevaluation of the Native Fishes of the Rio Yaqui in the United States," Proc. 54th Ann. Conf. West. Assoc. Game and Fish Comm. (1974):273–279.

[3] J. P. Hubbard, The Biological and Taxonomic Status of the Mexican Duck, New Mexico Dept. Game and Fish Bull. 16 (1977) (see table 6 in particular).

drainageways. Just looking at trees in my riparian woodland study plots, I find five or six species per 300-foot transect below 5,000 feet, eight to twelve above, and, at most, half as many on adjacent hillsides, depending on elevation. Moreover, breeding-bird species diversity increases with diversity in tree species, which represent resources, not merely with elevation in the 2,000-foot riparian gradient I investigate on six mountain islands.[4]

Five thousand feet is a workable dividing point in this gradient, since woodlands below are primarily deciduous, dominated by cottonwoods, walnuts, and willows, while conifers and evergreen oaks mix with deciduous species above. Furthermore, by using the five-thousand-foot mark to separate lowland from upland riparian avifaunas, I obtain the greatest dissimilarity in species composition (71 percent) and the least sharing of indicator species. Only the ubiquitous western wood pewee is shared. The ten best indicators of lowland sites are western wood pewee, black-chinned hummingbird, Cassin's kingbird, black-headed grosbeak, white-winged dove, lesser goldfinch, Lucy's warbler, warbling vireo, northern oriole, and yellow-billed cuckoo, in first-to-last rank order.[5]

I record sixteen to twenty-six species, with diversities of 3.80 to 4.39 in my lowland plots, twenty-one to twenty-eight species and 4.31 to 4.59 diversities in my upland sites. There are other distinctions, too. For example, the lowland avifaunas contain five to nine birds per acre, the uplands three to six. Mean species weight is 32 grams in the lowlands, 43 grams above. The lowlands support nearly twice the live weight, or biomass, of the uplands—275 to 360 grams per acre versus 110 to 255—calculated by multiplying mean weight by mean density of each species and totaling these products for each avifauna.

---

[4]The correlation coefficient (r) for male breeding bird diversity ($H' \log_2$) versus tree diversity ($H' \log_2$) is 0.75 ($P<0.01$), for the birds versus elevation, 0.28 ($P>0.05$). Linear fifteen-acre study plots of breeding birds and trees are: in Arizona, Sonoita Creek 4,000 ft., O'Donnell Creek 4,900 ft., south fork of Cave Creek 5,200 ft., Wet Spring, Pinaleno Mts. 6,000 ft., Miller Creek, Huachuca Mts. 6,100 ft.; and in New Mexico, Whitewater Creek, San Luis Mts. 4,800 ft. Bird species diversity ($H' \log_2$) is the mean of two to three years' censuses of territorial males per plot in 1971–1976.

[5]Indicator species are those with the largest products of mean density times frequency (number of sites). Dissimilarity is 100 percent minus the quotient of $2C/A+B$, where C is the number of species in common between the number in lowland (A) and upland (B) sites. For upland riparian indicators, see pp. 163–164.

Interestingly, high population densities together with great biomass production are characteristics associated with few species and low
diversities in immature communities. This is because only certain prolific creatures tolerate the relatively unstable conditions, hence they
have a corner on all the resources. Is it possible that lowland riparian
avifaunas are so disturbed by floods as to be comparatively immature?
Floodwaters from many mountain streams coalesce to inundate valley
creeks and river courses, and I observe the greatest flood damage at
my lowland study sites, where walls of water several feet high are not
uncommon during the summer rains.

Too much water in the lowlands is one possible explanation for the
differences in biomass production, but low temperatures in the uplands must also contribute. Upland riparian birds are on the average
1.3 times larger than lowland riparian species, a selective advantage in
the cooler environment where heat must be conserved. This means
fewer individuals per unit of area in the montane canyons, since larger
birds command larger territories, in accordance with their greater energy requirements.[6]

My curiosity about landscape patterns makes such leaps that my
feet cannot keep up. Does the large number of bird species persist as I
climb through the riparian-coniferous forest continuum around 7,000
feet? Certainly not, for a list of songbirds and other small vertebrates
in the Chiricahua Mountains reveals a decline in species richness.[7] My
canyon-bottom plots must represent rich avifaunal intrusions caused
by permanent water and the proliferation of tree species, while slopes
and canyon-head sites support increasingly depauperate avifaunas toward the highest elevations.

Horizontal patterns are no less interesting. I share a sycamore log
with its owner, a Yarrow's spiny lizard, pull out pencil and paper, a
hand calculator, and Joe Marshall's compendium on woodland birds,
and go to work. I will have to use a large computer eventually—what
would Edgar Mearns think—but I find it more inspiring to sit on a log

---

[6]T. W. Schoener, "Sizes of Feeding Territories among Birds," *Ecology* 49 (1968):
123–141.

[7]P. S. Martin, "Southwestern Animal Communities in the Late Pleistocene," in
Bioecology of the Arid and Semiarid Lands of the Southwest, ed. L. M. Shields and L. J.
Gardner, pp. 56–66, New Mexico Highlands Univ. Bull. 212 (1961).

with a spiny lizard and birds of two dozen kinds. Now that sophisticated electronic gear can be used in the field, I experience a new harmony between natural and unnatural history.

Latitude of a mountain island, its average distance from neighboring islands, approximate area of woodland, and variety of major woody plants in that woodland are variables that might logically affect the number of breeding birds. Marshall's maps and tabulations of species in pine-oak woodlands along the Arizona-Sonora border provide raw data.[8] Right now I can look at simple correlations, at the same time as I watch an elegant trogon—remarkable visual stimulation—detect the smell of javelinas shuffling by, an added effect, and enjoy the kaleidoscope of California sisters, Colorado hairstreaks, tripletail swallowtails, and other butterflies. Two birders looking for elegant trogons ask what I am doing. Balancing my checkbook? I explain.

Because there are more bird species in the tropics than in the temperate zone, I expect more breeding birds in southerly ranges. And because valley grasslands and deserts are barriers to woodland birds, except on migration, I expect a mountain to have more breeding species if it is closer to other mountains, potential supply depots. Finally, if a mountain has more woodland, it should have more birds, and these may represent more species if the woodland is richer in woody plant species. But is extent of woodland the primary determinant of the number of woody plant species, which in turn affect bird species, or is geographical position of that woodland more important?

A simultaneous analysis of all variables tells me that geography has little direct influence on birds, since 90 percent of the horizontal variation in bird species richness is explained by variation in plant species richness. Only an additional 3 percent is attributable to latitude and distance from nearby mountains. Woodland area adds essentially nothing. My findings are similar to those obtained on mountain islands in the Great Basin to the north, where habitat diversity accounts for 91

[8] J. T. Marshall, Jr., *Birds of Pine-oak Woodland in Southern Arizona and Adjacent Mexico*, Pacific Coast Avifauna 32 (1957). I analyze only the eight ranges censused for riparian and pine-oak birds in daylight and at night (quantitative data from Marshall's table 3). I include woody plants from his table 1. The Cananea Mountains are omitted, because severe logging badly upset their avifaunal diversity (the ratio of 1950's diversity to the theoretical maximum, the log of species richness, is 0.80 compared with 0.90–0.94 in the other ranges in table 3).

percent of the island-to-island differences .in number of breeding birds.[9]

Next I look at the determinants of plant species richness to comprehend this large measure of community structure, and I find that woodland area is the single most important factor. The more woodland on an island, the greater the variety of its major woody plants. To the meager 29 percent of explanation thus provided, mean distance from other mountains adds 17 percent and latitude 15 percent, leaving 39 percent unexplained by the natural factors I assay. The overall result is clear, though. Bird species diversity is governed primarily by plant species diversity, which in turn is determined by the extent of habitat available for housing and proximity to supply depots.[10]

One day at dawn, I lie in the riparian woodland of the south fork of Cave Creek Canyon, shaded by its sweet-smelling Arizona sycamores. My sleeping bag is a blind if I remain quiet, for I have been here enough hours to become a log or pile of leaves. Or have I? Mexican jays are suspicious. They always are. I can't outwit them. I learn their lifestyle only by living with their extended families long enough to condition them to my sleeping bag, coffee pot, binoculars, and the rest. This live-in approach to natural history is most rewarding.

Mexican jays exist in communal flocks of a few to perhaps two dozen individuals. If the flock is large, say a dozen jays, only one pair of breeding adults is present. The rest are offspring of previous years and possibly acquired "friends," all of which help defend a single territory. Two decades of jay watching have convinced me of this, but Jerram Brown proved it by color-banding each member of a flock.[11] Brown also

[9] N. K. Johnson, "Controls of Number of Bird Species on Montane Islands in the Great Basin," *Evolution* 29 (1975):545–567. See also R. P. Balda, "Vegetation Structure and Breeding Bird Diversity," in *Symposium on Management of Forest and Range Habitats for Nongame Birds*, ed. D. R. Smith, pp. 59–80, U.S. Dept. Agricult. Forest Serv. Genl. Tech. Rept. WO-1 (1975).

[10] In a multiple stepwise regression (MSR) analysis of bird species richness, r^2 additions of plant species richness, latitude, mean distance, and woodland area are 0.90 ($F = 60.0$), 0.02 ($F = 21.0$), 0.005 ($F = 0.2$), and 0.003 ($F = 0.1$) respectively. With 1–7 $d.f.$, F values are significant ($P<0.05$) except for the last two, and multiple correlation (R) = 0.96. Woodland area, mean distance, and latitude make r^2 additions of 0.29, 0.17, and 0.15, respectively, to plant species richness ($F = 1$–3, $P>0.05$, 1–7 $d.f.$), $R = 0.79$.

[11] J. L. Brown, "Cooperative Breeding and Altruistic Behavior in the Mexican Jay, *Aphelocoma ultramarina*," *Anim. Behav.* 18 (1970):366–378. See also J. L. Brown, "Al-

discovered that nests are built and incubating females and nestlings fed by all the flock. Actual parents contribute only a third to half the food and prefer to feed their own offspring as long as they remain in the nest. Once the young are fledged, however, parental food contributions drop to around a fourth of the total, as a flock exhibits increasing altruism.

Enhanced survival is the selective advantage of altruistic behavior, which may include the detection, group mobbing, and repulsion of predators so well known in jays. But delayed reproductive maturity and the raising of fewer, better-cared-for offspring are especially vital. Yearling jays may learn the arts of food and predator detection, nest construction, and family life in general from the older, breeding adults. All are hypothetical ingredients in natural selection for altruism. The communal life of the Mexican jay is a viable alternative to the familiar pair of breeding birds with little or no help nesting and no year-round models for learned behavior.

The acorn woodpecker may practice altruism also. I watched this species closely at the O'Donnell Cienega in 1974–1976 and found four to seven individuals attending a single nest and feeding fledglings. Of course, many birds have temporary helpers, including young of the previous brood or adult, unmated individuals.[12] But seldom are more than one or two helpers noted simultaneously, and I saw more. In addition, helpers do not stay with parents and offspring after the youngsters are fully grown and feeding themselves, but my extended family of acorn woodpeckers even roosted together at the nest site in a dead cottonwood limb.

Do acorn woodpeckers represent an early, perhaps facultative stage in the evolution of jaylike altruism? This seems possible along O'Donnell Creek, where some are communal and others not.[13] What if fledglings remain with their parents over winter because of communal

ternate Routes to Sociality in Jays: With a Theory for the Evolution of Altruism and Communal Breeding," *Amer. Zool.* 14 (1974):63–80.

[12] A. F. Skutch, "Helpers among Birds," *Condor* 63 (1961):198–226.

[13] P. B. Stacey and C. E. Bock, "Social Plasticity in the Acorn Woodpecker," *Science* 202 (1978):1298–1300. See also C. E. Bock and J. H. Bock, "Geographical Ecology of the Acorn Woodpecker: Diversity versus Abundance of Resources," *Amer. Natur.* 108 (1974):694–698; W. D. Koenig and F. A. Pitelka, "Relatedness and Inbreeding Avoidance: Counterploys in the Communally Nesting Acorn Woodpecker," *Science* 206 (1979):1103–05; H. Brandt, *Arizona Bird Life*, p. 659.

advantages including heat conservation in the roost cavity? Then year-lings are at hand to propagate the genes for togetherness if parents die. Yet the O'Donnell Creek situation, where food may be limiting, sug-gests that a commune may divide if it exceeds some critical mass in relation to the resource base. This reduces the deleterious effect of in-breeding already ameliorated by the prolonged nonbreeding role of most commune members.

Food must regulate the size and incidence of communal flocks in this acorn-dependent woodpecker. But the bird can exist without acorns, at least temporarily, which may explain winter survival in a commune subdivided by acorn shortage. On warm days in winter the acorn woodpecker remains as much a flycatcher as on the hottest sum-mer days, when it also sips nectar from agaves and my hummingbird feeders. Some individuals descend their mountain islands under stressful winter conditions and find insects and nectar at lower eleva-tions or these foods plus acorns and pine nuts at lower latitudes.

A male elegant trogon and his two dependent fledglings consume my time for awhile, since they represent the species' northern breed-ing limit. This showiest of local birds is an 1880's invader from Mex-ico.[14] I inventory the trogon's habits in Cave Creek Canyon, a conve-nient spot because the birds are somewhat used to flashing lights, blaring tape recorders, and people in cars grating up and down the gravel with sets of binoculars, asking, "Have you seen the trogon?" But it is sometimes disconcerting to observe trogons here because too often we bump into birders instead of the birds. Twice I stalked gen-uine ornithologists, lured by their tape recordings.

If I want conditioned trogons, though, I must put up with such nonsense. I might do so more easily if trogon listers would take time to sit with their quarry and learn its secrets instead of chalking it up and heading on to Rustler Park to "get" red-faced warblers, Mexican chick-adees, and yellow-eyed juncos. No other bird of the Borderlands is so easy to accompany, for an elegant trogon is quiet if a birder is too. It is an unhurried, unharried species normally, unlike so many others, which dash from place to place. While this male sits, I watch its winged and two-legged cohabitants fly by. Now in late August red-faced war-

[14]C. Taylor, *The Coppery-tailed Trogon: Arizona's "Bird of Paradise"* (Portal, Ariz.: Borderlands Productions, 1980).

blers, Mexican chickadees, and yellow-eyed juncos flock about me. I try to tell the birders, but they have directions from a guru.

The male gives one fledgling a three-inch caterpillar that has been beaten to death on a limb. The almost inert youngster holds it forty-five seconds before swallowing, as if practicing deliberacy. The same bird takes another caterpillar a half-hour later, the result of the adult's gleaning Arizona white oak leaves on the wing. Two caterpillars and a walkingstick in fifteen minutes constitute the fastest delivery to both young today. Birchleaf buckthorn berries are taken by the male but not fed to the young. Such selectivity must enhance the growth of nestlings and fledglings, for insects contain 13.0 times more protein and have 1.2 times more energy per unit mass than fruits.[15]

Are elegant trogons like other tropical birds in being slower growers than their temperate-zone cohabitants? Does their quietude bespeak a slower metabolism? After an eighteen- to twenty-day incubation period of two eggs, nestlings occupy old woodpecker holes or natural nesting cavities about two and a half weeks. Fledging in this canyon occurs between the last week of June and the first week of August, depending on when the eggs are laid, and trogon youngsters remain with their parents until migration in September–October.[16] Surely adult trogons pick large insects to feed their offspring while eating fruit themselves, because this not only fosters growth but broadens the food base, hence increases success during the long nesting and fledgling-dependency periods.

By the second day we confirm the absence of a female parent. The youngsters fly well and stay within 300 feet of each other. The male forages farther, often ranging out of sight in its twenty-acre territory.

---

[15] E. W. Morton, "On the Evolutionary Advantages and Disadvantages of Fruit Eating in Tropical Birds," *Amer. Natur.* 107 (1973): 8–22. Feeding observations reported in E. Steele, "Arizona's Mystery Bird," *Audubon Mag.* 68 (1966): 167–171, substantiate mine. On the comparatively slow feeding rate of nestling trogons among tropical birds, see table 12 in A. F. Skutch, *Parent Birds and Their Young* (Austin: Univ. Texas Press, 1976).

[16] This summary is based on three nesting sequences and sixteen other pairs or single adults with one or two fledglings, 1954–1979, in Cave Creek Canyon. Known or inferred clutch size differs from that in A. C. Bent, *Life Histories of North American Cuckoos, Goatsuckers, Hummingbirds and Their Allies*, U.S. Natl. Mus. Bull. 176 (1940), pp. 106–110. Bird plate 2 in Emory depicts a male elegant trogon, not a mountain trogon as indicated (W. H. Emory, *Report on the United States and Mexican Boundary Survey*, vol. 2, pt. 2, 34th Cong., 1st sess., 1859, U.S. House Exec. Doc. 135.)

The youngsters' begging is scarcely audible compared with that of the immediate postnestling period, but they do not forage for themselves. When one drops a mantis, though perched only 4 feet above ground, it just watches the insect's reflex kicking. When monsoon storm clouds part, the fledglings sun, spreading tail and back feathers. After ten minutes in the full sun, they begin to pant but remain exposed, quietly trogonlike, beautiful in their female-style plumages.

For a few hours we shift attention to a second trogon family, both parents and two fledged young. Twenty-five years of trogon watching have prepared me for the unexpected, which is why I keep on watching. All four birds are foraging in an abundantly endowed chokecherry. American robins accompany them. The offspring feed themselves, while the male feeds the female—not expressly, however. When the male plucks a cherry from his sitting position, the female flies over, takes it from his beak while sitting or hovering, and flies back to her perch several feet away. A safe distance from remonstration?

Still another trogon family includes two fledglings of similar size, which excite their parents with soft, mewing cries. I follow the cackling—complaining—male too closely perhaps, and the fledglings continue to call. So too, the peregrine falcons that echo loudly about the cliffs of Cave Creek Canyon. The male peregrine kills a small songbird, which it gives to the female in midair, despite loud protestations from the pair's fledged youngster and families of brown-crested flycatchers and acorn woodpeckers. Yet the male trogon ignores the world, flattens himself in a patch of dry streambed, spreads his feathers, cocks his head, and for nearly a minute becomes almost catatonic with eyes rolled upwards. He sunbathes.

A third day without an adult female near the first trogon family reminds me of someone who shot Cooper's hawks because they supposedly ate up all the trogons here a few years ago. Nearby, however, two fledgling Cooper's hawks are fed spiny lizards, cotton rats, and songbirds mostly smaller than trogons. For a bird hawk, the Cooper's certainly is generalized. I admire this creature that leads its young around, carrying a flopping black-headed grosbeak, forcing flying lessons instead of giving outright handouts. Does such movement contribute to its catholic tastes and reduce the chance of predation on elegant trogons?

Also, I have never seen Cooper's hawks hunt within sight of their nests. Once three young Cooper's hawks grew up in the Canelo Hills in an Emory oak grove frequented daily by white-winged doves that fed in safety there. For several years Cooper's hawks in Ramsey Canyon of the Huachuca Mountains nested twenty-five yards from the greatest feeder-induced concentration of hummingbirds and small songbirds I have seen and did so without incident, as far as I know. And Herbert Brandt recorded Cooper's hawks and elegant trogons nesting in proximity for several years without interaction in Miller Canyon of the Huachucas.[17]

The missing female trogon cues my recollection of a fleeting instant in the south fork of Cave Creek Canyon. Madrone berries invited a small flock of band-tailed pigeons, which fed noisily, displacing a male trogon to a dead sycamore limb over the creekbed. I perched on a rock by my swimming hole to revel in the late summer scene. A very large, brown accipiter, perhaps a female Cooper's, more plausibly a goshawk, barreled out of nowhere, up the open creekbed flyway within a few feet of the exposed trogon, over my head, and straight into the pigeons, which scattered far and wide. I learned that a trogon's subdued nature could conceal, despite its brilliant plumage.

Nesting elegant trogons have about doubled in number during my censuses of the 5,000 to 5,500-foot contour in Cave Creek Canyon. In 1954–1959 I recorded one to three pairs with eggs, nestlings, or fledglings but found three to six such pairs in 1971–1979. The actual number of adults is greater, usually, because unmated males are present. Once at Maple camp, Nancy spotted a chase involving three extras, as I watched a pair with young. Possibly the lone males function as reserves in case of losses to the first string, for I have not seen them help with nesting in the manner of Mexican jays and acorn woodpeckers. But I would not be surprised at any new turn of events.

I used to see a lot more trogons and coatis from my sleeping bag on the canyon floor than I do now. The present population of campground campers either scares wild animals away or conditions them to be panhandlers. *Chulos solitarios*, for instance, beg marshmallows and raid garbage cans at night. Before the 1970's I didn't know these solitary, male coatis could be nocturnal, since they always foraged around

[17] Brandt, *Arizona Bird Life*, p. 195. Cf. Taylor, *The Coppery-tailed Trogon*, pp. 26–28.

me in the daylight. But I soon discovered that some acquired the nocturnal habit in apparent response to nocturnally unattended trash cans
and diurnal campground hassle.

At Chiricahua National Monument I watched a fat, chocolate
brown *solitario* "table" seven campers in five seconds one evening.
When it began to rummage in a box of something left on the ground,
one defender of human rights climbed down on the opposite side of the
table, picked up a stick and advanced, warning the others to stay put
because "badgers" are vicious. That scene changed, for I left the au-
dience and lured the beast to my own campsite, where Gretchen and
Mark tamed it with marshmallows. I thought that either this species
hadn't been here long enough to acquire its own reputation, or those
campers had just arrived in Arizona.

The coati is, I believe, the largest native animal to invade the U.S.
Borderlands in the last hundred years. The first interior specimen
came from Fort Huachuca, Arizona, in 1891, although others had been
taken at the Border earlier—for example, an 1877 specimen from
Brownsville, Texas.[18] Yet no Boundary naturalist of the 1850–1853 period mentioned this diurnal, socially conspicuous mammal, while
harder-to-find species like the solitary, nocturnal cats of similar size
were collected or purchased and accounts of them were obtained from
mexicanos. Furthermore, other contemporary observers and hunters
like W. W. Price and John Springer did not mention coatis, and U.S.
fossil records are lacking.

By the 1920's coatis were abundant only in the Huachuca-
Patagonia mountains area of Arizona, though they had been present in
the Animas Mountains, New Mexico, as early as 1908. They seemed to
be pushing northward in fitful fashion then and continue to do so now.
Will evidence of a breeding population, females plus cubs, appear
north of the Galiuro Mountains, Arizona? Or are the peripheral records simply escaped and released pets or wandering *solitarios*, as I believe all the Texas records are? One must see a family band to confirm
the species' residency, and I know of none within a hundred miles of
the Texas border.

[18]J. H. Kaufmann, D. V. Lanning, and S. E. Poole, "Current Status and Distribution of the Coati in the United States," *J. Mammal.* 57 (1976):621–637; V. Bailey, *Biological Survey of Texas*, N. Amer. Fauna 25 (1905):192; V. Bailey, *Mammals of New Mexico*, N. Amer. Fauna 53 (1931):347. See also B. Gilbert, *Chulo* (New York: A. Knopf,
1973).

Like any species at its edge of range, coati populations exhibit extraordinary flux, as natural and cultural factors exert unusually stressful limiting or powerful enhancing effects. In 1960–1961 an epidemic of canine distemper reduced coatis everywhere in Arizona, while a thirty-two-inch snowfall in 1967–1968 drove the recovering Peloncillo-Guadalupe mountains population out of the southern portion of that cordillera. Three years later only a few *solitarios* had returned to Guadalupe Canyon, and I saw but a single male near Cloverdale in 1971. It is tempting, therefore, to say that coatis have always been in the United States but were at a periodic low in 1850–1853—too scarce for discovery. But why no folklore? Surely the irrepressible John Bartlett would have mentioned them.

Instead, I think the species is a culturally induced invader, an opportunist that responded to the heaps of carrion beef that littered south-central Arizona in 1891–1893. At least 360,000 head of cattle—perhaps even more than a million—had died by 1893 as a result of vastly overstocked ranges in the midst of a severe three-year drought. It is said that one could throw a rock from one carcass to another.[19] Why shouldn't the omnivorous coati, a known carrion eater, expand its range northward in this land of plenty? The twenty-five to fifty miles from the Ajo, Cananea, or Pinitos ranges in Sonora to the Huachuca and Patagonia mountains—eight to seventeen miles per year between 1891 and 1893—is a faster pace than the six miles per year of the armadillo, another recent invader from Mexico.

Coatis are vagile mammals, like most their size and larger. Certainly they can move easily across intermontane valleys through grassland and desert by following wooded riparian corridors. They may even cross some treeless stretches in their northward push, for I have seen them clamber over grassy south-facing slopes on feeding trips from wooded, north-facing exposures. However, tree-sized vegetation is a requisite for residency of this raccoonlike raccoon relative, whose U.S. breeding populations now extend from Baboquivari to the Catalina and Galiuro mountains, Arizona, and southeastward to the Animas and San Luis ranges in New Mexico.

I might learn something more about coati distributional dynamics by examining the horizontal patterns of less mobile, smaller, terrestrial

[19] J. R. Hastings and R. M. Turner, *The Changing Mile* (Tucson: Univ. Arizona Press, 1965), p. 41.

mammals and reptiles in woodlands and forests of mountain islands. After all, coatis eat mice, lizards, and snakes. I discovered this one morning, when a family band of seventeen taught me "sniff-root" foraging behavior, as they dug in leaf litter and turned rocks with herpetological fervor around my sleeping bag. A foot-long snake of some kind was unearthed and savored like a flaccid stick of licorice. Then a spiny lizard was extracted from a log, held like a popsicle, and consumed head to tail.

So I look at the variety of such prey in tree-dominated communities above 5,000 feet, the approximate lower limit of coati habitat. Utilizing faunas of the Chiricahua, Catalina, Pinaleno, Huachuca, and Santa Rita mountains, I analyze the dependency of species numbers on latitude, mean distance from neighboring islands, habitat area, and variety of woody plants, as I did for breeding birds.[20] Latitude explains 46 to 70 percent of the mountain-to-mountain faunal variation. Woodland area and plant species richness account for less. Simply put, small, terrestrial, vertebrate species decline toward the north, hence coatis will encounter fewer kinds of resources in their northward invasion. This, in concert with the colder climate, should put the brakes on.

Tree squirrels—*ardillas*—instruct me further on dispersal. Three species are isolated on seven exemplary mountain islands. The Chiricahuas are the only U.S. base of the Apache squirrel, a Sierra Madrean species with another isolate in the Sierra de San Luis, while the Catalinas, Huachucas, Santa Ritas, and Pajaritos house a second Borderlands specialty, the Arizona gray squirrel. The Pinalenos once hosted the red squirrel or chickaree of the Rocky Mountains. Random dispersal must have placed the Apache and Arizona gray squirrels, but lati-

---

[20] My experience is added to data from: D. F. Hoffmeister, "Mammals of the Graham (Pinaleno) Mountains, Arizona," *Amer. Midl. Natur.* 55 (1956):257–288; D. F. Hoffmeister and W. W. Goodpaster, *The Mammals of the Huachuca Mountains, Southeastern Arizona*, Illinois Biol. Monogr. 24 (1952); K. I. Lange, "Mammals of the Santa Catalina Mountains, Arizona," *Amer. Midl. Natur.* 64 (1960):436–458; J. T. Marshall, Jr., *Birds of Pine-oak Woodland*, table 1; Martin, "Southwestern Animal Communities"; M. A. Nickerson and C. E. Mays, "A Preliminary Herpetofaunal Analysis of the Graham (Pinaleno) Mountains Region, Graham Co., Arizona, with Ecological Comments," *Trans. Kansas Acad. Sci.* 72 (1970):492–505. In MSR analyses r^2 contributions of latitude, woodland area, and plant species richness to species richness of small, terrestrial mammals are 0.46, 0.44, and 0.10 ($F = 3$–8, $P<0.05$, $R = 0.99$); to species richness of reptiles, 0.70, 0.17, 0.11, respectively ($F = 6$–29, $P<0.05$, $R = 0.98$). Cf. B. D. Patterson, "Montane Mammalian Biogeography in New Mexico," *Southwest. Natur.* 25 (1980):33–40.

tude played its role in stocking the four southern ranges with these two and the northern range, the Pinalenos, with the single northern derivative. The chickaree might have traveled forest connections during the last pluvial period, while the Apache and Arizona gray squirrels may have waited for woodland pathways during warm-wet, postpluvial time.

Postpluvial dispersal of woodland species northward from Mexico is Paul Martin's hypothesis, and I find it fitting.[21] Martin points out that a glaciopluvial climate would eliminate the present midcontinental summer high-pressure center that generates the Borderlands monsoon. Concurrently, it would produce enough winter precipitation to keep the pluvial lakes full and the cooler temperatures necessary to lower the elevational limits of coniferous forest species and send them southward. So the southern species, adapted to warm temperatures and summer rain, would not find conditions favorable for dispersal during the pluvial but might in a warm-wet interval.

The postulated warm-wet interval must be comparatively recent, because a certain Sierra Madrean faunal element has not penetrated north of the Borderlands. Had the necessary conditions existed earlier, or had they been repeated during interpluvials, I would expect more extensive northward and lateral dispersal of the Apache squirrel, black-eared mouse, southern pocket gopher, and such Madrean reptiles as the bunch grass and striped plateau lizards and the twin-spotted and ridge-nosed rattlesnakes. It is significant in this regard that large, mobile Mexican mammals like the coati and armadillo lack pluvial fossil records and first appear north of the Border in historic time or in archaeological sites no more than a few thousand years old.[22] These invaders must surely be culturally induced.

[21] Martin, "Southwestern Animal Communities." Cf. P. V. Wells, "An Equable Glaciopluvial in the West: Pleniglacial Evidence of Increased Precipitation on a Gradient from the Great Basin to the Sonoran and Chihuahuan Deserts," *Quaternary Res.* 12 (1979):311–325.

[22] E. D. Lundelius, Jr., "Late Pleistocene and Holocene Faunal History of Central Texas," in *Pleistocene Extinctions: The Search for a Cause*, ed. P. S. Martin and H. E. Wright, Jr., pp. 287–319 (New Haven: Yale Univ. Press, 1967); E. H. Lindsay and N. T. Tessman, "Cenozoic Vertebrate Localities and Faunas in Arizona," *J. Arizona Acad. Sci.* 9 (1974):3–24; and J. S. Findley, A. H. Harris, D. E. Wilson, and C. Jones, *Mammals of New Mexico* (Albuquerque: Univ. New Mexico Press, 1975), pp. 342–344. The javelina might join the coati and armadillo as a recent invader, since there is but one questionable fossil record in Arizona and no appearance elsewhere until postpluvial time.

Abert's Squirrel (Emory)

Tree-squirrel scenery has been altered culturally. The Abert's squirrel was introduced into the Pinaleno and Catalina mountains between 1940 and 1943, as usual without considering what an exotic can do to a natural landscape. By 1951–1952 the chickaree was rare, and by 1966–1967 it was extirpated, apparently the victim of competition with the much larger Abert's. Ditto, or almost, for the Arizona gray squirrel in the Catalinas. By 1960 it was no longer reported, although I suspect that this essentially riparian species, a devotee of the Arizona black walnut, may remain a fugitive from competition at elevations below the coniferous forest habitat of the Abert's.[23]

The chickaree could not avoid the Abert's squirrel, for it too is strictly a coniferous-forest animal. Where both occur naturally, the Abert's specializes on ponderosa pine, the chickaree on Douglas fir and Engelmann spruce. They share only about 30 percent of a mixed-tree forest and exclude one another competitively. But where the widespread chickaree lives alone, it utilizes ponderosa pine besides fir and spruce in a manner typical of habitat expansion in the absence of competition. I envision the Pinaleno chickarees as such generalists originally, unprepared for and overwhelmed by Abert's squirrels in ponderosa pine. Then they must have been confined to comparatively small fir and spruce stands insufficient to sustain them.

Natural disturbances affect montane faunas too, though I tend to overlook such factors, since their creative influences are often masked by our landscape tinkering. Fire is of prime importance, for the results of woodland and forest fires are shown by contrasting tree-dominated communities in the U.S. Borderlands with their counterparts in Mexico. There is no fundamental difference in climate or extent of livestock grazing to explain the open, parklike woods of Mexico within a hundred miles of sapling-choked, brushy vegetation of similar species composition at the same elevations across the Border. The difference in vegetative structure is attributable to unchecked fires in the mountain islands of Mexico and Smokey the Bear in the United States.[24]

The message of Smokey—not just no man-caused fires but no fires whatsoever—is another case of unnatural history. Before the twentieth

[23] Human impact on tree squirrels is noted in Hoffmeister, "Mammals of the Graham Mountains"; Lange, "Mammals of the Santa Catalina Mountains"; and W. L. Minckley, "Possible Extirpation of the Spruce Squirrel from the Pinaleno (Graham) Mountains, Southcentral Arizona," *J. Arizona Acad. Sci.* 5 (1968):110. See also J. W. Ferner, "Habitat Relationships of *Tamiasciurus hudsonicus* and *Sciurus aberti* in the Rocky Mountains," *Southwest. Natur.* 18 (1974):470–473.

[24] J. T. Marshall, Jr., "Fire and Birds in the Mountains of Southern Arizona," *Proc. Tall Timbers Fire Ecol. Conf.* 2 (1963):135–141. My substantiating observations extend to a comparison of the Chisos Mountains, Texas, with the Sierra del Carmen, Coahuila.

century lightning must have set mountain fires with sufficient frequency to burn leaf and wood litter, seedlings, and saplings and produce grassy glades, especially in ponderosa pine forests. I have often
seen an old snag ablaze or smoldering in late spring or early summer,
the tinder-dry fire season, and just as frequently the U.S. Forest Service has put the fire out. In June, 1974, I saw this in the Huachuca
Mountains, while a sister fire burned in naturally controlled fashion
only twenty miles away in the Sierra San José, Sonora.

Results for the U.S. mountain islands have been degeneration of
woodland and forest, if not outright disaster. First, overgrazing re-
moves grass and oak seedlings, permitting junipers to invade. And degeneration follows if the junipers outnumber oaks and pines because
fire is not allowed or there is insufficient grass to carry it. Then when
wood accumulates, building up a fuel more concentrated and explosive
than dry grass, there will be a conflagration.[25] Whether touched off by
lightning, spontaneous combustion, or man, the resulting fire is bigger
and hotter than otherwise, destroying mature trees normally resistant
to ground fire and hence the whole community.

Smokey the Bear retired in the 1970's after "saving" so many
woodlands and forests that we may never be able to manage them naturally. Now, by allowing lightning fires to burn unchecked, we risk big
ones and the consequent destruction of many summer houses and
other recreational facilities that should not have been built in fire-
climax communities to begin with. But tree managers are awake at
long last and have decided that some prescribed and controlled burns
are preferable to the raging blazes that result from overprotection.
Small acreages with backfired or otherwise cleared borders can be
burned when litter and moisture conditions are proper for moderate
heat.

The avifaunal consequences of natural or prescription burns can
be predicted by analysis of Joe Marshall's quantitative data. Specifically, I look at birds of roadrunner size or smaller because they are less
mobile hence more prone to be affected by fire than the larger species.

---

[25] M. Dodge, "Forest Fire Accumulations—A Growing Problem," *Science* 177
(1972):139–141. As could have been predicted, a 9,000-acre, man-caused fire burned
upper Ramsey, Carr, and Miller canyons in the Huachuca Mountains, Arizona, in June,
1977. By August, 1979, most evergreen oaks and deciduous trees on slopes had basal
sprouts three to five feet high, but conifer replacements were not apparent.

And I multiply mean density by number of mountain ranges or frequency to obtain indicator values for each species in open, parklike versus brushy timber. Fortunately, Marshall studied so many mountain islands in southern Arizona and northern Sonora that ten ranges represent each vegetative structural condition, and fifty-two birds of appropriate size nest in each.

Just over half of the species, or 56 percent, are more important in open vegetation. The ten top birds, in first-to-last rank order, are buff-breasted flycatcher, western and eastern bluebirds, purple martin, house wren, Mexican chickadee, American robin, olive warbler, greater pewee, and Montezuma quail. Conversely, 42 percent of the species seem to benefit from or prefer closed vegetation. Elf, flammulated, and screech owls, ash-throated flycatcher, roadrunner, Scott's oriole, blue-gray gnatcatcher, Hutton's vireo, rufous-sided towhee, and black-headed grosbeak are the ten leading species of this group. Only the Cassin's kingbird shows no difference in importance related to vegetation type.

There is no statistical difference in the number of birds preferring open or closed woodland or forest. Fire does not appear to affect avifaunal richness, but geography might, since fire-conditioned vegetation occurs south of the Border and twenty-three of the fifty-two birds are primarily tropical in breeding distribution. The effect of latitude is easily corrected by removing these species from consideration—subtracting the buff-breasted flycatcher, Mexican chickadee, and elf owl, for instance. Still I find no statistical difference and conclude that fire is neither beneficial nor harmful to avifaunal richness.[26]

Indeed, I postulate that fire cycles in woody vegetation are much like drought cycles in their effect on community composition.[27] Certain species dominate community structure under one regime and not the

[26] From table 3 in Marshall, *Birds of Pine-oak Woodland*, I find that twenty-nine species are most important in open vegetation, twenty-two in closed or brushy vegetation, and one shows no difference. With a 2×2 contingency comparison of the fifty-one species showing a difference, $\chi^2 = 1.40$ ($P>0.05$); after eliminating twenty-three tropical species, $\chi^2 = 0.30$ ($P>0.05$).

[27] The fire history of evergreen woodland and coniferous forest along the Border is poorly known, but in trans-Pecos, Texas, cyclic frequencies averaging twelve (Guadalupe Mountains) to seventy (Chisos Mountains) years may be linked to the presence versus infrequent occurrence, respectively, of aboriginal man (data supplied by William Moir and Gary Ahlstrand).

other. Those adversely affected are replaced by close competitors, only to return as the cycle is repeated. Thus, for example, I might expect the whiskered owl, more important in open woodland, to replace the screech or flammulated owls, which occur in closed vegetation. Similarly, the dusky-capped flycatcher, prevalent in open, fire-caused community structure, may trade places with the ash-throated flycatcher, an indicator of brushy vegetation. Altogether, I find seven pairs of such potential competitors.

Clearly, though, there are other pairs of potential competitors, both species of which may benefit from fire-cleared vegetation. Western wood and greater pewees, eastern and western bluebirds, and rufous-crowned and chipping sparrows are such pairs. Moreover, the screech and flammulated owls and Hutton's and solitary vireos exemplify pairs that seem to respond positively to the absence of fire. I look closer. These situations do not contradict my hypothesis of competitive replacement at all, because in each case the second bird is segregated from the first by its higher, wetter position on mountain islands. These creatures remind me that, while simple threads run through the landscape carpet, the carpet pattern is always complex.

11. *And Canyon Trails*

AMONG my favorite cues for walking is the olfactory essence of Arizona sycamores after a washing. I am stimulated to unlimber, as the creatures around me become more active following the rain. Beneath the trees, shuffling through the leaf litter, wet feet in draws, I join the hosts of smaller beasts whose foraging is triggered by monsoon weather. For a long time I have looked for one particular animal among the others on these walks. A greenish species of the grapevine tangles, it matches the hue of riparian vegetation. It is diurnal. A young man in a hurry ran over one on his bicycle this morning, thinking it was but a crack in the pavement.

Today is not much different from the other August days—rain in the early afternoon and then the clearing. I have been waiting on a log for an hour in the rain, under my poncho. A fledgling elegant trogon sits some feet away, as immobile as its ancestors. A *chulo solitario* crouches in the protection of an Arizona cypress. A black-tailed rattlesnake, coiled between a rock and a log, is discovered by Gretchen who, at age ten, hardly ever sits. I must move cramped muscles.

The creek runs more vigorously, and its speckled dace disperse downstream with me. I stick to the creek because it is as far from the asphalt as I can get inside the confines of this canyon bottom. The leaf litter crawls before my eyes. My imagination moves it. Or does it? And then my discovery, straight as a sycamore sapling, basking on a flat rock in the returning sun. Its tail vibrates a warning as I reach. I am supposed to be dissuaded but am bitten instead. No matter—I admire new-leaf green flecked with yellow. This uniform coloration, the narrow head, and the laterally compressed body fit the green rat snake beautifully for life above ground.

It was not always thus in the life of this serpent, for its hatchlings are colored like the earth and leaf debris. They are olive brown with blotches on body and tail plus a trident mark, or spots suggestive of such, on the top of the head. These youngsters blend well with their terrestrial environment, the place where the species' eggs are laid. Blotches obliterate their serpentine form in the light and dark shadows. Try catching a moving blotched snake in leaf litter. I suspect that juvenile green rat snakes are more earthbound than the arboreal adults, judging from their very different kind of concealing coloration.

Before they reach thirty inches, green rat snakes have lost the blotched pattern. I know of other, similar changes in coloration that reinforce my idea of different selective forces in the lives of juvenile versus adult snakes. Baird's rat snake of the Big Bend in Texas is a sister example. Its youngsters are blotched, the adults striped. Young Mexican racers and indigo snakes along the lower Rio Grande are strongly banded and quite secretive compared with the conspicuous, unicolored adults. However, these two species are snake eaters, and I theorize that the disruptive coloration and retiring behavior of their offspring are adaptations that deter cannibalism, among other things.

Shall I release this green rat snake or keep it alive to note any further change in color and behavior? Another preserved, faded body would be redundant. Road kills suffice for morphological records, and there are at least a dozen pickled specimens to substantiate this particular locale—Cave Creek Canyon in the Chiricahua Mountains. Twenty years ago there would have been no question. The snake would have succumbed to this arch predator, who would have been a bit more ignorant of the exciting differences in meaning between juvenile and adult coloration.

After walking for several daylight hours, I am ready for less strenuous learning. Perhaps I shall try a strictly modern transect, a night drive for snakes down the canyon. Although I am sure to find subjects for observation, I am strongly aware of skimming the surface of natural communities. One favorite drive is from 5,500 feet in Cave Creek Canyon down into the San Simon Valley toward Rodeo, New Mexico, at 4,000 feet. In the 1950's this road was gravel to the canyon mouth and asphalt beyond, the kind of surface that makes the sinuous bodies of serpents silvery in a car's headlights.

Two decades later the road is entirely paved, a thoroughfare dangerous to passing snakes. It is crowded with night drivers catching snakes instead of observing them. I am frightened away, and I guess a number of my subjects are, too. Gasoline has tripled in price, as have the values of the few luckless species that fall prey to the army of commercial road hunters. Yet this road is only a transect, a thin line across a wild landscape replete with snakes. Until Cave Creek Canyon and the San Simon Valley are entirely urbanized or agriculturally over-simplified, local snake populations should not be threatened.

I stopped night driving by the mid-1960's, about the time Harvey Pough completed his study of rattlesnakes on the transect from Cave Creek to Rodeo.[1] He found the same species I did and on essentially the same community stages. Both of us marked and failed to recapture any specimens. Perhaps this is because the serpents do not remain on or near a road night after night but only cross it in their travels. High road temperatures, compared with those of the surrounding soil and air, are said to attract and hold nocturnal snakes. But I find that the body temperatures of several species are more strongly determined by soil than by road surface temperatures over a variety of hourly and monthly conditions.[2]

Rattlesnakes, *cascabeles*, appear to dominate the local serpent fauna, with better than 70 percent of all individuals observed. How-ever, I think they are simply seen more readily than nonvenomous species because of their comparatively great bulk. Also, ease of obser-vation could relate to the typical stationary position of a rattler on pavement, whereas harmless species usually are crawling across a road. Certainly the rattlers could be basking, the harmless snakes sim-ply traveling, but I cannot discover any closer correlation between road and rattler temperatures than between road and other snake temperatures.

The three local rattlesnakes are good teachers of species-specific evolutionary roles, because they segregate spatially in the transect of deciduous woodland to desert grassland. Black-tailed rattlers, beau-tifully gold and brown, are almost confined to the woodland, while the salmon-pink western diamondback predominates in mesquite and tar-

---

[1] H. Pough, "Ecological Relationships of Rattlesnakes in Southeastern Arizona with Notes on Other Species," *Copeia* (1966):676–683.

[2] Using data from table 9 in B. H. Brattstrom, "Body Temperatures of Reptiles," *Amer. Midl. Natur.* 73 (1965):376–422, a multiple stepwise regression (MSR) of snake body temperature against soil, road, and air temperature gives r^2 additions of 0.90 ($F = 8$, $P<0.01$), 0.03 ($F = 4$, $P<0.05$), and 0.01 ($F = 1$, *n.s.*), multiple correlation (R) = 0.97. Regarding road versus snake thermal relations specifically, for rattlers, $r = 0.82$ ($P<0.05$, 4 *d.f.*); for other snakes, $r = 0.93$ ($P<0.001$, 8 *d.f.*).

Western Diamondback Rattlesnake (Emory)

bush-invaded grassland. The drab tan Mojave rattlesnake prefers the shortest grass and fewest shrubs at lowest elevations. Even so, spatial overlap between the diamondback and Mojave in the mesquite-tarbush zone is twice that in the other environments jointly occupied, and Harvey Pough thinks this results from an invasion by the Mojave over the last one hundred years. I quite agree.

The most logical scenario of invasion evokes the all-too-familiar theme of desertification. As San Simon Valley grassland is degraded into shrubland, the shrub-adapted diamondback prospers, while the Mojave rattler, the most dry-adapted of the three species, moves into the newly made desert. Because the diamondback is larger than its new cohabitant and eats larger animals, food competition is reduced, and the invasion is successful initially. Whether or not stage space will place limits on the Mojave's new act remains to be determined.

Recently, I read a similar tale of local mule and white-tailed deer.[3] Apparently the desert-adapted muley is moving into the montane domain of the white-tail. This historic upward range expansion seems to be related to the desertification of montane woodland because of over-grazing, fire suppression, and perhaps a dryer, hotter climatic trend. Moreover, the muley is supplanting the white-tail, and I wonder if this might not happen to one member of the Mojave-diamondback act.

The culturally induced movement of one species into the area of another, and the resulting adverse influence of the invader on the resident is not unique to deer or rattlesnakes. Remember the longfin dace that invaded speckled dace territory in the upper Gila River? Surely this resulted from aquatic desertification, the watershed deterioration–soil erosion–siltation syndrome. Think too of the increasing influence of mallards on Mexican ducks along the upper Rio Grande. Are such man-related faunal shifts as reversible as those connected with natural climatic or fire cycles? Or are they strictly unidirectional?

Sometimes I traipse up and down canyons simply counting trees in the floristic relay between 5,200 and 7,000 feet. In five canyons of the Peloncillo, Pinaleno, Chiricahua, and Huachuca mountains, I record the number of individuals of each tree species, using 300-foot

[3]R. G. Anthony and N. S. Smith, "Ecological Relationships between Mule Deer and White-tailed Deer in Southeastern Arizona," *Ecol. Monogr.* 47 (1977):255–277.

transects near streams. I want to learn more about foliage changes as certain trees give way to others, since foliage type must be one important factor that specifies food, foraging, and nesting space for birds.

Tree species richness rises and falls. Eight species per average transect at 5,200 feet become twelve at 6,000 feet and then nine at 7,000. The variety of conifers, the needle-leaved structural component, seems to follow this trend. Oaks and the Arizona madrone, broad-leaved evergreens, exhibit a reverse trend, while broad-leaved deciduous trees show no significant correlation with elevation. Which foliage type determines the most change in structural diversity? I run a computerized simultaneous analysis of the three types to answer this question and discover that 78 percent of the variation is attributable to conifers alone. Broadleaf evergreens add 12 percent; broadleaf deciduous trees, only 8 percent.[4]

In the Huachuca Mountains, Miller Canyon tells a similar story. Conifers determine the major share of vertical change in riparian woodland between 5,000 and 6,700 feet.[5] Their variety and hence the structural contribution of needle leaves determine 92 percent of the total variation in woody-plant species richness. Here too, maximum richness is reached at 6,000 feet, at the ninety-year-old Tombstone, Arizona, waterworks, where I am diverted by long-spurred columbines and Madrean wood-nymph butterflies. Unlike the synthesis in other canyons, broadleaf deciduous trees contribute the only other important share of foliage change in Miller Canyon, but it is a paltry 4 percent.

Since conifers are the major factor in vegetative structural change and decline toward a canyon mouth, and because woody vegetation exerts the primary control over breeding-bird richness, which also de-

[4]Transect samples of woody plants are from Turkey Creek (7,000 ft.) and the south fork of Cave Creek, Chiricahua Mts. (5,200 ft.), Miller Canyon, Huachuca Mts. (6,200 ft.), Clanton Canyon, Peloncillo Mts. (5,400 ft.), and Wet Canyon, Pinaleno Mts. (6,000 ft.). An MSR of total species richness on conifer, oak-madrone, and deciduous species richness gives r^2 additions of 0.78, 0.12, and 0.08 respectively ($F = 74$, 21, 15, $P<0.01$); $R = 0.99$. Conifers exert a negative influence on other foliage types, according to D. C. Glenn-Lewin, "Species Diversity in North American Temperate Forests," *Vegetatio* 33 (1977): 153–162.

[5]An MSR of data from table 1 in O. C. Wallmo, "Vegetation of the Huachuca Mountains, Arizona," *Amer. Midl. Natur.* 54 (1955): 466–480, gives r^2 contributions of conifers and deciduous trees as 0.96 ($F = 59$, $P<0.001$) and 0.04 ($F = 3$, *n.s.*) with respect to total species richness.

clines down-canyon, I am left with the hypothesis that most breeding birds depend mostly on conifers in riparian woodland. When I look at nest position, though, only the number of ground-nesting birds is positively and significantly affected by conifers. Foliage nesters are not especially influenced by any vegetative structure but respond most strongly to deciduous trees. Cavity users are constrained by broadleaf evergreens in a significantly positive fashion.[6]

These results are not really surprising, for birds are quite exposed when certain trees are leafless. Deciduous trees are leafless over the winter months, of course, and evergreen oaks are bare for a few weeks during the April–July leaf-replacement period. Yet several riparian birds initiate nesting before all oaks have new leaves, so leaf fall is not a strong deterrent to their use of these trees.[7] By comparison, conifers are never completely bare. Because ground nesters are potentially even more exposed than foliage nesters, they are the most dependent on coniferous cover. And the dependence of cavity nesters on broadleaf evergreens may involve the many natural hollows in oaks and their hard wood hence long cavity life.

To further check my ideas, I compare the incidence of cavity, ground, and foliage nesters in each canyon avifauna with their frequencies at lowland riparian sites.[8] Because oaks and conifers decline relative to deciduous trees below 5,000 feet, I expect significant declines in cavity and ground nesters plus compensatory increases in foliage-nesting birds. Indeed so! Cavity nesters drop from between 31 and 44 percent to between 18 and 29 percent; ground nesters, 10 to 19 per-

[6] Number of birds in each nesting guild from the localities in footnote 4 is regressed (MSR) against number of plants of each foliage type. Plants are counted in 300-foot intercept transects located in fifteen-acre plots in which bird counts are means of two to three years (1971–1979). Significant ($P<0.05$) r^2 additions are: for ground nesters, conifers = 0.75 ($F = 11$); for cavity nesters, oaks-madrones = 0.89 ($F = 24$); $R = 0.75$–0.97. Compare with D. R. Stauffer and L. B. Best, "Habitat Selection by Birds of Riparian Communities: Evaluating Effects of Habitat Alterations," *J. Wildl. Mgmt.* 44 (1980):1–15, for lowland riparian contrast.

[7] R. S. Balda, "Effects of Spring Leaf-fall on Composition and Density of Breeding Birds in Two Southern Arizona Woodlands," *Condor* 72 (1970):325–331.

[8] Lowland riparian bird data are from: my plots at Sonoita (4,000 ft.) and O'Donnell (4,900 ft.) creeks, Arizona, and Whitewater Creek (4,800 ft.), New Mexico; plus S. W. Carothers, R. R. Johnson, and S. W. Aitchison, "Population Structure and Social Organization of Southwestern Riparian Birds," *Amer. Zool.* 14 (1974):97–108; and T. A. Gavin and L. K. Sowles, "Avian Fauna of a San Pedro Valley Mesquite Forest," *J. Arizona Acad. Sci.* 10 (1975):33–41.

cent in the uplands, virtually disappear below 5,000 feet. Simultaneously, foliage nesters increase from between 41 and 53 percent of canyon avifaunas to between 68 and 77 percent of lowland riparian avifaunas.

Food and foraging space are other parameters of bird life potentially influenced by vegetation and, for analysis, I can look at guilds of birds, groups of species that search and feed in similar ways and places. I will make the following guild assignments, therefore: air-insect (fly catchers), foliage-insect (vireos, warblers, tanagers, and others), foliage-seed or fruit (acorn woodpecker, elegant trogon, jays), foliage-nectar (hummingbirds), timber-search (nuthatches, creepers), timber-drill (certain woodpeckers), ground-insect (flicker, small owls, wrens), and ground-seed (finches). Air-sweepers like the whip-poor-will and also the larger raptors are too few for consideration at present.

Next I observe the simultaneous determination of a guild by conifers, broadleaf evergreens, and deciduous trees. Number of birds per guild is statistically related to number of trees of each foliage type at five elevational positions in my 1,800-foot vertical gradient. I expect the best positive correlations with foliage-use birds, and I get them. Both the foliage-insect and foliage-seed or fruit guilds are primarily and positively governed by conifers and secondarily, in the case of the insect eaters, by broadleaf evergreens. Foliage-nectar species are not highly dependent on any of the three types, for these hummingbirds feed mainly at the flowers of shrubs and smaller plants.[9]

Among the remaining guilds, only the ground-insect and timber-search groups are governed in any significant manner by tree foliage. Conifers are most important in the first case, but their influence is negative. Broadleaf evergreens exert primary and positive control over timber searchers. It is obvious that timber drillers are not determined by foliage types, because they do not feed on foliage in a major way. Furthermore, the ground-seed guild of finches depends mostly on the seeds of herbaceous plants, not those of trees. Why the air-insect guild

[9]See footnote 6 for methods and note 4 for study sites. Only the significant ($P<0.05$) contributions of r^2 are given, as follows: for foliage-seed or fruit birds, conifers = 0.94 ($F = 50$), and oaks-madrones = 0.05 ($F = 15$); for foliage-insect birds, conifers = 0.65 ($F = 6$), and oaks-madrones = 0.31 ($F = 16$); for ground-insect birds, conifers = 0.62 ($F = 6$), and deciduous trees = 0.21 ($F = 13$); for timber-searchers, oaks-madrones = 0.72 ($F = 5$). In each of these guilds $R = 0.96-0.99$, compared with $0.44-0.72$ in the others.

is not significantly related to foliage types is a mystery, since foliage feeds certain insects that in turn feed these birds.

By now I am overwhelmed with details and must take stock of my general findings. First, I have learned that conifers represent most of the change in foliage structure over the elevational gradient of riparian canyons in southeastern Arizona and adjacent New Mexico. Next, I have determined that these needle-leaved trees exert chief control over the number of ground-nesting and ground–insect eating birds and all foliage-feeding birds except the hummers. The presence of broadleaf evergreens, principally oaks, governs the number of cavity nesters and timber-searchers, some of which are one and the same species. Finally, deciduous trees appear to be the least important structural element from my "bird's eye" point of view.

On a cool March evening I huddle by my fire at the headspring of the Río de la Concepción in Arizona, the only U.S. locality for the Sonora chub and a dozen species of flowering plants. I camp near adobe ruins at the Hank Bartlett and Yank Hewitt ranch site of 1880. Trash litters the ground under a grand Emory oak that the Apaches and band-tailed pigeons visit every other year for acorns. The U.S. Forest Service tells me to keep this place clean or they will close it—"love it or lose it"—so my family takes six grocery sacks of cans, plastic, and paper into Nogales. Apache litter of 1880 did not accumulate this way. Nor did the white man's in those less profligate days.[10] The Bartlett-Hewitt Ranch was burned out by Apaches in its first year.

Poor-wills sing at 7:45 P.M.; whiskered owls, at 8:00. Immediately a screech owl sounds off. No elf owls yet, but April will add that species. All four insectivores nest here in the Pajarito Mountains at 4,000 to 5,000 feet. Sometimes I find a northern pygmy or flammulated owl, but I'm uncertain of their nesting. Wait a minute. The screech owl's song does not bounce as it should. Or is that the paced, primary song of the whiskered? It must be a screech owl, because the same tone and cadence turn into bouncing later. Do the first, measured notes help to adjust territorial borders between screech and whiskered owls?

The screech owl has its bouncing-ball notes, the whiskered owl its telegraphic tooting, but the two species seem to use the same paced

[10]This assertion might be argued, based on observations of litter in C. Lumholtz, *New Trails in Mexico* (New York: C. Scribner's Sons, 1912), pp. 15, 239.

vocalizations tonight. Does this enhance division of resources in the manner of mockingbird mimicry? Still I cannot be certain whose voice is whose without specimens in hand. Screech and whiskered owls are so similar in their protective coloration that confirmation of a caller requires a close look. I must return with mist nets for capture and a luring tape recorder to verify my hypothesis of convergent vocalization. Meanwhile, I'll reconsider basic elements of this ecologic stage and evolutionary play.

An evolutionary role or niche is, of course, a species' place on stage plus its function there. The broader the role, the more resources utilized. And an appearance in many scenes of the play, a broad niche, should mean greater overlap with other species. But is a presumed habitat generalist like the screech owl, a transcontinental species, also a food generalist? Is it displaced locally by competition with habitat specialists like its whiskered cousin, a species confined to woodlands of Sierra Madrean affinity? Or does the whiskered owl give way in the presence of the widespread screech? I'll look closer.

In these Borderlands, where they occur in the same sierras, the whiskered owl's niche is 1.2 times broader than the screech owl's. In space alone the whiskered outdoes the screech by a margin of 1.2 to 1.0, whereas the food difference is slightly less (1.1 to 1.0). I judge spatial niche width by calculating a diversity value from the abundance and distribution of the two species at sixteen study sites in New Mexico, Arizona, and Sonora. Food-niche width is the diversity of food items plus that of their mean lengths as determined by stomach contents analysis.[11] The big-footed screech owl eats more large arthropods and small vertebrates but not as many differently sized items as the small-footed whiskered owl.

The narrowed niche of the screech owl locally and my field experience suggest that this larger species is displaced downward in elevation by competition with the smaller whiskered owl. How peculiar, since both species are nonmigratory and the larger bird should fare

---

[11] Spacial niche width is $1/\Sigma p_i^2$, where p_i is individuals per mountain canyon from table 3 in J. T. Marshall, Jr., *Birds of Pine-oak Woodland in Southern Arizona and Adjacent Mexico*, Pacific Coast Avifauna 32 (1957). Food niche width is calculated with the same formula, using data from tables 1–4 in A. Ross, "Ecological Aspects of the Food Habits of Insectivorous Screech Owls," *Proc. West. Foundtn. Vert. Zool.* 1 (1969):301–344.

Original Monument 19, Pajarito Mountains (Emory)

better in the cooler, upland climate. While the two overlap between roughly 4,000 and 6,500 feet, I find most screech owls below 5,500. Despite the overlap, abundances are negatively correlated in riparian canyons, and a summed niche overlap value for space and food is less than all but one of the comparable values between each species and the elf, flammulated, and northern pygmy owls that occur with them.[12] If song mimicry does happen, surely it reinforces the ecological segregation of screech and whiskered owls.

The place of the mimicking owls is Sycamore Canyon—called Bear Valley in the 1800's—appropriately in the Pajarito, or Little Bird, Mountains. Although my little owls are widespread, their vocal antics may be peculiar here. Hybridization between the southern and Botta's pocket gophers is a local event, for example. These two species are a similar upland-lowland pair locally and in the Patagonia, Santa Rita,

[12] Using data in table 3 in Marshall, *Birds of Pine-oak Woodland*, $r = -0.58$ ($P = 0.06$) for screech versus whiskered owl numbers in canyons with brushy vegetation and -0.60 ($P<0.05$) in canyons with fire-cleared woodland. In the Chisos Mountains, Texas, and Sierra del Carmen, Coahuila, where the whiskered owl is absent, the screech owl prevails to at least 7,000 feet. The table 3 data and those on food from table 2 in N. F. Snyder and J. W. Wiley, *Sexual Size Dimorphism in Hawks and Owls of North America*, Amer. Ornithol. Union Monogr. 20 [1976] are used to compute niche overlap, using the formula $\Sigma p_{ij} p_{ik}/\sqrt{(\Sigma p_{ij}^2 \Sigma p_{ik}^2)}$. The summed overlap of 0.84 between screech and flammulated owls is the only one lower than the 0.92 value between screech and whiskered owls.

and Animas mountains. Perhaps they hybridize in Sycamore Canyon because of man's landscape alterations begun a century ago.

Botta's pocket gopher is an eight-inch burrowing mammal of deep, silty soils in valleys around the Pajaritos, although it inhabits canyons and parks at higher elevations elsewhere. The southern pocket gopher, a slightly smaller species, chooses shallow, rocky soils in evergreen woodlands but also occurs in coniferous forest in the higher mountains eastward. Curiously, these *tuzas* seem to avoid one another except in Sycamore Canyon, where they overlap between 4,100 and 4,700 feet. In the early 1970's, hybridization was limited to about 15 percent of the total population in this zone.[13]

Not only are the hybrids rare, suggesting the effectiveness of local ecological segregation—Botta's gophers primarily in the floodplain, southerns on adjacent slopes—but the male hybrids are sterile or essentially so and the females reproductively inferior to either parental type. This reduces backcrossing, the breeding of hybrids with the parental species. Moreover, little if any intermediate or hybrid environment exists in Sycamore Canyon, where the floodplain-slope interface is rather abrupt. Also, the hybridization could be relatively recent, since pre-mating isolating mechanisms seem poorly developed.

I think the Botta's pocket gopher is a newcomer in Sycamore Canyon, invited by soil eroded from its slopes and deposited in the floodplain, beginning in the 1870–1890's era of overgrazing. Deepened soil would allow the Botta's to travel up-canyon, meet, and then hybridize with the southern pocket gopher because of the initially small Botta's population. If the invasion began between 1870 and 1890 at a point just below the known lower limit of the southern gopher, movements of less than 100 feet per year would take the invader one and a half miles to its present upper limit. Indeed, Botta's pocket gophers can disperse this fast.[14]

Since the hybrids exhibit little "acting potential" on the Sycamore

[13]J. L. Patton, "An Analysis of Natural Hybridization between the Pocket Gophers, *Thomomys bottae* and *Thomomys umbrinus*, in Arizona," *J. Mammal.* 54 (1973):561– 584. See also D. F. Hoffmeister, "The Species Problem in the *Thomomys bottae– Thomomys umbrinus* Complex of Pocket Gophers in Arizona," in *Contributions in Mammalogy—A Volume Honoring E. Raymond Hall*, ed. J. Knox Jones, Jr., pp. 75–91, Univ. Kansas Mus. Nat. Hist. Misc. Publ. 51 (1969).
[14]T. A. Vaughan, "Movements Made by Two Species of Pocket Gophers," *Amer. Midl. Natur.* 69 (1963):367–372.

stage, I think their theater run is about over. But with continued grazing, complemented by drought, slope erosion might permit the Botta's gopher to continue its incursion, and a small, unstable batch of hybrids might continue to mark the invasion front. Personally, I would like to verify my first hypothesis a few decades hence, but Sycamore Canyon must be protected from all grazing for that to be possible. Although designated as a research natural area by the U.S. Forest Service in the early 1970's, it is commanded by an antagonistic black Angus bull, fenced in, feeding on, and trampling the streamside flora and fauna.

My walk this morning discloses a mashed vine snake, and I wonder whether man or beast is responsible. This yard-long serpent is truly bizzare, but only in life. It is a slim, gray, pike-headed eater of lizards, with predatory behavior that baffles the human eye—and apparently the lizard eye as well. I count it the canyon's most unusual reptile. Today I witness the vine snake's unique approach-and-capture scheme from start to finish, for I am seated twenty-five feet from a Sonoran spotted whiptail, hoping to see whether it digs termites in the manner of its cousins. The act I am about to witness, however, was not on this day's program.

As the curtain lifts on the scratching lizard, I am aware that the tangle of vegetation above it is not entirely botanical. Animateness is revealed in the slow, arrowlike descent of a branch without leaves. Fascinating! Now I behold the snake's head, a mere inch-long extension of its body and not at all distinct therefrom. A lateral dark stripe runs exactly through the eye and beyond into space. Into space? Could that be its tongue? But I see no flicker.

Almost imperceptibly the vine snake descends, perhaps a yard from its arboreal ambush. Time disappears—seconds, minutes I do not record and have no feeling for at all. (My notebook entry is so terse, when I re-read it five years later, that I believe I was mesmerized by the slow pace of that special scene.) Eventually the snake's tongue—straight and rigid, the dark stripe in space—seems almost to touch the busily engaged whiptail. My back begins to tingle, and the spell is broken. I am sweating in the humid summer air, and the vine snake holds the lizard fast. The predator's toxic saliva, imparted through enlarged, grooved teeth at the rear of the upper jaw, apparently benumbs or kills its prey.

Having swallowed its meal, the five-foot vine snake repairs to a manzanita bush, allowing me time to recover my wits and my camera. As I approach closely, the beast gapes widely, suddenly displaying a jet black mouth and throat lining. If I back up and stand still, the black void disappears. If I advance again, the black reappears, magically, for the rest of the snake blends perfectly with the gray-green manzanita foliage. Moreover, the snake actually thrusts its black-void startle display toward my head, and I note that its binocular vision seems directed toward my own. Why should it focus on my eyes or head, the smallest part of my potentially dangerous bulk?

How often have I seen that before? Never the black-void startle display, but the binocular stare certainly is not unique among large diurnal serpents of the Borderlands. I have walked along a trail, stopped with the onset of that peculiar feeling of being stared at, looked around, and discovered a Sonoran whipsnake or coachwhip looking me squarely in the eyes. Usually the observer's head is on a lower plane, but if it is at eye level in a shrub or small tree I feel a bit peculiar, to say the least. I guess my false sense of superiority dictates that I see other creatures before they see me, and all should flee, not stand and stare.

In the Pajarito canyons, I look for a reptile that disappeared from naturalists' eyes between the time of its discovery on the Carl Lumholtz expedition to northern Sonora in 1890 and its rediscovery near Cananea, Sonora, in 1970.[15] This three-inch beast, the rock horned lizard, is a thick-jawed relative of the widespread short-horned lizard, but apparently more specialized. To date it is known only from evergreen woodland on rocky slopes in the Sierras Manzanal and Baviácora, Sonora. Here its spatial niche is above that of the short-horned lizard in the grasslands.

Events in the rediscovery story remind me of my own search for the rough-footed mud turtle in Texas. One method was the same as mine, namely to study the route of the historic expedition and follow it to a "spot marked X." Simultaneously, however, Vincent Roth undertook a novel approach, a study of the stomach contents of two old specimens, with the hope that specific identities would pinpoint habitat and locale. Horned lizards are confirmed ant eaters, of course, and the his-

---

[15]C. H. Lowe, M. D. Robinson, and V. D. Roth, "A Population of *Phrynosoma ditmarsi* from Sonora, Mexico," *J. Arizona Acad. Sci.* 6 (1971):275–277.

toric specimens held ants and other insects that told Roth they were eaten among evergreen oaks at 5,000 to 6,000 feet on the side of an open canyon between Naco, Agua Prieta, and Fronteras, Sonora.[16]

Although the known localities are slightly west and south of Roth's Sonora triangle, that doesn't preclude finding the elusive creature in the hypothesized area. Who knows, maybe someone will find the mythical two-legged lizard instead. I rather suspect that local folks notice mountain skinks or Arizona alligator lizards crawling in serpentine fashion with their hind legs pressed tightly to their bodies, when they mention these animals. But some naturalists consider the possibility of burrowing amphisbaenid lizards in the area. I'm not completely skeptical; there are more secrets than certainties in the living landscape.

For instance, we don't always find critters where we expect to, simply because we don't know enough about them. I recall the first bunch grass lizard I found in plains grassland at 5,000 feet in the Sulphur Springs Valley, Arizona, a few thousand feet below the montane grassland where it should have been.[17] While I muddled that particular discovery with another mislabeled specimen, erroneously reported from desert country, my vindication came with the later finding of bunch grass lizards over the 4,500- to 5,500-foot contour in plains grasslands of the Empire and San Rafael valleys, Arizona, the Animas Valley in New Mexico, and near Cuauhtémoc, Chihuahua.

After lunch I give up the search for terrestrial hideaways and wade down Sycamore Canyon to see my swimming companions, the Tarahumara frogs. Recently, they too surprised me by turning up in several canyons of the Santa Rita Mountains, including Gardner, whose watercourse I have traversed several times.[18] These pustular, olive-brown creatures are the Sierra Madre's native answer to bullfrogs, for they are as large as five inches and equally wary of terrestrial and aerial predators. When I go swimming, if I am quiet, I cohabit a medium

[16] V. D. Roth, "Food Habits of Ditmars' Horned Lizard with Speculations on Its Type Locality," *J. Arizona Acad. Sci.* 6 (1971): 278–281.

[17] F. R. Gehlbach, "Annotated Records of Southwestern Amphibians and Reptiles," *Trans. Kansas Acad. Sci.* 59 (1956): 364–372.

[18] S. F. Hale, F. Retes, and T. R. Van Devender, "New Populations of *Rana tarahumarae* (Tarahumara Frog) in Arizona," *J. Arizona Acad. Sci.* 11 (1977): 134–135.

where they have no innate adverse image of man. I enjoy a particular deep pool in which Tarahumara frogs perch on my head and shoulders, and canyon treefrogs, plucked from streamside boulders, crawl methodically to concealment behind my ears.

A black-necked garter snake has just the opposite effect, since it eats frogs. Carefully released black-necks may dive to the bottom of the pool but soon surface, and no frog swims freely or remains about the shoreline during such maneuvers. Once I had some soft rubber snake models. One was plain olive in color, quite unlike the brightly striped, black-necked garter snake. I placed it on the shore, slipped carefully into the water, and with a thread drew it sinuously across the surface near some Tarahumara frogs ensconced in rock niches in the pool's boulders. The effect was electric. Frogs fairly "flew" into the pool. Did they recognize the serpentine form? A stick of similar proportions, pulled across the water, elicited no such response.

Where Tarahumara frogs live among large boulders of the living stream, black-necked garter snakes also abound, but at lower gradients, especially around large pools and stock tanks, I find the Mexican garter snake and its prey, the leopard frog. I note similar habitat distinctions between the two snakes in O'Donnell and Scotia canyons, respectively in the Canelo Hills and Huachuca Mountains to the east. The situation is a mosaic, not an up-canyon versus down separation, as in whiskered versus screech owls and southern versus Botta's pocket gophers. Vertical structural differences, conferred by water depth, are governing factors here, reminding me that natural communities are organized vertically, not horizontally.

Whatever vertical structure distinguishes adjoining communities, a blend zone or continuum always exists between them. Usually the continuum is broad, and intercommunity changes are gradual. The Borderlands are this kind of mix between the temperate United States and tropical Mexico. Sometimes, however, rapid changes are associated with abrupt geologic-climatic transitions, as between floodplains and hillsides. Then frequent physical disturbance characterizes the continuum, and weedy describes certain species that typify it.

As the term implies, weedy species grow rapidly and reproduce prodigiously, so they are common and resistant to disturbance. Weeds are really the pioneers of community succession that persist on constantly disturbed sites. Especially distinctive is the fact that many weedy plants and some animals, especially whiptail lizards, are discernible as the self-perpetuating products of past hybridization. And they are polyploids, their genetic makeup being half again or double the usual diploid condition of presumed parental species. This added genetic wherewithal may enable them to survive the considerable flux of disturbed environments.

While I walk slowly back to camp, refreshed in body and spirit by my swim with the frogs, I frighten myriad Sonoran spotted whiptails from my path. They are animate weeds in the flood-scoured streambed. Moreover, they reproduce parthenogenetically. That is, their eggs develop with only female genes—each hatchling a copy of the female parent—because there are no males. Of sixteen species of whiptails in the Border continuum, nine are similarly unisexual, and at least five of these typify naturally disturbed habitats, such as floodplains and playas, and culturally altered sites like overgrazed desert grasslands.[19]

Perhaps the weedy reproductive life of unisexual whiptails can be clarified by comparing it with the reproductive features of other egg-laying lizards in the same local environments. I will look at the interrelations of average female size, minimum size at maturity, age of first reproduction, average egg and clutch size, and clutch frequency. To do so, I must computerize the manifold data I have on nineteen iguanid lizards, three skinks, a gecko, and three unisexual plus four bisexual whiptails that live along the Border between 3,000 and 5,000 feet.

Principal components analysis is the statistical technique I use. In nontechnical terms, it identifies species with common traits and specifies those features which are most important in distinguishing them from other species. Thus, most of my lizards cluster together in one of four groups, three of which display different reproductive tactics.[20] Tree, lesser earless, and side-blotched lizards represent the first assemblage: small creatures that lay an average of five small eggs three

[19] J. W. Wright and C. H. Lowe, "Weeds, Polyploids, Parthenogenesis, and the Geographical and Ecological Distribution of All-female Species of *Cnemidophorus*," *Copeia* (1968):128–138. See also O. Cuellar, "Animal Parthenogenesis," *Science* 197 (1977):837–843; C. J. Cole, "Chromosome Inheritance in Parthenogenetic Lizards and Evolution of Allopolyploidy in Reptiles," *J. Heredity* 70 (1979):95–102.
[20] In the principal components analysis (PCA), factor 1 (major loadings: maximum size 0.94, maturity size 0.94, egg size 0.83) explains 61 percent of the variance, while factor 2 (major loadings: clutch size 0.64, clutch frequency −0.53) explains another 18 percent. Clusters visually distinguished in the PCA matrix are significantly different,

times a year. The second contains large species, such as the collared, leopard, and desert spiny lizards, which average four, larger eggs only twice a year. Texas and regal horned lizards plus the Great Plains skink are instructive members of the third group, whose species have tripled their average clutch to twelve eggs while cutting oviposition to once a year.

I expect unisexual whiptails to stand out reproductively, but I cannot separate them from bisexual whiptails and the western banded gecko, all of which comprise the fourth group. Furthermore, this one is characterized strictly by its intermediacy between the first two.[21] So it appears that all-female whiptails lack reproductive distinctions aside from the basic premise that they can colonize new habitats with only one individual and out-reproduce bisexual lizards by a geometric factor of two.

Unisexual whiptails should be quite fit in disturbed environments, since their accelerated reproductive capacity should permit fast recovery of optimum population size following catastrophic mortality from such stresses as fire and flood. At the same time, however, the rapidly expanding numbers might make unisexuals attractive prey, resulting in mortality proportional to increases in density. Thus their populations should end up being no larger than those of bisexual whiptails on the same ecologic stages, and this seems to be the case in the Willcox Playa, a Registered Natural Landmark in southeastern Arizona.[22]

The quick-recovery tactic may be characteristic too of the lizards of group one. After all, they are comparatively easy prey because of their small size, are limited to small food items, and cannot conserve

---

as seen when both factors are submitted separately to one-way analysis of variance (ANOVA) ($F = 22, 21$, respectively, $P<0.001$). Data for the PCA are from many sources, especially H. S. Fitch, *Reproductive Cycles in Lizards and Snakes*, Univ. Kansas Mus. Nat. Hist. Misc. Publ. 52 (1970); and D. W. Tinkle, H. M. Wilbur, and S. G. Tilley, "Evolutionary Strategies in Lizard Reproduction," *Evolution* 24 (1970):55–74.

[21] Tukey-HSD tests of mean factor scores of the clusters provide a similarities matrix ($P>0.05$) involving the whiptail-gecko group twice with the small iguanids (factors 1, 2) and once with the large iguanids that have few eggs per clutch (factor 2). Confirmatory evidence of similar reproductive strategies among all whiptails is given by J. J. Schall, "Reproductive Strategies in Sympatric Whiptail Lizards (*Cnemidophorus*): Two Parthenogenetic and Three Bi-sexual Species," *Copeia* (1978):108–116.

[22] J. C. Mitchell, "Ecology of Southeastern Arizona Whiptail Lizards (*Cnemidophorus*: Teiidae): Population Densities, Resource Partitioning, and Niche Overlap," *Canadian J. Zool.* 57 (1979):1487–99.

energy and water as efficiently as large lizards by reason of their high ratio of skin surface area to body volume. Their mortality must be considerable. Large lizards, on the other hand, are more mobile, less prone to be eaten, and so can afford to lay fewer, larger eggs that hatch into larger juveniles more successful in finding food and resisting energy and water losses. Their lives are less risky.

But what of those large species that lay more eggs less often? The difference lies in what a lizard can accomplish reproductively, relative to other life-history demands.[23] Group-two lizards are fast, wary animals that rely on speed for prey capture and escape. Some, like the leopard lizard, customarily eat group-one inhabitants. They simply can't afford to haul a lot of eggs around. Group-three lizards are more deliberate predators, often cryptic in color and behavior, even secretive by comparison. The skinks brood their eggs, protecting them against desiccation, fungus, and even vertebrate predator attacks. All can afford more eggs per clutch hence require fewer clutches.

The trail beckons, but I must linger awhile to satisfy my curiosity about birds. They too lay eggs, remember, and their scaly legs and nitrogenous waste packages are so reptilian that their reproductive tactics may be also. I will find out. A new principal components analysis includes the familiar reproductive features of 100 local species, except that egg incubation time is substituted for minimum size at maturity. The latter makes little strategical sense now, for birds do not grow throughout life and lay more eggs with increasing body size as do lizards. Incubation time is similar nonsense among lizards, who do not incubate their eggs.

I am astounded at the results. Three distinct clusters of species emerge in almost the same relation to each other as the three major lizard groups.[24] Songbirds, woodpeckers, and some shorebirds are pri-

[23] L. J. Vitt and J. D. Congdon ("Body Shape, Reproductive Effort, and Relative Clutch Mass in Lizards: Resolution of a Paradox," *Amer. Natur.* 112 [1978]:595–608), also conclude that reproductive strategy is adaptively integrated with nonreproductive elements of lizards' lives.

[24] This PCA shows that factor 1 (major loadings: egg size 0.96, incubation period 0.88, body size 0.82) explains 53 percent of the variance, while factor 2 (only major loading: clutch size 0.97) explains another 17 percent. Clusters visually determined in the PCA matrix are significantly different relative to both factors submitted individually to one-way ANOVA ($F = 60, 32$, respectively, $P<0.001$). Data for the PCA are from many sources. See A. F. Skutch, *Parent Birds and Their Young* (Austin: Univ. Texas Press, 1976), for background.

mary inhabitants of the first, distinguished by small body and egg size plus an average clutch of five eggs incubated fourteen days. Cluster two contains raptorial and water birds, generally larger species with correspondingly larger eggs, three-egg clutches, and twenty-seven-day incubation periods on the average. Waterfowl and gallinaceous birds like the turkey and quail comprise cluster three, wherein species are also large but average ten large eggs per clutch incubated twenty-seven days.

Of the six reproductive features, only clutch frequency is not an important component of avian life style. Maybe it is too labile. Most birds can lay a new clutch, one or more times a season, to compensate for losses that prevent successful incubation of average clutches. And they do this regardless of group affiliation, although group one and group three birds lay more compensatory eggs per season, probably because they lay more eggs to begin with and lose more to unfavorable weather and predation. Most lizards cannot respond this way, since the fate of their eggs is unknown to them. Their clutch frequency must off-set adult mortality, not egg mortality as it apparently does in birds.

Since there are no significant differences between the similar bird and lizard assemblies, only among assemblies within the separate bird and lizard analyses, I conclude that avian and saurian reproductive modes are similar.[25] To reiterate: there are small species, whose individuals and their eggs live at great risk, so the females produce medium-size egg clutches or replacement clutches several times a year. And there are large species of two diverse strategies, based on different activity and exposure levels, which promote their populations in a less risky environment. But wait!

The hawks, gulls, herons, and others of bird cluster two are active predators, to be sure, but they also nest in exposed places and protect their small clutches and nestlings, unlike group-two lizards. Furthermore, the ducks, geese, and gallinaceous birds of cluster three are not necessarily inconspicuous foragers like group-three lizards, but secretive about nesting and less active in defense of their more independent offspring. Thus, elements of the large bird and lizard strategies are really more analogous than alike, with fundamental differences linked to the complex parental behavior of birds.

[25] Sheffé tests of factor 1 and 2 mean scores, respectively, of the bird versus lizard clusters show no significant differences ($t = 1.3, 3.3, P>0.05$).

Certainly not all large or small species conform equally to the three groups, for each is a unique actor, capable of utilizing a special suite of props to occupy a certain stage position. For instance, nightjars, hummingbirds, and doves orbit group one in my principal-components space but do not cluster, which means they exhibit divergent tactics. Models like my bird and lizard assemblies are but first approximations of landscape patterns and should stimulate naturalists to refine or disprove them. With this in mind, I will walk farther on the canyon trails—in search of better information.

12. *Cienega Summer*

LIGHTNING splits the San Pedro Valley sky, and I sit watching on the west side of the Huachuca Mountains, my back against the adobe bricks of a house built in the 1870's. I am grateful to be living in a Canelo Hills sanctuary, a Registered Natural Landmark owned by the Nature Conservancy. This is one of three border places that are special favorites, a refuge for study and writing seventeen miles by gravel road from town. My family and I, plus a live-in colony of Arizona alligator lizards, caretake the old adobe dwelling, for it is a monument of Arizona territorial architecture and a landmark of the Boundary survey period, when natural landscapes began to wash away.

Beneath me lie the remains of the original builder, William Whitehill, or so they say. The slope in front is mostly ragweed and Johnson grass. Plowing eliminated plains grassland long ago, and when irrigation agriculture ceased Botta's pocket gophers invaded the loosened soil, eating all attempts at revegetation by native grasses. Below the slope is a cienega, only three acres, but the last nearly natural one I know of in the Borderlands. Its Madrean ladies tresses are grazed only by white-tailed deer. Springs feed this marsh and seep into O'Donnell Creek, a headwater tributary of the San Pedro River. Gila chubs, coarse-scaled suckers, and longfin dace still live here. It is a vignette of the vanishing San Pedro.

I rethink my theories on the desiccation of this river and its watershed as I contrast nine years of protection at the sanctuary with overgrazing on National Forest leases roundabout. In 1883 there were 68,000 cattle in this region. Three years later, as unprecedented floods hit the San Pedro and the nearby Santa Cruz, cattle numbered 156,000. By then channeling had begun at the mouth of the San Pedro and along the Santa Cruz. James Hastings suggests that seven inches of summer rain and 68,000 cattle in 1883 produced no unusual floods, whereas five inches and 156,000 in 1886 did.[1]

[1] J. R. Hastings, "Vegetation Change and Arroyo Cutting in Southeastern Arizona

San Pedro River Valley and Huachuca Mountains (Emory)

However, when John Bartlett crossed the San Pedro River near Benson in 1851, he had to cut a road through eight- to ten-foot banks to let his wagons down to river level. By 1946 this particular channel was twenty-five feet deep. Elsewhere in the 1850's the river was broad and shallow, for beaver dams created overflows that became densely timbered marshes. Beavers still remained on the upper San Pedro in 1892, when Edgar Mearns recorded the first specimens of the Sonoran subspecies in the Mexican portion of the river.[2] Probably channelization had begun at some points and not others in the last half of the nineteenth century. Beavers are gone now, regardless of the timing.

I cannot erase the hordes of cattle from my mind. As grass is removed through overgrazing and trees are cut, the controlled, transpired water loss of plants is reduced, and atmospheric moisture buildup, the stuff of summer convectional storms, slows down. Rain is less frequent, allowing the bare ground to dry out more quickly and completely. The hard, dry soil surface, compacted by hooves, sheds water

during the Past Century: A Historical Review," in *Arid Lands Colloquia*, ed. R. M. Turner, pp. 24–39 (Tucson: Univ. Arizona Press, 1959). See also R. U. Cooke and R. W. Reeves, *Arroyos and Environmental Change in the American South-west* (Oxford: Clarendon Press, 1976).

[2] J. R. Bartlett, *Personal Narrative of the Explorations and Incidents in Texas, New Mexico, California, Sonora, and Chihuahua, Connected with the United States and Mexican Boundary Commission during the Years 1850, '51, '52, and '53*, vol. 1 (New York: D. Appleton and Co., 1854), pp. 379–381; E. A. Mearns, *Mammals of the Mexican Boundary of the United States*, U.S. Natl. Mus. Bull. 56 (1907):350–359.

like the proverbial duck's back. This, then, increases runoff at the expense of penetrating, percolating ground moisture, and we get the gully washers or "toad stranglers"—flash floods—that channelize the landscape.

Perennial grasses depend primarily on summer rainfall. Winter rains have no consistent effect on their growth, despite local folklore.[3] Also, mesquite invasion of grasslands is favored at low levels of summer rainfall, and mesquites depress the growth of grasses. So when overgrazing and trampling remove grass and compact soil, reducing the incidence of convectional storms and the benefit of what little rain falls, grasslands slowly degenerate into mesquite shrublands. The long taproot of the velvet mesquite permits its survival as upland sites are desertified. Now, with increasing channelization, mesquites may be removed from their floodplain *bosque* headquarters, but they find new refuge in degraded grassland. The velvet mesquite is the coyote of woody plants.

John Bartlett's Boundary survey came very near or through our sanctuary via Babocomari Wash. This major tributary of the San Pedro supported a cienega and beaver colony as late as 1893. Bartlett mentioned that the creek was lined with cottonwoods and willows, and the grass was luxuriant about seven miles upstream from the San Pedro.[4] In July, 1974, when George Bradt and I went the length of the Babocomari on the abandoned Southern Pacific railbed, below the concrete dam, we found only scattered clumps of cottonwoods, mostly second growth, essentially no grass, and a fifteen-foot trench on the dry creek near Bartlett's campsite. Was this the same area in which malaria was the scourge of frontier days? Geographically yes, ecologically no, we concluded.

The extinction rate of native fishes in the San Pedro River between Benson and the mouth of Babocomari Wash, gives another picture of the rate of landscape change. Between 1846 and 1904, roughly the first half-century of record, four of the eleven species were lost, and a fifth became rare.[5] Between 1904 and 1950, the second half-

---

[3] D. R. Cable, "Influence of Precipitation on Perennial Grass Production in the Semidesert Southwest," *Ecology* 56 (1975): 981–986.

[4] Bartlett, *Personal Narrative*, p. 396.

[5] R. R. Miller, "Man and the Changing Fish Fauna of the American Southwest," *Papers Michigan Acad. Sci., Arts, Letters* 46 (1961): 365–404.

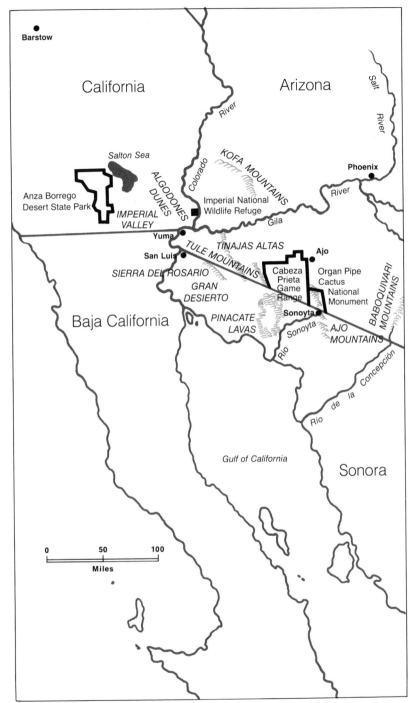

MAP 3. Western Section of U.S.–Mexican Boundary

century, four more disappeared, so it seems that deterioration of the natural river has accelerated. The first species to go included the largest two, one of which—the humpback sucker—had been earlier marketed in Tombstone as buffalo fish. This food fish and the huge Colorado River squawfish were lost before the turn of the century. The small desert pupfish disappeared after its original discovery here in 1851, perhaps in response to the demise of its beaver hosts and cienega-type habitat. Then the flannel-mouth sucker went extinct locally, followed by the speckled dace, Gila chub, and coarse-scaled and Gila mountain suckers.

Between 1904 and 1950 the San Pedro south of Fairbank lost 57 percent of its local natives, a figure comparable to the 60 percent loss from the Gila and Colorado rivers at Yuma, Arizona, and somewhat less than the 79 percent attrition from the Salt River at Tempe. Typically, the large squawfish went first or coincidentally with suckers and chubs. Then smaller species were extinguished. The seriousness of the Salt River debacle, associated with the mushrooming of a megalopolis, is approached by a 75 percent loss from the Río Chihuahua at Ciudad Chihuahua in the same period.[6] Big cities and diverse native fishes just don't mix.

Because the San Pedro River fishes are almost gone, I cannot investigate the evolutionary roles of the eight locally extirpated species. I cannot reconstruct a vanishing community from a few impact-tolerant survivors, and there is no surrogate worth studying in these Borderlands. How did the eleven species in nine genera manage the San Pedro's riffles and pools in times of drought, normal flow, and flash flood? To gain even a partial answer I must travel northward a hundred miles to the headwaters of Aravaipa Creek, a disjunct tributary of the San Pedro, protected in a Defenders of Wildlife sanctuary. Six of eleven natives still live there.[7]

My seine hauls in August, 1975, disclose three to six species in six

[6] W. L. Minckley and J. E. Deacon, "Southwestern Fishes and the Enigma of Endangered Species," *Science* 159 (1968): 1424–32; S. Contreras-Balderas, "Speciation Aspects and Man-made Community Composition Changes in Chihuahuan Desert Fishes," in *Symposium on the Biological Resources of the Chihuahuan Desert Region, United States and Mexico*, ed. R. H. Wauer and D. H. Riskind, pp. 405–431, U.S.D.I., Natl. Park Serv. Trans. and Proc. Ser. 3 (1977).

[7] My investigations in Graham County substantiate W. E. Barber and W. L. Minckley, "Fishes of Aravaipa Creek, Graham and Pinal Counties, Arizona," *Southwest.*

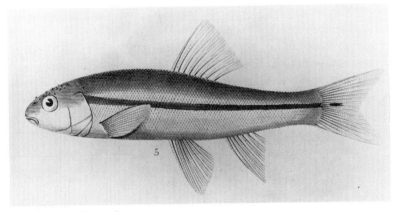

Longfin Dace (Emory)

genera, whose individuals contribute to species diversity calculations of 0.86 to 1.97. I now recall similar headwaters sites in the Devils rivers of Texas with two to nine species in up to six genera and 0.59 to 2.11 diversities in the spring and summer. Are most such creeks structured similarly in the Border country? Heat, drought, and swells from monsoon rains may be such rigorous environmental problems that comparatively few species adapt to them. Are the species obligate specialists, therefore, bound to evolve to generic levels of distinction?

The longfin dace has the leading role in the Aravaipa play, pretty much as elsewhere in southeastern Arizona. Its spatial niche is 1.3 times broader than that of the Gila mountain sucker, the second most abundant and widespread species here. The coarse-scaled sucker is third among actors, then the roundtail chub, spikedace, and loach minnow. Average niche overlap of the longfin dace with the cast is 0.29 on a scale of 0.00 to 1.00—none to complete overlap—compared with the 0.64 mean value of all other species combinations. Together with its broader use of space, this suggests that the longfin dace is patchily distributed along the stream, offering but little competition to its cohabitants.

The five other species are largely pool or riffle fish, seldom occurring in shoals where longfin dace are common. I note similar relations

Natur. 11 (1966):313–324. Niche width and overlap are computed with p_i = individuals/ species/seine haul using formulas given in footnotes 11 and 12 of chapter 11. Fishes were returned alive to the creek.

among the actors of O'Donnell Creek—Gila chubs and coarse-scaled suckers concentrated in pools, longfin dace between pools. Here in Aravaipa, loach minnows are strictly riffle inhabitants, analogues of darters in the East. Spikedace command fast water below riffles, and Gila mountain suckers dominate both pools and riffles. Of course these habitat distinctions are not absolute, as revealed by my computed niche overlaps among all six fishes, and I do not account for food, time, and other resource specializations.

To save a perennial stream and cienega in this era of overgrazing, one must build a dam to prevent the stream from cutting headward and draining its watershed. This, fortunately, was done in time to protect portions of the Babocomari and O'Donnell cienegas, but similar marshes on Aravaipa Creek in the 1870's and 1880's are long gone. So too are their desert pupfish and Gila topminnows. Moreover, the cienega on the San Ignacio del Babocomari Land Grant has been grazed continuously, its upstream sacaton grass burned purposely each winter, and the creek behind the dam planted with black bass and sunfish. Longfin dace and Gila chubs were found there as late as 1950, but in 1974 I caught only the dace and exotics.[8] By contrast, the O'Donnell Creek cienega has not been grazed by large herds in forty years. Although its borders were farmed, sacaton has reoccupied many of the swales, retarding soil erosion of the kind that has inundated Babocomari Creek.

Who cares? "We came to see the Montezuma quail," many visitors say. Then they may leave our sanctuary without having really seen anything. Judging by visitor interests, native fishes have few champions. This is unfortunate. Gila or roundtail chubs, for example, were tasty to aborigines and certainly are palatable to me. They make fine sport fish on a fly rod. The energetic Edgar Mearns fished for them in 1885 in the Verde River of central Arizona, and I caught one measuring eight inches in O'Donnell Creek. W. L. Minckley advocates giving trophies for the largest chub and other native fishes that can sustain sport fishing.[9] I believe it would be less costly to manage appropriate Boundary

[8]The 1950 collections are reported in R. R. Miller and C. H. Lowe, "An Annotated Check List of the Fishes of Arizona," in *The Vertebrates of Arizona*, ed. C. H. Lowe, pp. 133–151 (Tucson: Univ. Arizona Press, 1964).

[9]W. L. Minckley, "Native Fishes as Natural Resources," in *Native Plants and Animals as Resources in Arid Lands of the Southwestern United States*, ed. J. L. Gardner,

waters for chubs, squawfish, and perhaps Gila trout than for "put-and-take" hatchery rainbows. And to naturalists who are fishermen it would be more pleasing.

Fifteen miles west of O'Donnell Creek is Sonoita Creek with a representative, though depauperate, native fish community.[10] The longfin dace remains, the most tolerant and presently the most abundant of native species in upstream portions of Sonoita Creek near the Patagonia sewage settling pond. Speckled dace and Gila mountain suckers live downstream from this unnatural headwater. Sometimes these two are scarce, sometimes common, but if pollution from the sewage pond continues I have little hope that they can hold out. Three of the four remaining original species were confined to Monkey Spring and its outflow pond in recent years, but repeated introductions of black bass eliminated the new species of pupfish and Gila chub in 1969, leaving only the Gila topminnow.

Until the first quarter of this century, the little Gila topminnow was widely found in the U.S. Borderlands from Frisco Hot Springs, New Mexico, to the Colorado River at Yuma, Arizona. Now it finds its best and nearly last U.S. refuge in Monkey and Cottonwood springs along Sonoita Creek. The Arivaca Creek story tells why. This Pajarito Mountains creek originally was fishless, so in 1936 it was stocked with Gila topminnows to control mosquitos during a malaria outbreak. Ironically, the Arizona State Health Department thought it was stocking the common mosquitofish, an aggressive exotic that eats up topminnows wherever the two are in contact. In 1957 topminnows were thriving in Arivaca Creek, but in 1959 common mosquitofish of unknown provenance had completely eliminated these native, no-cost mosquito predators.

Fearing total extermination of the endangered Gila topminnow, W. L. Minckley attempted to reestablish the species within its former range.[11] His work was discouraging. Four introduced populations were

<hr />

pp. 48–60, Contrib. 8, Southwest. and Rocky Mtn. Div. Amer. Assoc. Advanc. Sci. (1965).

[10] W. L. Minckley, *Aquatic Biota of the Sonoita Creek Basin, Santa Cruz County, Arizona*, The Nature Conservancy, Ecol. Studies Leaflet 15 (1969). See also Minckley and Deacon, "Southwestern Fishes."

[11] W. L. Minckley, "Attempted Re-establishment of the Gila Topminnow within Its Former Range," *Copeia* (1969): 193–194.

eliminated by flooding, two by common mosquitofish, and one by pesticide poisoning between 1965 and 1968. O'Donnell Creek is within the species' range, so I decided to introduce topminnows from Monkey Spring in August, 1974. Fate may intervene, however, as I discovered a black bass below the cienega dam in 1976 and learned that a rancher upstream, in the normally dry portion of the O'Donnell drainage, had two stock ponds containing these exotic predators. Unless the bass are destroyed, another flash flood may provide the lone predator with mates, and the result will spell disaster for my introduced topminnows and for the other natives as well.

Success in introduction of a species, either by man or by natural agency, often results from the species' increased growth and reproduction following its use of new resources in the new environment. This is nicely demonstrated in a study of the Gila topminnow in a concrete canal, for the planted population grew larger and had more young than the natural spring population from which it came.[12] In the spring small crustaceans were scarce, whereas these food items were abundant in the canal. So topminnows in the spring took decomposing biotic materials primarily, while their siblings in the canal ate crustaceans and turned the added energy into added growth and reproduction. Such ecologic plasticity, the ability to capitalize on novel situations, serves Gila topminnows well since their native streams fluctuate from resource-poor pools in the dry season to freshets teaming with life after the summer rains begin.

Gila topminnows still inhabit the Santa Cruz, San Bernardino, and Sonoyta rivers plus Cajón Bonito Creek in the Sonoran Borderlands. But the Santa Cruz, parent stream of Sonoita Creek, is biotically depauperate in Arizona. This small river begins in the San Rafael Valley a few miles south of O'Donnell Creek and develops perennial surface flow toward the Border. Sometime between 1950 and 1956 native fishes were eliminated there, but I found the topminnows, longfin dace, and coarse-scaled and Gila mountain suckers in the Sonoran portion of the river three miles south of the town of Santa Cruz in July, 1971. I also found song sparrows nesting in yew-leaf willows, hiding, it

[12] G. D. Constantz, "Reproductive Effort in *Poeciliopsis occidentalis* (Poeciliidae)," *Southwest. Natur.* 19 (1974):47–52. Also note Constantz' "Life History Patterns of a Livebearing Fish in Contrasting Environments," *Oecologia* 40 (1979):189–201.

seemed, from the fate of their brethren on the Santa Cruz at Tucson, Arizona.

Both Boundary surveys describe the Río Santa Cruz as flowing, alternately above and below ground, after it rounds the southern end of the Patagonia Mountains in Sonora and heads back into Arizona through Nogales. By 1950, however, Arizonans had pumped its water supply 300 feet below the entrenched riverbed and eliminated river-bank willows, song sparrows, and local populations of five native fishes. The fishes, four of which remain in Sonoita Creek, albeit ten-uously, cannot return to the dry river, but the song sparrow has staged a comeback. Between May, 1895, and May, 1962, no song sparrows nested in the Santa Cruz watershed at Tucson, Arizona, but thereafter several pairs nested amid tamarisk bushes fed by irrigation water.[13]

Anyhow, sparrows are like nongame fishes in being low-priority conservation items. They are too "plain Jane," though I personally en-joy the challenge of identifying them in the field. With song, identifi-cation is easy. But only a few species are readily discerned by means of plumage, while many species are difficult, and some are downright im-possible. The Santa Cruz basin, especially the pristine plains grassland of the San Rafael Valley and its mesquite-dominated variant of Sonoita Creek, furnishes five sparrows of varying degrees of difficulty. The five-striped sparrow is the distinctive newcomer from Mexico, firmly established as a breeding species along Sonoita Creek and westward to the Pajarito Mountains in 1969–1970.[14] Song and grasshopper spar-rows, the latter abundant in the San Rafael Valley, are less colorful, and the Botteri's and Cassin's sparrows are almost impossible to distinguish from each other by plumage features alone. Their songs give them away.

At dawn in late July Nancy and I listen to a Botteri's sparrow on territory in a sacaton swale just below our adobe house. Common yel-lowthroats sound off in the green Johnson grass at the septic tank drainage, a curious place for these cienega birds. Yet this spot is a man-made mini-marsh. Acorn woodpeckers come noisily—no other way for

[13] R. S. Crossin, "The History and Breeding Status of the Song Sparrow near Tuc-son, Arizona," *Auk* 82 (1965): 287–288. This species persisted until the mid-1940's along the Santa Cruz River near Patagonia.

[14] G. S. Mills, "New Locations for the Five-striped Sparrow in the United States," *Western Birds* 8 (1977): 121–130.

them—to the Mexican blue oaks around the house. Ash-throated fly-catchers quarrel there with brown towhees, while black-chinned hum-mingbirds vie with broad-tailed hummers at our feeders. The days be-gin with natural and unnatural history. We resist getting up, when we have been out late chasing western spadefoot toads, but we must get going if we are to understand the breeding bird composition of decid-uous woodland below the mountains. We must have data from O'Don-nell Creek.

Few naturalists conduct breeding-bird studies in the Borderlands, and fewer still gather quantitative data for natural-history interpreta-tion. So off we go, because we don't know of any published information we can use and because dawn is just a fine time to be out. It is fun to see community visitors—the rufous-backed robin that arrived on my birthday, for instance—and it is good for one's morale to have his quan-titative data verified after three or four census mornings.[15] Then too, census results change and surprises are in store as the summer mon-soon arrives, usually between the Mexican Día del San Juan (June 24) and U.S. Independence Day (July 4).

The first week of our study is the last week of June. There has been almost no rain since January, and the creek has dried to pools be-low the dam, ceasing to run altogether a short distance north of the sanctuary. Few plants are green outside the cienega. A late freeze in May devastated many woody species, and the seasonal drought com-pounds the problem. Arizona walnuts are leafless, or nearly so, as are most of the Mexican blue and Emory oaks on adjacent hillsides. They will sprout again in July. Despite the drought, large predatory birds have already finished nesting, for there are young common ravens, great-horned owls, and red-tailed hawks about. Two other species of the mountain canyons, western flycatchers and band-tailed pigeons, linger around the scarce resource, the permanent water supply.

Surprisingly few small birds are breeding, but the hole nesters are an exception. Acorn woodpeckers, a pair of flickers, and two pairs of white-breasted nuthatches feed young. The acorn clowns include a

[15]The rufous-backed robin at O'Donnell Creek, July 4–5, 1974, is a first summer record in the United States. The study plot in deciduous woodland along O'Donnell Creek is fifteen lineal acres and requires about twenty man-hours of observation to achieve stability of data (no new species added and no increases in number of territorial males per species).

mated pair and five helpers, perhaps young of previous years, a typical entourage in this highly social bird. I cannot tell about elf owls, but I suspect they still quarrel over unused nest holes; two pairs are all over our study plot, yelping like puppies at dusk and dawn, apparently adjusting territorial borders. A pair of screech owls has young about ready to fledge. Whiskered and barn owls visit for water but do not stay.

¡*Verdad*! San Juan's Day brings a tenth of an inch of rain, the first in six months. But this moisture is not enough even to dampen the grass, as evidenced by a lightning strike that becomes a fire in the Mustang Mountains north of us. We see the smoke by day, the red and yellow glow by night for two days, until the fire burns itself out of fuel on a rocky ridge. Sprinkles continue about every other day, but it remains very hot, in the high nineties. Then on July 6, the day the rufous-backed robin disappears, we get another tenth of an inch. By this time the western flycatchers are gone, and the band-tailed pigeons have increased to twenty-seven. On July 10 an omen in the form of a canyon treefrog comes hopping out of the vegetable garden. If anything beyond a frog, it is a rain god, not a prince. And on July 15 the Botteri's sparrow begins to sing—another signal.

New life begins July 18. It rains all day—two inches—and the same birds start doing different things. Now we discover how four pairs of black-headed grosbeaks can occupy the same nesting space as four pairs of blue grosbeaks. The black-heads have been nesting, incubating eggs in the last week of June, and presently feed young, most of which have left their nests. This species catches insects on foliage or in the air of the deciduous and evergreen woodlands. The blues have been paired and defended nesting territories centered on grape or currant tangles in the deciduous woodland where the black-heads were nesting. But blue grosbeaks feed in the cienega and plains grassland to a great extent. With the rain the two species change positions and activities. Blue grosbeaks take over the woodland and lay eggs, while the families of black-heads move partially into the grassland to feed.

The temporal divisions of nesting and feeding space no doubt allow the two grosbeaks to coexist, but, more than this, the timing of reproduction to coincide with summer rainfall is survival strategy. And it is done in a manner that benefits both species. Just as black-headed grosbeaks have additional mouths to feed, the rains come, dormant plants start to grow, and insects feeding on these plants increase accordingly. Food is more abundant at every level in a community's energy-transfer system. Similar benefits accrue to blue grosbeaks, as more energy is now available for their egg production, as well as for feeding young later on.

Many other species time their reproduction to coincide with summer rainfall.[16] After all, in the evolutionary play, survival of additional companies of actors, the offspring, is most likely when additional stages and props are available. Among woodland birds this summer, delayed reproduction is true of all but cavity nesters, large predators, and selected species like the black-headed grosbeak and black-chinned hummingbird. On our deciduous woodland study plot, nineteen of the twenty-five breeding species seem to wait for the monsoon. The delay characterizes all three grassland species of another census plot—eastern meadowlark, common yellowthroat, and Botteri's sparrow. Western spadefoot toads and canyon treefrogs conform, as do lesser earless lizards, Sonoran spotted whiptails, and the short-horned, tree, and Clark's spiny lizards. These amphibians and reptiles lay eggs or have young from July 18 through August 10.

The day after the first deluge I catch a Clark's spiny lizard, muddy, beneath a rock on a grassy hillside 200 feet above its normal riparian abode. My excavation reveals eleven eggs. They hatch August 20. Another Clark's spiny in another summer disappears from her territory on our barn, although her male consort stays. When last seen July 11, she is gravid, heavy with eggs. Not so July 30, upon her return home. Heavy rains begin July 11–12 this year. Do other lizards respond to the stimulus with equal punctuality? Gretchen has marked fourteen gravid lesser earless, tree, and Clark's spiny lizards around the buildings. By July 15 two recaptures have laid their eggs, by July 19 two more, and no new gravid females are in the sample.

Eggs laid and young born during the monsoon have a better chance of survival, because they avoid desiccation as well as starvation. Amphibian, reptile, and bird eggs, respectively, require more to less moisture for development. Newly metamorphosed toads are especially

---

[16]Appropriate references are many and diverse, among them: A. S. Leopold, "Adiós Gavilán," *Pacific Discovery* 2 (1949):4–13; and R. E. Ballinger, "Reproductive Strategies: Food Availability as a Source of Proximal Variation in a Lizard," *Ecology* 58 (1977):628–635.

vulnerable to drying out, since their skin is little barrier to water passage. Young lizards fare better by virtue of their scales, partly resistant to water loss, and birds add feathers as insulation to a partially permeable skin. But all young animals have relatively more skin surface area than adults, because they are so much smaller; they therefore lose water more readily.

A more complex reproductive strategy is evident in the Mexican garter snakes that abound in the cienega and O'Donnell Creek and in the southwestern leopard frogs and fishes they eat. These animals have a constant source of water, so I do not expect them to time reproduction to midsummer rainfall. Indeed, they do not, at least, not strictly. Newly born garter snakes, recently hatched fish, and transforming leopard frogs are present in late June, but the frogs and fishes reproduce again following monsoon floods. I believe the frogs have a two-year larval period in the cold creek water, so June froglets might have hatched from eggs laid the previous summer. Nonetheless, small garter snakes have plenty of small food in June, and uneaten prey grow up to sizes that can better withstand the physical stress of monsoon flooding.[17]

The rain continues—two more inches, then four, and by early August brown plains grassland becomes a chameleon green carpet. Emory and Mexican blue oaks, delayed in leafing out, form dark green threads in a landscape dotted by the perennially green cienega and lined by summer green, riparian woodland. Blue flax colors the rock outcrops, and Mexican gold poppies plus barrel cacti blaze without burning on naturally dryer hillsides. They are a living complement to the fire that released nutrients tied up in dead poppy bodies of the previous summer. As a reminder of all seasons, harlequin grasshoppers meld brown with green, gold, and red.

For comparison with the O'Donnell Creek avifauna, I censused breeding birds in deciduous woodland at Sonoita Creek, another Registered Natural Landmark, but one 900 feet lower than O'Donnell at 4,900 feet. I revisited fifteen-acre plots in June and July, 1974 and 1976. Originally I intended to secure data to make lowland versus upland comparisons of riparian avifaunas. But soon I became inter-

[17]K. R. John, "Survival of Fish in Intermittent Streams of the Chiricahua Mountains, Arizona," *Ecology* 45 (1964):112–119.

ested in whether these lowland communities were temperate or tropical in nature, since some tropical birds nest in them. And I wondered if they were fundamentally different from comparable avifaunas in Arizona north of the Borderlands. Would these bird communities present a picture similar to the one I had seen in the lower Rio Grande Valley of Texas?

Sonoita Creek is a special experience, since it serves as an avian highway from Mexico for such tropical lowland birds as the gray hawk, tropical and thick-billed kingbirds, northern beardless tyrannulet, black-capped gnatcatcher, and rose-throated becard. It is good fortune that 300 acres of the deciduous woodland and creek are preserved as another Nature Conservancy sanctuary and strange that no one regularly conducts breeding-bird inventories here. My study plot at the south edge of the sanctuary contains twenty-six breeding species on the average, just one more than the O'Donnell Creek plot. The mean diversity value is 4.34, so close to that of O'Donnell (4.38) that the two avifaunas may be considered essentially the same in structure.

I would love to extoll the thrill of assaying tropical Mexico at Sonoita Creek, thus encouraging birders to mark off a plot and count territorial males as they add names to their lists. This would permit naturalists to look at community makeup with more data than my meager two censuses. In fact, I hope the Nature Conservancy will mark several fifteen-acre plots, and register their locations and regular survey procedures in the many bird guides that focus footsteps in the direction of Sonoita Creek. Then serious students could record data to send to a central repository for analysis at such time as sufficient amounts accumulate. If we knew the number of individuals per species throughout the year, not just territorial males at nesting time, we could judge the seasonality of its avifauna, an important feature in considering its stability and its temperate versus tropical nature.

But I can't promise more than one pair of gray hawks and a pair of northern beardless tyrannulets in a study plot, for this is what I found. What were the other species? Such relatively widespread deciduous woodland constituents as the brown-crested flycatcher, Gila woodpecker, warbling vireo, western wood pewee, and black-headed grosbeak. My thrills come from watching gray hawks court or brown-crested flycatchers drive a gopher snake from their nesting tree. I do not miss the daily excitement of a common black hawk or rose-throated becard, because the Fremont cottonwoods are spectacular with or without bird ornaments.

What interests me most, however, is the temperate structure of the bird community despite the tropical input. Comparisons reveal that riparian lowlands in the eastern United States support an average of twenty-two to twenty-four bird species with species diversity values averaging 3.94 to 4.03. The smaller values are in the northeast, larger ones in the southeast. Tropical counterparts in Mexico and Central America average forty species, with a mean diversity of 4.93.[18] Thus with twenty-five or twenty-six species and diversities of 4.34 and 4.38, Sonoita, and O'Donnell creek avifaunas are closer to the temperate model. Apparently, though, the temperate-to-tropical shift begins in the Borderlands.

In case eastern and western bird communities are different and comparisons with the east inappropriate, I examine a study of breeding birds in deciduous woodland along the Verde River and its tributaries 200 miles north of Sonoita Creek.[19] From this I calculate an average of twenty-one species and diversity of 3.94, values like those of the northeast. Or, if I look at known and probable nesting species in the San Pedro River Valley, eighty miles north of O'Donnell Creek, there are twenty-one, with a diversity of 3.53.[20] Again, the avifauna resembles temperate North America, and I conclude that lowland riparian avifaunas of the east and west are essentially alike, having fewer species and lower diversities in their northern sectors.

While the number and diversity of species are higher in the Borderlands, the most impressive feature is that overwhelming densities of a few species give way to more equal representation of all. In my Sonoita and O'Donnell plots, densities of the most abundant and rarest

[18] F. R. Gehlbach, D. O. Dillon, H. L. Harrell, S. E. Kennedy, and K. R. Wilson, "Avifauna of the Río Corona, Tamaulipas, Mexico: Northeastern Limit of the Tropics," *Auk* 93 (1976):53–65.

[19] S. W. Carothers, R. R. Johnson, and S. W. Aitchison, "Population Structure and Social Organization of Southwestern Riparian Birds," *Amer. Zool.* 14 (1974):97–108. Extrapolating breeding males from table 2, I computed diversity indices (Shannon-Weiner H' log$_2$). A complementary study is by N. E. Stamp, "Breeding Birds of Riparian Woodland in South-central Arizona," *Condor* 88 (1978):64–71.

[20] T. A. Gavin and L. K. Sowls, "Avian Fauna of a San Pedro Valley Mesquite Forest," *J. Arizona Acad. Sci.* 10 (1975):33–41. I extrapolated breeding males as a mean of the June–August data in table 2, using table 3 as a guide.

birds differ by a factor of no more than six. In the Verde and San Pedro valleys, however, this difference is four to twenty-eight, averaging ten for natives. If the superabundant starlings of the Verde Valley are considered, the average jumps to fourteen. Starlings alone reach breeding-season densities three times those of the most abundant native birds and up to thirty-six times those of the rarest species.

Starlings settled in Arizona in 1946, as elsewhere in edificial places or along streams with cottonwoods featuring abundant nesting cavities.[21] Woodpeckers provide many nest holes, of course, and starlings preempt such space from native hole drillers and other users, causing severe inequities in an avifauna. Cavity-dependent birds are 2.1 to 3.3 times more abundant than woodpeckers ordinarily.[22] But at three starling-invaded sites in the Verde Valley the ratio is 4.4 to 1.0, while it is 2.8 to 1.0 at four other spots lacking starlings. After subtracting starling numbers from the data on infested sites, I find a ratio of only 2.0 cavity-dependent birds for every woodpecker, so I assume that the reduction in natives followed superior competition for cavities by starlings.

Someone is watching me through binoculars, while I bird-watch with the collector of the first black-capped gnatcatchers in the United States. The specimens were taken on Sonoita Creek, adjacent to my study plot the week before. But someone is more interested in my behavior than in the family relations of the birds we watch. I am disappointed in being spied upon and, when quizzed about my purpose, realize that certain birders are excessively disturbed about "the killing"—like Cassin's kingbirds around a Cooper's hawk with a gnatcatcher in its talons. They feel that the taking of specimens precludes their adding the black-capped gnatcatcher to their lists, though I assure them the species occurs commonly in Sonora just 100 miles away.

Of all the birds I studied from my sanctuary vantage points, perhaps none stirred so much furor as the black-capped gnatcatchers that

[21] A. Phillips, J. Marshall, and G. Monson, *The Birds of Arizona*, (Tucson: Univ. Arizona Press, 1964), p. 141.

[22] Averages based on six riparian avifaunas personally studied (footnote 4, chapter 10), plus the first five avifaunas from table 2 in J. T. Marshall, Jr., *Birds of Pine-oak Woodland in Southern Arizona and Adjacent Mexico*, Pacific Coast Avifauna 32 (1957); and figure 32 in J. A. D. Flack, *Bird Populations of Aspen Forests in Western North America*, Amer. Ornithol. Union Monogr. 19 (1976).

White-throated woodrat.

Woodrat midden in cholla.

Desert pocket mouse.

Arizona gray squirrel.

Coatimundis (tails marked).

Pygmy mouse.

Left: Leon Spring pupfish, ♀ *right*, ♂ *left*. *Right*: Comanche Spring pupfish, ♀ *left*, ♂ *right*.

Left: Big Bend mosquitofish, ♀ *right*, ♂ *left*. *Right*: Tiger salamander (larva).

Rough-footed mudturtle.

Tarahumara frog.

Rio Grande chirping frog.

Bunch grass lizard.

Chuckwalla.

Yarrow's spiny lizard.

Sonoran fringe toed lizard.

Vine snake in threatening posture.

Ridge-nosed rattlesnake.

Ringneck snake in defensive tail display.

invaded the United States along Sonoita Creek in 1970.[23] June, 1971, held an interesting experience for me, unwitting mediator, squarely in the middle of a raging controversy between birders, who abhor collecting, and ornithologists, who demand study skins as evidence. Especially in Ramsey Canyon of the Huachuca Mountains, in another Registered Natural Landmark, where birders rallied around hummingbird feeders, I was caught up in a colossal lack of communication between the amateur and professional lovers of birds.

How the pursuit of natural history has changed since Boundary-survey days! When Edgar Mearns birded, he did so with a shotgun, because many species were new to science, others were in novel plumages or locations, and one simply could not identify most birds without a specimen in hand. Field guides and binoculars did not exist. Between Mearns and Frank Holzner, his assistant, 4,448 birds and 2,515 mammal specimens were taken on the Second Boundary Survey in 1892–1894.[24] Yet not one study skin or pickled critter represents a species that has disappeared or changed locations because it was exterminated by naturalists, while birds like the turkey and mammals like the elk have been extirpated from the Borderlands by the public and many species have retreated or advanced because of our landscape tinkering.

That we do not castigate professional ichthyologists and herpetologists for preserving fishes and snakes or mammalogists for skinning bats and rats is typical arch-predator behavior. I doubt too that many birders would cry out against collecting cowbirds, whose "ethics" and "propriety" are suspect in certain ornithological circles.[25] But I realize that the creatures thus studied are most unlike us and so considered

[23] A. R. Phillips, S. Speich, and W. Harrison, "Black-capped Gnatcatcher, a New Breeding Bird for the United States, with a Key to the North American Species of *Polioptila*," *Auk* 90 (1973):257–262. Note views by A. R. Phillips, "The Need for Education and Collecting," *Bird Banding* 45 (1974):24–28; and J. B. Tatum, "On Killing Birds," *Bird Banding* 45 (1974):315–319. See also R. C. Banks, *Human Related Mortality of Birds in the United States*, U.S. Fish and Wildl. Serv. Spec. Sci. Rept. 215 (1979).

[24] This assessment of bird and mammal skins is based on my visit to the U.S. National Museum, June, 1972, and on U.S. Boundary Commission, *Report of the Boundary Commission upon the Survey and Remarking of the Boundary between the United States and Mexico West of the Rio Grande, 1891–1896*, pt. 2, 55th Cong., 2nd sess., 1898, Senate Doc. 247, p. 205.

[25] A. R. Phillips, "The Instability of the Distribution of Land Birds in the Southwest," in *Collected Papers in Honor of Lyndon Lane Hargrave*, ed. A. H. Schroeder, Papers Archaeol. Soc. New Mexico 1 (1968), p. 145.

least deserving of protection in our man-centered universe. Maybe some day our conservationist attitudes about collecting will mature to the point where we finally measure up as the earth stewards we fancy ourselves to be.

By the first of August, many birds along O'Donnell Creek have ceased singing except at dawn and dusk. So we cease counting birds and start thinking more about what we have counted. Bronzed cowbirds, for instance, reveal their preference for brown towhees as foster parents for their offspring. The towhees may not appreciate this welfare system. I watched one towhee nest under construction at the end of June. The builders were also watched by a bronzed cowbird, which got underfoot and was driven away several times. When the towhees finally abandoned their efforts, the nest contained a single, untolerated bronzed cowbird egg. A second towhee pair, building the first week of July, allowed three bronzed cowbird eggs to be laid by the fifteenth, evicted two of these, laid three of their own by the eighteenth, and had one hatchling cowbird and one towhee to feed on the twenty-sixth. Where the fallen eggs went I never knew, but on the first of August only a hefty cowbird remained in the nest.

A bird-watching visitor suggests that I make specimens of all cowbird eggs and nestlings, but I will not manipulate this evolved parasitism and man-caused increase in bronzed cowbirds, this fascinating mix of natural and unnatural history. I will discover little if I do. I am not above meddling, especially if it will aid certain kinds of studies, but to choose friends and enemies subjectively at this time will reduce my effectiveness as an observer. I am reminded of a certain brown-crested flycatcher that acquired the "bad habit" of eating black-chinned hummingbirds at feeders.[26] While I discovered that hummingbirds have unusual predators in unnatural environments and rediscovered the concept that predators eat the most abundant and most easily caught prey, the bird judges yelled for a shotgun. I have often wondered whether they carried through and, if so, whether they saved the specimen.

Also by the first of August the fall migration is well underway, al-

---

[26] A similar observation is by G. J. Gamboa, "Predation on Rufous Hummingbird by Wied's Crested Flycatcher," *Auk* 94 (1977): 157–158.

though a number of local breeding birds are just beginning to nest. Grace's warblers and western tanagers are down from the coniferous forest of the Huachuca Mountains, and rufous hummingbirds have been here three weeks already. Yet lesser goldfinches begin to court for the first time this summer, and a common nighthawk incubates a single egg among pebbles eroded from conglomerate rock on a sanctuary hilltop. Did this camouflage expert produce the characteristic two-egg clutch earlier? It does not move its egg when discovered, although such behavior is recorded in the lesser nighthawk.

Lesser nighthawks suddenly appear in early August and join the common nighthawks in evening cienega flights, possibly in response to our pestiferous mosquitoes. If man wishes to preserve cienegas, he must expect to preserve mosquitoes. I see other potential mosquito hunters, pallid bats that roost abundantly in crannies of the old adobe house. They make little difference in the number of mosquito bites, though, for now they feed on the sudden swarms of small June bugs that are August bugs in the Borderlands. Bats and nighthawks obtain more food energy per unit of capture effort by concentrating on the larger June bugs, and this makes sense in the evolution of a successful predator.[27]

Despite mosquitoes, watching insects attracted by porch light is pleasurable activity. A metallic green walnut beetle or the silver-striped juniper beetle may visit. They are living gemstones of the Borderlands. And I might find that click beetle whose phosphorescent thoracic "eyes" snap on when I disturb it. The pallid bats find wild cotton moths and imperial moths, bring them to porch roosts, eat their succulent bodies, and shower us with the wings. Elf and screech owls come to feed on insect handouts. Arizona alligator lizards forage at dusk this time of year. We have marked no less than seven individual adults in the house the past four weeks, and each warm, damp night number three patrols the same window screen for June bugs.

Two antelope jackrabbits lope along the dirt road in front and pause. They are improbable creatures, definitely the inspiration for certain postcard hoaxes perpetrated on travelers from the East. Their ears are longer than six inches, longer even than the long ears of the

[27] D. Griffiths, "Prey Availability and the Food of Predators," *Ecology* 56 (1975): 1209–14.

Arizona alligator lizard (Emory)

more familiar black-tailed jackrabbit. The antelope jack's body appears larger by a third, and this giant species often travels in pairs or trios in the summertime. In this respect it is like the equally large white-sided jackrabbit of Whitewater Creek on the New Mexico–Chihuahua border.

I am puzzled why Mexicans customarily leave these large jacks alone while killing black-tails for sport and dog food.[28] Anglos will kill all indiscriminately, thinking they are preserving the grass for cows. Perhaps the *ganaderos*, Mexican cattlemen, observe and utilize the habits of wildlife in their ranching activities, while Anglos don't. Although inconclusive, my information suggests that *ganaderos* believe the antelope and white-sided jackrabbits inhabit well-tended grassland, whereas the black-tailed jackrabbit lives in overgrazed country. Historically, might Mexican cattlemen have associated the larger jacks with plains grassland or open oak woodland and the black-tail with desert grassland or desert communities? This is a fair though not absolute breakdown of the species' ecologic niches and conforms with better and worse grazing potential, respectively.

The summer begins to wane in August with rasping cicadas and fawns born in the cienega, like so many other creatures in harmony with the monsoon's life-giving tune. We record the first white-tail fawn July 30, the second August 7, about as Edgar Mearns predicted nearly seventy years ago. The cienega is a deer nursery. The Coues' white-tail deer is the locally distinctive subspecies of the only really large man-

[28] S. Anderson, *Mammals of Chihuahua: Taxonomy and Distribution*, Bull. Amer. Mus. Nat. Hist. 148 (1972), p. 267, corroborates my experience.

tolerant and man-tolerated wild mammal of the Borderlands. It was Mearns's favorite, "the most beautiful species known to me," even though in September, 1893, a doe nursing twin fawns frightened him into thinking Apaches were stalking close by.[29] My own love of these deer, these *venados*, relates to their ability to thrive in unnatural landscapes and their appreciation by men who look for beauty as well as those who look for trophies.

One hot August afternoon Gretchen, Mark, and Tommy, the eighty-pound Labrador retriever, are swimming in O'Donnell Creek. A week-old white-tail fawn is discovered, and Tommy instinctively pins it down, inadvertently breaking its foreleg. Surely it is appropriate to try to save this *venadito* in our sanctuary, even though the arch predator may kill it later outside the fenced sixty acres. So the broken leg is set by a young veterinarian, who says the fawn befits his month-old practice since he has yet to see a case he learned about in school. And Nancy, aided by George and Holly Pilling, nurses it back to health and independence.

Again I lean against the old adobe house, thinking about the management required here. It is not enough to buy a piece of natural history and let it sit, remain natural, and be enjoyed. A fence alone just slows the deterioration, for it is really just man's territorial symbol. Bass come in gullywashers under the fence, and cowbirds expand over it from adjacent cattle pens, while the cows break down our fences to get at the lush grass. Well-meaning but ignorant visitors release their unwanted pets. Just last week feral dogs ate one of our Coues' white-tails. These few acres lose their nature, as they extract energy from less exciting lands. Without management, the sanctuary slowly becomes like the culturally altered landscapes that surround it.[30]

[29] Mearns, *Mammals of the Mexican Boundary*, p. 183.

[30] R. Margalef ("On Certain Unifying Principles in Ecology," *Amer. Natur.* 97 [1963]:357–374) expresses this concept, critical to conservation: "When two systems of different maturity meet along a boundary that allows an exchange, energy (production) flows toward the more mature subsystem, and the boundary or surface of equal maturity shows a trend to move in an opposite direction to such energy flow."

13. A Walk in Time

REPEAT photography is a most convincing way to study the vegetative aspects of landscape change. To do it one finds a historical picture, locates the site, judges the angle of the original photo, and snaps a new copy of the same scene. Then if possible trees, shrubs, and certain other plants are identified, counted or measured, and compared between photos. Ideally, the season should be the same as depicted originally, since leaf fall and annual vegetation can confound attempts at interpretation. Dozens of rephotographed sites in one region like the western Borderlands can furnish enough information on the frequency of occurrence of natural versus invader plants for analysis of vegetative trends.

A potent modification of then-versus-now photography is to mark each photo plot permanently and recensus it regularly. Repeated visual evidence pinpoints dates of change and allows a more precise determination of causes than the two-shot approach. Furthermore, I suspect that most cyclic changes are missed by historical-modern photo evidence spaced more than a half-century apart, since there are shorter cycles linked to weather, fire, and flood. I remember the experiences of creatures in rivers, in valley jungles, and on mountain islands roundabout.

Some frequently rephotographed study plots do exist to confirm the cyclic nature of vegetation in these western Borderlands. In southern Arizona and adjacent Sonora, for instance, burroweed and jumping cholla come and go in the desert grassland, while saguaro cactus fluctuates similarly in succulent desert. The cyclic ups and downs are about two to five decades apart.[1] But unidirectional changes are equally ap-

[1]S. C. Martin and R. M. Turner, "Vegetative Change in the Sonoran Desert Region, Arizona and Sonora," *J. Arizona Acad. Sci.* 12 (1977):59–69. For climatic cycles see H. E. Thomas, *The Meteorologic Phenomenon of Drought in the Southwest*, U.S. Geol. Surv. Prof. Paper 372-A (1962); and J. R. Hastings and R. M. Turner, *The Changing Mile* (Tucson: Univ. Arizona Press, 1965), pp. 278–283.

parent—the invasion of mesquite, for example—and seem linked to continuing human impact in contrast to cyclic ties with natural factors.

Luckily for my curiosity, all 258 Boundary monuments between the United States and Mexico, from El Paso, Texas, to the Pacific, were photographed by the Second Boundary Survey in 1892–1894.[2] The Rio Grande's deepest channel is a natural boundary in the eastern Borderlands, so there are no similar markers in that section. In March–May, 1971, I located seventy-three of the historical picture sites between El Paso and the Colorado River and packed the nine-pound original volume of photos, my camera, and other equipment to 68 monuments that I rephotographed. At certain locales I dared not climb with the fragile photo album and was prepared with photographic copies of the historical scenes.

A first appraisal of the original pictures confirmed the severe drought of the early 1890's and indicated overgrazing. Since then, summer rains have increased in five of seven decades, and winter precipitation has declined. Also, cloudbursts have become less frequent compared with light-intensity rains. Although no significant change in total annual precipitation can be found in southern Arizona and adjacent New Mexico, a one- to two-degree increase in annual temperature over the past century suggests that aridity is slightly more prevalent these days.[3] At the same time unnatural factors like overgrazing have been reduced or shifted geographically, so I expected that my new pictures would tell some interesting stories.

Analysis of the photo pairs required categorization of the pictorial evidence as increases, decreases, or no change in dominant life forms, such as oaks, paloverdes, and grasses in grasslands. Subdominants like short willows, bursages, and grasses in woodlands were treated in the same manner, grouped for analysis, because specific identities were not always certain in the historical pictures if the original plants had disappeared. Fremont cottonwoods, saguaros, and ocotillos were unmistak-

[2] U.S. Boundary Commission, *Album: Views of the Monuments and Characteristic Scenes along the Boundary between the United States and Mexico West of the Rio Grande, 1892–1895*, 55th Cong., 2nd sess., Senate Doc. 247 (1898). See also plates 3, 5, 6, 9–12 in E. A. Mearns, *Mammals of the Mexican Boundary of the United States*, U.S. Natl. Mus. Bull. 56 (1907).

[3] R. U. Cooke and R. W. Reeves, *Arroyos and Environmental Change in the American South-West* (London: Oxford Univ. Press, 1976), pp. 65–79; Thomas, *Meteorologic Phenomenon of Drought*; Hastings and Turner, *The Changing Mile*.

Representative Rephotography (1892–1894 photos *left*, 1971 *right*), Selected To Show a Variety of Natural and Unnatural Effects. *Top*: Boundary Monument 60 in desert grassland, Playas Valley, New Mexico (reduced grass cover, weedy plant invasion, and trap effect of fence). *Middle*: Boundary Monument 111 in plains grassland, San Rafael Valley, Arizona (recovery of grasses, shrub and grass invasion of adobe rubble, and appearance of deciduous woodland behind hill). *Bottom*: Boundary Monument 170 in succulent desert near Quitobaquito Spring, Arizona (death of jumping cholla cactus and ironwood tree, appearance of mature saguaros, and persistence of small shrub cover).

able, as were most white-thorn acacias, creosote bushes, and mesquites. Such indicators could be assayed separately and grouped. To the three categories each of natural dominant and subdominant plants, I added the same ones for succulent-semisucculent, mesquite, and other shrubby invaders. Thus, I assembled a list of fifteen categories for each of six natural communities.

A 10 percent difference in numbers or measured coverage of grasses was the arbitrary minimum for assignment to a change category. Anything less was considered no change, for minor differences between the old and new photos could be caused by season and human error. The number of pertinent scenes determined the eventual size or frequency value of each category in each natural community, and correlations among categories provided an assessment of community dynamics as well as broad vegetative trends regardless of community affiliation.

Overall, the most common vegetative change is an increase in dominant plants. This category receives top ranking in deciduous woodland, succulent desert, and plains grassland (evergreen woodland, shrub desert, and desert grassland are the other communities illustrated by the photo pairs). The second most frequent trend, an increase in subdominants, is negatively correlated with a woody shrub invasion, the third category noted. No change in dominants is the fourth trend and is negatively associated with a mesquite invasion, itself fifth in the frequency hierarchy. Complicated threads in the landscape carpet begin to merge, as I observe that mesquite and woody-shrub invasions usually counter increases in or the stability of dominant and subdominant plants.[4]

Simply stated, the western Borderlands of today are much brushier than they were seventy-seven years ago. This thicker or denser aspect results from increases in woody vegetation of both natural and in-

[4] Spearman correlation values (r) are -0.68 to 0.87 ($P<0.05$, 10–14 $d.f.$). Because of the many significant correlations and unequal numbers of photos among the six natural communities, category frequencies are converted to percentages, arc sine–transformed, and submitted to factor analysis. Factor 1 (major loadings: no change in subdominants 0.97 and dominants 0.89, increase in dominants -0.81, mesquite and woody shrub invasions -0.79) explains 52 percent of the variance, and factor 2 (major loadings: woody shrub invasion 0.87, mesquite invasion 0.52, decline in dominants 0.49, increase in subdominants -0.81) explains another 23 percent.

San Rafael Valley Seen from Canelo Hills (Bartlett)

vader types, augmented specifically by a regionwide proliferation of mesquite. Moreover, brush development must have started by about 1880, since certain invading mesquites were ten to fifteen years old in 1892, according to evidence like the original picture of Monument 77. Apparently some invaders got the upper hand early and have not relinquished it, despite the recovery or stability of dominant species in recent years.[5]

Often the invaders are associated with past human disturbance, as exemplified by Boundary Monument 111 in the plains grassland of the San Rafael Valley, Arizona-Sonora. This monument, like certain others, is built from the stones of one of fifty-three monuments erected by the First Boundary Survey in 1853–1855. The old photo shows an adobe building behind the monument, while the new one depicts a sacaton and mimosa thicket amidst adobe rubble at the former building site. Grass was almost absent in the original picture but is lush in the new copy, as in most rephotos of plains grassland west of the Continental Divide. Monuments 99 and 109 are further examples. Eastward, as at Monuments 20 and 60 in New Mexico–Chihuahua, plains and desert grasslands were in better shape historically. Deterioration there contrasts with increased grass cover to the west.

[5] Hastings and Turner, *The Changing Mile*, p. 288. See also D. H. Harris, "Recent Plant Invasions in the Arid and Semi-arid Southwest of the United States," *Ann. Assoc. Amer. Geogr.* 56 (1966):408–422. Elsewhere, invaders may have become established during the Spanish cattle period (see chapter 7).

Saguaro Cactus (Emory)

Trees cannot be seen behind the hill in the midground of the historical photo of Monument 111, whereas cottonwoods, delineating the Santa Cruz River, are evident in 1971. Today's profusion of Fremont cottonwoods and Goodding willows is amazing elsewhere, at Monuments 73 and 118, for instance. Were the original trees too small to be seen, hence recent colonists, or were they cut or poorly adapted to flowing rivers and therefore scarce on the high water tables of yesteryear? Despite the local destruction of deciduous woodland because of irrigation agriculture, native riparian trees are more abundant now than nearly a century ago.

The recent appearance of mature saguaros in succulent desert is equally spectacular. Apparent increases up to 83 percent are noted at monuments like 170. Even Monument 167 at Lukeville, Arizona, corroborates this change while illustrating the demise of another cactus, the jumping cholla. The large saguaros must have been unobservable youngsters historically, since they require twenty to thirty years to reach the photographable height of about three feet and these individuals have had enough time to attain six to fifteen feet.[6] Some are even larger. But where were their parents seventy-seven years ago? At the bottom of a natural cycle, perhaps.

A slight shift to denser, subdominant species is suggested at Boundary Monuments 78, 196, and others in the shrub desert. Creosote bushes once commanded both sites, respective sectors of the Chihuahuan and Sonoran subdivisions of this community. My new pictures indicate that the stable creosote-bush populations may be upstaged by white-thorn acacias or tarbushes in the Chihuahuan region and, to a lesser extent, by white bursages in the Sonoran. This change in leading actors could be temporary, since at least white bursage has one-fifth the life expectancy of creosote bush.[7] Again, natural cycles may be involved.

A dozen paloverdes or mesquites graced the historic landscape at

[6] W. R. Steenburgh and C. H. Lowe, *Ecology of the Saguaro: 2*, Natl. Park Serv. Sci. Monogr. Ser. 8 (1977). See also W. A. Neiring, R. H. Whittaker, and C. H. Lowe, "The Saguaro: A Population in Relation to Environment," *Science* 142 (1963): 15–23; J. Vandermeer, "Saguaros and Nurse Trees: A New Hypothesis To Account for Population Fluctuations," *Southwest. Natur.* 25 (1980): 357–360.

[7] F. Shreve and A. L. Hinckley, "Thirty Years of Change in Desert Vegetation," *Ecology* 18 (1937): 463–478; F. Shreve, "Changes in Desert Vegetation," *Ecology* 10 (1929): 364–373.

Monument 196. They are gone now, save for a few eroded stumps. Sandblasted stems might remain if the plants had died naturally. Perhaps they were cut for firewood or charcoal manufacture, a familiar fate of desert trees today. In fact, mesquite is the favorite charcoal candidate among Mexican woodcutters, who still raid Organ Pipe Cactus National Monument in search of it. Although the mesquite-decline category ranks last among trends in both shrub and succulent deserts, it doesn't even register in my appraisal of grasslands and woodlands. In general, mesquite has increased, not declined.

Woodcutting once had a similar effect on the oaks, pines, and junipers of evergreen woodland. Now these trees flourish with the closing of mines, substitution of coke for wood in local smelters, and elimination of small homesteads that required wood for fuel and construction.[8] Yet oaks in particular have expanded naturally above 4,500–5,000 feet, as at Monuments 100 and 105. At lower elevations, however, the oak groves in certain draws have declined, although their counterparts remain on adjacent slopes and ridge tops. Monument 123 exhibits this peculiar circumstance, possibly attributable to the concentrated grazing and trampling of oak seedlings in the draws.

But the abnormally cold winter of 1978–1979 revealed another cause of mortality. Groves of Emory oaks were decimated in many draws and on flats between the Chiricahua and Pajarito Mountains, Arizona, whereas a few hundred feet away on elevated exposures, the trees were only damaged. Mexican blue and Arizona white oaks were less affected, alligator and red-berry or one-seed junipers untroubled entirely. Some manzanitas were killed, while mesquites were dead to ground level but had sprouted by late August, 1979. Apparently cold air drainage and stagnation during one to two weeks of below-freezing weather were the causes.

More pervasive than any change in oaks are increases in their shrubby subdominants over the last seventy-seven years of evergreen woodland history. Red-berry or one-seed junipers at Monuments 31 and 104 plus manzanitas at Monument 127 are examples at various elevations. Also, ocotillos have moved into low-elevation woodland and

[8] Hastings and Turner, *The Changing Mile*, pp. 52–56; and C. J. Bahre and D. E. Bradbury, "Vegetation Change along the Arizona-Sonora Boundary," *Ann. Assoc. Amer. Geogr.* 68 (1978):145–165. See also R. C. Tyler, *The Big Bend: A History of the Last Texas Frontier* (Washington, D.C.: U.S. Natl. Park Serv., 1975), p. 136.

grassland, as at Monument 132, while vacating their historical desert at Monuments 171 and 194 and elsewhere. Have they followed the course of desertification due to overgrazing? Monument 102 reveals the decline of another native subdominant, Wheeler sotol, while Monument 133 illustrates its stability, both under the onslaught of ocotillo.

Historical photos that show direct human disturbance invite me to compare the incidence of invader plants versus recovering natural dominants or subdominants. The Boundary survey camp at Monument 66, construction refuse at 106, and wagon tracks at 19 are representative of disturbances of the 1890's landscape. In some places, as at Monument 193, the original wagon trail has become a bulldozed dirt road that parallels a Border fence, and the fence concentrates grazing and focuses other alterations, such as the accumulation of modern litter I observe at Monument 60. Significantly, invading species are now dominant at 80 percent of these monuments, accenting the role of man as a major influent.[9]

Two particular monuments inside cities reveal the ongoing replacement of natural with unnatural history. No permanent edifices were visible originally from Monument 1 on the Rio Grande floodplain in El Paso–Juárez, but metal-smelting and refining operations flank the monument at present. Monument 122 in Nogales, Arizona-Sonora, was shaded by Fremont cottonwoods and bordered by a frame building in the historical picture. But progress replaced the wooden structure with an asphalt parking lot and the cottonwoods with exotic crepe myrtles. A chain-link fence visible here and in other border towns gives way to barbwire fence in the countryside, but neither barrier impedes man and his changed vegetation, as far as I can see.[10]

Nevertheless, the landscapes I study have experienced fewer man-made upheavals than others north and south of the Arizona-Sonora border rephotographed by James Hastings and Raymond Turner in

[9] Assuming unnatural invaders and natural species have equal chances of reoccupation, $\chi^2 = 3.6$ ($P<0.06$) at ten rural sites and $\chi^2 = 4.7$ ($P<0.05$) at these plus four urban sites, excluding Monuments 1 and 122.

[10] Supposed differences between U.S. and Mexican treatments of vegetation given in Bahre and Bradbury, "Vegetation Change," are not confirmed by my factorial analysis of variance (ANOVA) of their table 1 data ($F = 0.28$, $P = 0.61$, for U.S. versus Mexican sites; $F = 2.3$, $P = 0.08$, for sites versus vegetative cover type).

1960–1965. Excluding cities, only 19 percent of my seventy-three photo pairs depict edificial influence, by contrast with 52 percent of sixty-four matched pairs from the Hastings and Turner study. The Hastings and Turner sites show more declines than increases in most dominant and subdominant vegetation, while Boundary monuments depict the opposite. Only deciduous woodland exhibits similar trends.[11]

Within the past century, I am convinced, vegetative changes linked primarily to human influence have been unidirectional. The invasions of woody shrubs and especially mesquite, which date from the drought-stricken and overgrazed landscapes of the late 1800's, remain glaringly apparent on continually abused sites. Native indicator plants have declined generally on such sites, whereas the same vegetation has revived where original disturbances have been rectified. Man's landscape tinkering has been more influential than climate in creating unidirectional trends, although aridity may magnify such changes.

The thickening of deciduous woodland, for example, may be tied to man. Excessively large herds that overate grass in the late 1800's must have contributed to soil erosion, flash flooding, and channelized rivers in a major way. I suspect the lower water tables plus longer dry spells fostered riparian growth by providing more germination sites—seeds rot in water—and allowing time for growth to sizes that withstand severe floods. Local extirpation of the beaver and disappearance of the human woodcutter also favored an increase in trees. Short-term climatic change is not dismissed as a factor, of course, as drought contributes to the destruction of grasses instigated by overgrazing. But unfavorable climate only worsens an otherwise controllable situation.

Neither is climate the primary influent in the desertification of low-elevation evergreen woodland. The decline of oaks, rise of subdominant trees and shrubs, and invasion of ocotillos must be traced to overgrazing, since a proliferation of oaks and subdominants is manifest above the 4,500 to 5,000-foot contour. The higher slopes are steeper, the woods naturally thicker, and the grass less abundant, so cows have never been as influential there. I do not discount climatic stress, be-

---

[11] Plates 1–57 and 82–88 in Hastings and Turner, *The Changing Mile*, which evidence is categorized according to my scheme for Boundary-line comparisons. Spearman r is 0.28 ($t = 0.65$) for plains grassland and 0.10 ($t = 0.20$) for evergreen woodland (6, 10 $d.f.$, $P>0.05$); $r = 0.79$ ($t = 3.20$, $P<0.02$, 6 $d.f.$) for deciduous woodland.

cause it favors drought-resistant and cold-hardy plants like junipers compared with their oak associates. At the same time, however, junipers are unpalatable to livestock, and oaks are not.

Conversely, climatic cycles could be the prime determinant of the vegetative cycles that occur in desert communities. Grazing is not as concentrated in deserts as in low-elevation woodlands and grasslands, because the grass cover is less dense. And, except for local mining and use of its river courses, the desert was less used historically. Still, the hand of man may be in the synergistic "pie." For instance, largely mature saguaro populations could alternate with primarily immature ones to the tune of dry versus wet cycles, respectively. The large individuals withstand drought, even trampling, while the small ones require moisture and the shade of associates like foothill paloverde. As paloverdes are cut and the desert grazed, man modifies the natural cycle.

Adverse climatic conditions must have only temporary effects unless compounded by the heavy hand of man. In the historical perspective, grasslands are especially illustrative, because their dominant plants wax and wane more rapidly than woody species. Consider the San Rafael Valley, in which an 1892 photograph of the Boundary Survey camp near La Noria (Lochiel) illustrates abject destruction of vegetation, while the modern landscape is the best example of plains grassland on the Arizona-Sonora border.[12] Grazing was regulated here during the severe 1942–1956 drought, hence man's animals did not overgraze the landscape as they had done in the late 1800's.

At the end of my brief walk in time, the photographic evidence converges upon man as a removable or modifiable agent of vegetative change. Perhaps man's impact is a more important finding than the nature of change itself. Other repeat photographers have variously named overgrazing, a hotter, dryer climate, fire suppression, or rodents and rabbits as primary adverse influences, and most have dismissed fire and the small mammals.[13] Like them, I believe that over-

---

[12] Figure facing p. 189 in U.S. Boundary Commission, *Report*.

[13] Similar repeat-photography studies employing up to thirty-six Boundary monuments are by R. R. Humphrey, "The Desert Grassland: A History of Vegetational Change and an Analysis of Causes," *Bot. Rev.* 24 (1958):1–62; Hastings and Turner, *The Changing Mile*; N. M. Simmons, "Flora of the Cabeza Prieta Game Range," *J. Arizona Acad. Sci.* 4 (1966):92–104; Bahre and Bradbury, "Vegetation Change"; C. R. Ames, "Along the Mexican Border—Then and Now," *J. Arizona History* 18 (1977):431–446. Charles Ames loaned me his repeat-photos for the present analysis.

grazing is especially critical but suggest that short-term climatic cycles, not fundamental climatic change, have exacerbated man-made vegetative changes. Man can cycle his demands on vegetation in harmony with natural climatic cycles, but he cannot control those cycles, at least not yet.

Finally, I believe that damage to natural vegetation and its environment, such as the degeneration of desert grassland into shrub desert, may modify climate. I remember a dream I had, wherein cattle erased grass, which slowed down transpiration, which reduced summer thunderstorms (for which there is evidence), while the cows compacted the soil so that runoff increased as percolation declined. All of this would compound desertification. The resulting soil erosion and lowered atmospheric humidity would certainly limit the kinds of plants that grow, and this would in turn affect climate. Once started, desertification may be self-perpetuating.[14]

[14]C. Sagan, O. B. Toon, and J. B. Pollack, "Anthropogenic Albedo Changes and the Earth's Climate," *Science* 206 (1979):1363–68. While this book was in press, an important new work was published: D. Sheridan, *Desertification of the United States* (Washington, D.C.: Council on Environmental Quality, 1981).

14. *El Gran Desierto*

Six o'clock, and the full moon rises. A kit fox trots briskly over the sand dunes at my camp in Sonora, Mexico, near Boundary Monument 198. I sit in a swale, reveling in the rosy solitude—soaking up the heat of today's 100 degrees, as the mercury plummets toward the 50's. For the most part, this is wilderness, *despoblado*, protected by its average daily maximums of over 100 degrees Fahrenheit eight months of the year. But there are vehicle tracks on the hardpan nearby, paralleling the toe prints of kangaroo rats and pocket mice on some windblown sand. Already the moving sand erases our footmarks. The soft breeze that rippled mirage waters in the afternoon now gently tumbles this great desert.

I see the Sierra del Rosario, where no measurable rain has fallen in three years.[1] Two to three inches annually is about the average in this most severe of Boundary landscapes. The kit fox doubles back to sniff my water bag. Does she know freestanding water? Does *la zorra* lick the dew? The kangaroo rats I trap live without drinking. All their body water is made internally, metabolized, from the seeds they eat. Neither they nor their lizard compatriots will even touch "the stuff" in captivity. The amount of water I carry could exceed that kit fox's lifetime experience.

The rose fades to purple and silver, as I dream the history of the Gran Desierto. From his camp at the Tinajas Altas, Edgar Mearns rode here and back February 14, 1894. I can make that trip tomorrow, for this is the only border stretch without a fence. No livestock here to transmit hoof-and-mouth disease, because there is no water—only a few hardy souls dodging the U.S. Border Patrol on their way north and some small quadrupeds, which interest me especially. The solitude and its rodents are of concern tonight.

[1] September, 1969–August, 1972, according to Larry May (personal communication).

Yet the full moon is unsuitable for livetrapping desert creatures, who travel cautiously under the bright, reflective lighting. Rodents stick to the shadows, perhaps instinctively because their ancestors did and survived. I put out my Sherman live traps anyway. Certain nocturnal species may be more intrepid than others. If I catch some venturesome species in disproportion to its abundance at another season, I will learn something new. "If you don't keep your line in the water, you won't catch anything," my father used to say, when bird-watching distracted me from my fishing.

It is springtime, nights are getting shorter, seed supplies are relatively scarce, and hence the seed-eating kangaroo rats and pocket mice may sacrifice some sneakiness. If this were fall, after the monsoon— such as it is in this deprived land—seeds would be more abundant, nights longer, and these rodents might not have to be active. I suspect the critters expend energy and expose themselves to potentially unfavorable environments only when necessary to obtain food, shelter, or mates.[2]

Suddenly heaven becomes hell, as flares light up the sky and rockets explode in midair. My wilderness is a mock battleground. On the U.S. side of the Border below Yuma, Arizona, the Cabeza Prieta portion of this desert remains desolate, in part because it is an aerial gunnery range. Yet the commotion reverberates far to the south, experienced by even the few desert rats. This paradox of preservation is practically a duplicate of the White Sands ecologic theater in New Mexico. And I am acutely aware that wilderness is simply a temporary state of mind.

Zero catch next morning. Wary creatures must have been as jumpy as I during that unexpected Fourth of July. On other full-moon occasions I have caught a kangaroo rat or less often a pocket mouse, but I need more data to verify their differential activity. Large, top-of-the-head eyes and bounding locomotion are the kangaroo rat's special features for life in the open, where it may see its predators first. Conversely, pocket mice are shrub scurriers that should be more inhibited by moonlight. In the San Pedro River Valley, Arizona, Michael Rosenz-

[2]R. B. Lockard and D. H. Owings, "Seasonal Variation in Moonlight Avoidance by Bannertail Kangaroo Rats," *J. Mammal.* 55 (1974):189–193. See also M. L. Cody, "Optimization in Ecology," *Science* 183 (1974):1156–64.

Ord Kangaroo Rat (Emory)

weig learned that the Merriam kangaroo rat chooses open ground, while the desert pocket mouse prefers dense vegetation.[3]

These two species and other heteromyid rodents dominate shrub desert communities. At seven of my eight trapping sites these mice with cheek-pouch "seed baskets" outnumber cricetid rodents, the similarly small mammals without cheek pouches. I catch two to four species of heteromyids, 15 to 115 grams in weight, all of which are confirmed seed eaters. Is their actor's guild limited by food or spatial resources? Will I find certain casts more frequently than others, just as I reencounter the seven to ten indicator birds of shrub deserts?

Indeed so. The heteromyids divide up seeds by sizes directly proportional to their particular body sizes, although Merriam's kangaroo rats and desert pocket mice are apparent exceptions to this rule. At Tucson, Arizona, for example, five of six interspecific comparisons—all except the Merriam's rat with the desert pocket mouse—show significant differences in sizes of seeds harvested. Only three of the six demonstrate comparable distinctions in choice of vegetation structure, and

[3]M. L. Rosenzweig, "Habitat Selection Experiments with a Pair of Coexisting Heteromyid Rodent Species," *Ecology* 54 (1973):111–117.

again the Merriam's rat–desert pocket mouse duo reveals no important difference.[4]

If shrub deserts are poor in resources as suggested by their simplistic vegetation, in turn restricted by the lack of water, perhaps the most successful heteromyid groups comprise species that converge upon the limited resources. Understandably, then, the Merriam's kangaroo rat–desert pocket mouse combination is found most frequently. In fact, it is trapped twice as often as the next most common assembly, which includes both species with the Arizona pocket mouse. Additional common casts of characters include these three rodents with Bailey's pocket mouse or just the first two with the Bailey's.[5]

All four heteromyid assemblies must be considered common, because altogether they are trapped more often than seven others in local shrub deserts. What is the secret of their success? Is it the use of similar seed types revealed by similar body sizes? If so, body-weight ratios between the species of these groups should be smaller than the ratios of comparatively rare groups. However, mean weight ratios of the common and rare assemblies are not especially different—2.3 versus 2.4, respectively. It may be that very similar bodies engender too much competition, because they make seed harvests that are too much alike. Rodents of very different sizes, on the other hand, may require dis-

[4]J H. Brown, "Geographical Ecology of Desert Rodents," in *Ecology and Evolution of Communities*, ed. M. L. Cody and J. M. Diamond, pp. 315–341 (Cambridge: Harvard Univ. Press, 1975) (cf. C. A. Leman, "Seed Size Selection in Heteromyids," *Oecologia* 35 [1978]: 13–19); R. T. M'Closkey, "Niche Separation and Assembly in Four Species of Sonoran Desert Rodents," *Amer. Natur.* 112 (1978): 683–694.

[5]My data on eight flat shrub desert sites between the Baboquivari Mountains and the Colorado River, Arizona-Sonora, sampled 60–150 trap nights each in April–July, 1971, are compared with relevant data from other sources to analyze assembly frequencies and body-size ratios (Brown, "Geographical Ecology"; M'Closkey, "Niche Separations"; M. L. Rosenzweig and J. Winakur, "Population Ecology of Desert Rodent Communities: Habitats and Environmental Complexity," *Ecology* 50 [1969]: 558–572). The four common assemblies with six or more records each occur a total of thirty-four times; seven others with three or fewer records occur sixteen times, so $\chi^2 = 6.5$ ($P<0.05$) if expected frequencies are equal. Body-size ratios fit a normal curve ($\chi^2 = 6.2$, *n.s.*; $\bar{x} = 2.29 \pm 0.09$) and are the same ($t = 1.02$, *n.s.*, 45 *d.f.*) as those of the Chihuahuan desert region ($\bar{x} = 2.19 \pm 0.33$) based on a synthesis of my data and that from H. H. Genoways, R. J. Baker, and J. E. Cornely, "Mammals of the Guadalupe Mountains National Park," in *Biological Investigations in the Guadalupe Mountains National Park, Texas*, ed. H. H. Genoways and R. J. Baker, pp. 271–332, U.S.D.I., Natl. Park Serv. Trans. and Proc. Ser. 4 (1979).

parate seed supplies so rare that the assemblies themselves are rare.

Nevertheless, some sharing of seed types occurs within the four common assemblies. This must be a productive activity in a relatively unproductive landscape, for I find the highest densities correlated with the greatest similarity of body sizes. The relationship disappears when rare groups with mean weight ratios smaller than those of the common groups are added but not when rare assemblies with larger ratios are added. Therefore, within the bounds of some limiting similarity, about a twofold average difference in body weight, convergence in body size must permit the sharing of seed types, which fosters larger rodent populations.[6]

But how is the resulting competition handled? Does another environmental factor like space separate the species if food size does not? My data on spatial distributions and densities of the various heteromyid groups indicate that as the basic two-species unit adds species, average interspecific overlap shrinks. This must reduce competition, as the additional rodents harvest seeds in different areas. Simultaneously, however, average niche width increases.[7] Intriguing. Larger assemblies use more of the desert but with less overlap among the users.

A bracing walk this fine April morning gives me further insight. The heteromyids use creosote bushes and white bursages for food and cover, and the vegetation is patchily distributed. Some plants are clumped, others scattered, but the clumps and scatters are focused on the crests and lees of dunes or along drainage channels in adjacent hardpan. Kangaroo rats and pocket mice can be interspersed among the plant groupings and bare ground with minimal overlap, since they segregate according to differences in the openness of horizontal space.[8]

[6] For densities corresponding to the common body-size ratios of 2.0–2.5, $r = -0.46$ ($P<0.05$, 17 $d.f.$); for densities versus 1.6–2.5 ratios, $r = -0.17$, $n.s.$, 20 $d.f.$); for densities versus 2.0–3.2 ratios, $r = -0.52$ ($P<0.05$, 20 $d.f.$). G. E. Hutchinson ("Homage to Santa Rosalia: Or, Why Are There So Many Kinds of Animals," *Amer. Natur.* 93 [1959]: 145–159) introduces the idea of limiting similarity.

[7] The correlation (Pearson r) is -0.53 for mean niche overlap and 0.15 for mean niche width versus number of species. Though insignificant because of small sample size (4 $d.f.$), the trends support E. R. Pianka ("Niche Overlap and Diffuse Competition," *Proc. Natl. Acad. Sci. USA.* 71 [1974]: 2141–45), whose formulae I use. Cf. Brown, "Geographical Ecology."

[8] Rosenzweig, "Habitat Selection Experiments." See also J. T. Wondolleck, "Forage-area Separation and Overlap in Heteromyid Rodents," *J. Mammal.* 59 (1978): 510–518; R. T. M'Closkey, "Spatial Patterns in Sizes of Seeds Collected by Four Species of Heteromyid Rodents," *Ecology* 61 (1980): 486–489.

The greater the variety of such space, then, the more heteromyid species that use it.

And what of the cricetid rodents I so handily dismissed as being scarce? After all, they do eat seeds, although their tastes are catholic compared with heteromyids'. I may not have the whole story locally, for my experience in the Chihuahuan desert region indicates that cricetids increase in numbers and invade the shrub desert coincidentally with the summer monsoon. Around the Guadalupe Mountains, Texas–New Mexico, my trap samples from July–September contain more cricetids than those of April–June. Perhaps the seasonal increase in green vegetation stimulates reproduction and invites the additional consumers.[9] Here in the Gran Desierto, however, the monsoon is not the same outstanding feature.

Cricetid rodents may respond more quickly than heteromyids to a monsoon landscape because their reproductive potential is greater. Six small species average 3.5 offspring per litter, whereas six kangaroo rat and pocket mouse neighbors average 2.1 in the Guadalupe lowlands.[10] Species in both groups have one or two litters per year, the first in a spring flush of green if winter rain has been substantial, the second during or after the monsoon. Low winter rainfall may explain the comparative rarity of spring cricetids locally, for it seldom generates the kind of greenery associated with the monsoon.

I think heteromyids are less affected by insufficient winter rains or the monsoon's largess. All build deep burrows, stock them with seeds,

[9] A split-plot analysis of variance (ANOVA) of cricetid versus heteromyid numbers in April–June versus July–September (six samples of sixty to ninety trap-nights each season in shrub desert, 1960–1963) gives but one significant effect: cricetids with season ($F = 9.2$, $P<0.05$, 7 df.). W. G. Whitford ("Temporal Fluctuations in Density and Diversity of Desert Rodent Populations," *J. Mammal.* 57 [1976]:351–369) provides similar information. From his figure 9 on prebreeding numbers, I compute the following mean coefficients of yearly variation: heteromyids, 0.71 ± 0.15; cricetids except woodrats, 1.06 ± 0.13; woodrats alone, 0.47 ± 0.12 ($F = 3.56$, $P = 0.07$, 1–17 df.). Cf. table 3 in W. Conley, J. D. Nichols, and A. R. Tipton, "Reproductive Strategies in Desert Rodents," in *Symposium on the Biological Resources of the Chihuahuan Desert Region, United States and Mexico*, ed. R. H. Wauer and D. H. Riskind, pp. 193–215, U.S.D.I., Natl. Park Serv. Trans. and Proc. Ser. 3 (1977).

[10] From the data on pp. 289–298 (excluding woodrats) in Genoways, Baker, and Cornely, "Mammals of the Guadalupe Mountains," $F = 17.1$, $t = 5.4$, $P<0.001$. Litter frequency is a rough estimate that fluctuates widely with year-to-year differences in productivity. See also table 1 in Conley, Nichols, and Tipton, "Reproductive Strategies in Desert Rodents."

and so create favorable microenvironments for themselves year-round. Several if not all species become inactive in these retreats during stressful times, even daily, but especially in winter. Thus ensconced, they are relatively independent of unfavorable temperatures, humidities, and reduced food supplies. Among desert cricetids, only the cactus mouse seems capable of this avoidance tactic, so most cricetids appear to be but temporary, seasonal competitors.

As the sun climbs to an uncomfortable angle, I ask myself what I may have missed in looking at rodents as guilds of actors. I must not overlook one special performance. Surely the woodrat or packrat has one of the longest theater runs in space and time, as I discovered several hundred miles ago in the Big Bend of Texas. Its midden house or den, typically a pile of sticks, leaves, cactus parts, and sometimes cow patties, is a successful way of avoiding extreme temperatures that has been in use at least forty thousand years.[11]

Building one's own thermal environment has been man's answer, too. But modern man costs the desert dearly. By mining fossil fuels that he must burn to be cool or warm, man transforms the landscape with wells, pits, roads, and pipelines and then abandons it when the resource is expended. Water mining may have the same effect eventually. Meanwhile, the woodrat gathers litter in building its den. Of course the beast is infamous for packing off unnatural litter. But more importantly, I believe this rodent inadvertently plants a living litter supply and thus creates a self-sustaining environment.

The white-throated, desert, and southern plains woodrats live in desert communities along the Border. All three typify prickly pear or cholla cactus stands, although agaves and yuccas are substitutable. The thicker the cactus the denser the woodrats become, because they depend on succulent, spiny plants for food, water, and protective building material.[12] I will bet that harvested cholla joints occasionally root themselves, for I have seen prickly pear pads do so after being dis-

[11]A. K. Lee, "Adaptations to Arid Environments in Woodrats of the Genus *Neotoma*," *Univ. California Publs. Zool.* 64 (1963):57–96; P. V. Wells, "Macrofossil Analysis of Wood Rat (*Neotoma*) Middens as a Key to the Quaternary Vegetational History of Arid America," *Quaternary Res.* 6 (1976):223–248.

[12]J. H. Brown, G. A. Lieberman, and W. F. Dengler, "Woodrats and Cholla: Dependence of a Small Mammal Population on the Density of Cacti," *Ecology* 53 (1972): 310–313; G. C. Raun, *A Population of Woodrats* (Neotoma micropus) *in Southern Texas*, Bull. Texas Mem. Mus. 11 (1966).

carded by the southern plains woodrat. And what of cactus left in an unused den? Is it in a ready-made plant growth chamber?

The cycle of a woodrat population may be a special desert theme, perhaps as follows: favorable rainfall builds a cactus patch that attracts woodrats in proportion to its density; the woodrats are culled by predation or other factors and thus remain within the support capacity of the cactus; a drought or severe freeze kills most of the cactus, thinning the woodrats accordingly; the number of unoccupied dens increases; some cactus pads and joints, sheltered in empty dens, grow into new plants with the return of normal rainfall and temperatures; the woodrats revive.

Boom-and-bust characterizes small rodent populations, but perhaps the woodrat-cactus connection is so advantageous that it moderates the cyclic ups and downs. Certainly woodrats do not usually experience the extreme flux of their rodent associates. For example, in a south Texas cactus patch, 1958–1961, they were the most stable of three cricetid species.[13] And between 1971 and 1974, woodrats were comparatively stable in a shrub desert and adjacent desert grassland in southern New Mexico. These builders showed the least flux among six cricetids in both communities. Although six heteromyids made up the most stable group, woodrats were more stable than even the average heteromyid.[14]

By the time I return to camp for a drink, about 11 A.M., the April sun has heated the sand to an uncomfortable level. My thoughts move from rodent habitat to lizard behavior, for only the lizards are moving now, from bush to bush. In mid-August of 1855, Nathaniel Michler of the First Boundary Survey rode his horse from Sonoyta to Fort Yuma under similar circumstances, "the most dreary and tiresome [ride] I have ever experienced. . . . not even the wolf or the hare to attract the attention, and, save the lizard and horned frog, naught to give life and animation to this region."[15]

Sonoran fringe-toed lizards furnish excitement, though, as they run over the dunes on their hind legs, hotly pursued by this unnatural

[13] Raun, *Population of Woodrats.*

[14] My calculations, from Whitford, fig. 9, "Temporal Fluctuations."

[15] W. H. Emory, *Report on the United States and Mexican Boundary Survey,* vol. 1, 34th Cong., 1st sess., 1857, House Exec. Doc. 135, p. 115.

biped. When pressed, they dive beneath the surface and "swim" in the sand with the aid of enlarged scales along the edges of each toe. Similar scale festoons around the eyes deflect blowing sand. Furthermore, the creature's eyelids overlap when closed, firmly sealing them against abrasion in the burrowing process. The shovellike snout aids burrowing, during which sink-trap nostrils and earflaps keep sand out of the respiratory and auditory tracts. Highly specialized beasts, these six-inch "fringe-tones," as my children once called them. I wonder if Michler saw any?

Most lizards forage all day now but will retreat underground at midday in late May to August, as the ground heats to the intolerable point, just as in the white sands of New Mexico. Nevertheless, lizard foraging time increases into June before declining. The creatures simply get up earlier, retire later, and take an increasingly long midday nap. Then, as the days shorten, the same species arise later and retire earlier, finally disappearing for several days to weeks at a time beginning in September or October. Hatchlings remain active longest, since their small bodies most quickly heat to activity levels in the retreating sunlight of autumn.

Because time is my own scarcest resource, the lizard time niche is especially interesting. I note, for instance, that large species like the desert iguana emerge from their burrows later this morning than smaller ones like my fringe-toed favorites. And the large lizards seem to forage longer. Perhaps my groups of lizards with similar body sizes and reproductive and activity styles can be used to clarify the temporal niche. By determining how length and hourly apportionment of daily activity is affected by average get-up time, body-operating temperature, and group affiliation, maybe I can reduce a complex web of factors to something understandable.

Later, far from this educational desert, I undertake a simultaneous analysis of the three variables among nine local lizards.[16] Not surprisingly the one synthetic factor, group affiliation, has the only significant influence on time-niche dimensions and allows me to predict

[16] Group affiliation by number plus data from tables 1 and 2 in E. R. Pianka and W. S. Parker ("Ecology of Horned Lizards: A Review with Special Reference to *Phrynosoma platyrhinos*," *Copeia* [1975]:141–152) are used in a multiple stepwise regression in which $r^2 = 0.30$ ($F = 5.9$, $P<0.05$; $r = 0.54$) for the effect of galaxy on time niche width. Other r^2 values are insignificant.

that this niche broadens as a species evolves larger size together with fewer, larger egg clutches and more sedentary behavior. It is the smallest lizards, those with the highest reproductive rates, that have the narrowest time niches. But why the difference?

Large, relatively sedentary lizards possess broad time niches, because they are sit-and-wait predators. This applies to plant eaters like the desert iguana besides insect eaters such as the desert horned lizard. Large, active foragers like the desert spiny and leopard lizards need less time. They eat on the run, in a hurry, in spurts, compared with the more even division of hourly activity among the slow-moving predators. Yet these fast movers take more time than the small side-blotched and brush lizards, for example, because their larger bodies require longer to heat to activity temperatures. And the smallest lizards are most susceptible to predation, overheating, and water loss, so they are active only as long as necessary to get the chores done.

With all of its natural advantages—fewer predators, less heat and water flux, more food sizes to choose from, and more time to choose— large body size requires much food to sustain the bulk. Thus I find it intriguing that two of the largest local lizards, the desert iguana and chuckwalla, are confirmed plant eaters as adults, while their youngsters eat some insects. Insect flesh contains more energy per unit consumed than plant material, hence promotes fast growth to the relatively safe adult size. However, in terms of energy expenditure, insects are more costly to run down and subdue than plants. Perhaps the result is a net cost to large species that exceed a certain bulk, which, evolutionarily speaking, forces the switch to herbivory in adulthood.[17]

For every rule there is an exception, and the gila monster is one different actor. Nathaniel Michler described the *escorpión* as "a large, slothful lizard, in shape a miniature alligator, marked with red, black, and white belts—a hideous-looking animal."[18] Nothing like it had been seen by the surveyors before 1854, when Arthur Schott found the first one near Boundary Monument 146. A venomous lizard, to be certain, but only two such species would be discovered in all the world. The

[17] F. H. Pough, "Lizard Energetics and Diet," *Ecology* 54 (1973): 837–844.

[18] Emory, *Report*, p. 121. See also C. M. Bogert and R. M. Del Campo, *The Gila Monster and Its Allies: The Relationships, Habits and Behavior of the Lizards of the Family Helodermatidae*, Bull. Amer. Mus. Nat. Hist. 109 (1956).

gila monster is a specialized predator on bird and reptile eggs plus nestlings of ground-dwelling birds and rodents. From these energy-rich foods, fat is manufactured and stored in a plump tail, which obviates any need to munch on green plants.

With its own energy-storing tail and banded coloration, the western banded gecko sometimes is mistaken for a baby gila monster. But at three to four inches, this lizard is little more than half the length of a hatchling *escorpión*. It does not even behave in the same manner. When pestered, banded geckos raise their tails and wave them laterally, rather than hissing and biting. They also wave their tails when confronted by their natural predator, the spotted night snake. As with uninitiated man, the night snake orients toward the movement and grabs the tail, which abruptly leaves the gecko's body, and the little lizard escapes. In one experiment, more geckos with tails avoided capture than were eaten, whereas no tailless geckos escaped.[19]

Curiously, a fracture plane in the center of most tail vertebrae facilitates tail loss. Moreover, regeneration of a complete tail requires only seven weeks in captivity, hence is twice as fast as in other lizards that lose their tails in escaping predators. All of the evidence points toward the tail as an antipredator device, but, in addition, whole and regrown tails contain more stored energy per unit weight than bodies or even eggs. The gecko tail is thus doubly advantageous. Special allocation of energy to it permits the rapid regrowth necessary for the predator-escape function, but, if unsacrificed, the tail accumulates an emergency energy supply like that of the gila monster.

When one looks for patterns, the plot may thicken. That's why the search is so stimulating. The lizard time niche is a major plot: the optimum use of energy in a land that is often too hot and always too dry. But that investigation has led to others. By observing all local lizards, I note large ones that eat plants, another large one that doesn't but stores fat in its tail, a small lizard that houses energy likewise and waves its tail in self-defense, and small snakes that also use their tails

---

[19]J. D. Congdon, L. J. Vitt, and W. W. King, "Geckos: Adaptive Significance and Energetics of Tail Autotomy," *Science* 184 (1974):1379–80; L. J. Vitt, J. D. Congdon, and N. A. Dickson, "Adaptive Strategies and Energetics of Tail Autotomy in Lizards," *Ecology* 58 (1977):326–337.

defensively, somewhat in the fashion of the black-striped and ringneck snakes I saw in the eastern Borderlands.

The western and Sonoran shovel-nosed snakes and banded sand snake are serpentine versions of the fringe-toed lizard in their special adaptations to these shifting sands. Of equal interest is the possibility that they are unrecognized behavioral mimics of the venomous Arizona coral snake, since all wave their tails at potential predators. The brightly ringed coral snake is said to advertise its dangerous nature to predators, who avoid it because their ancestors learned to do so. Some predatory birds instinctively fear the coloration, to be sure, but certain hawks eat coral snakes on occasion. The theory also says that any non-venomous snake resembling a coral snake may be avoided. This is called Batesian mimicry.

There are problems with the warning coloration and mimicry story among local species. Coral snakes and their supposed color mimics are secretive burrowers. If they surface, it is generally at night. Of course the snakes could be recognized by owls. Or they could be attacked by nocturnal mammals, although many if not all such beasts are color-blind. To this color-sensitive arch predator the alternating rings or bands of different colors produce a light and dark blur, blending the snakes with the ground litter through which they crawl. The color-pattern is disruptive in light and dark shadows, even in daylight. It diffuses the snake's outline, providing concealment.

Whatever the species, when a snake is discovered, its first line of defense is to crawl away rapidly. If it is restrained, thrashing may ensue, whereupon the disruptive coloration becomes especially effective. But tail-waving behavior is equally likely. If I look discerningly at a pestered coral snake, its head is tucked beneath body coils, and the tail is raised with a coiled end that looks like the head. The tail may even strike. Marvelous—self-mimicry. This may be better defensive behavior than merely displaying a brightly colored subcaudal surface in the manner of black-striped and ringneck snakes.

There are no red rings on coral snake tails, and I have an idea why. The head is also banded in black and yellow, so the defensively coiled and waving tail mimics the head with color pattern as well as behavior. If the red ring sequence were strictly a warning, I think it would be continuous, because the more repetition, especially at the active head and tail ends, the more strongly the message would be transmitted. But if coloration has only a minor defensive role compared with behavior, the length of ring sequence doesn't matter. A tail that acts like a hidden head is of primary importance.

For that matter, the cadre of possible color mimics among nonvenomous snakes exhibits a diverse array of color patterns. Think of western shovel-nosed, western ground, and long-nosed snakes among desert and grassland species that live alongside the Arizona coral snake. None matches this presumed model, and all range far outside the geographic limits of coral snakes. In fact, the only coloration they have in common with coral snakes is a disruptive pattern of bands or rings. Yet all wave their tails, and this may have a unique group influence on predators.

Consider the plight of a small, burrowing serpent confronted by a band of rooting, trampling snake eaters like coatimundis or javelinas. If nosed out of the ground or jabbed by one of these mammals, a waving tail that strikes at clawed or cloven feet might deter predation. To dispel the notion that the tail invites attack, as in geckos, I recorded tail injuries and missing tails in several hundred museum specimens of both tail wavers and nonwavers and found the fewest in tail-waving snakes. Than I presented rubber coral and plain-colored snake models to wild and captive coatis and javelinas that were used to man. I manipulated the models remotely with a thread to simulate self-mimicry plus serpentine crawling and observed that mimicry in particular deterred the mammals.[20]

Now consider the multitude of possibilities for confrontation with sham-aggressive tail-waving snakes. The more species besides coral snakes that wave their tails, the more likely potential predators or tramplers are to encounter and be frightened by this behavior. Consequently, the more likely they are to learn to avoid such snakes. While it is advantageous for any snake to become a tail waver, by virtue of the demonstrated antipredator effect, it is doubly strategic for a species to evolve this behavior if a neighbor already has done so. This

---

[20] F. R. Gehlbach, "Coral Snake Mimicry Reconsidered: The Strategy of Self-mimicry," *Forma et Functio* 5 (1972):311–320. See also H. W. Greene, "Defensive Tail Display by Snakes and Amphisbaenians," *J. Herpetol.* 7 (1973):143–161.

Senita Cactus and Sierra de Sonoyta (Emory)

group effect is a novel exposition of Mullerian mimicry, wherein repugnant species evolve similarity because it enhances avoidance learning by predators.

Time now to depart these blowing sands. My water supply is exhausted, and my body too well adapted to wetter climates. I must leave the desert to its own creatures. It is well for the land; man must not linger here. If a river or springs provide water, as at Yuma and Sonoyta, man survives in the long run only if he restricts his water-rich behavior. The smaller animals remind him, but he does not follow their lead. Mexican farming communes called *ejidos* spring up along the road west of Sonoyta, shrinking its springs by drilling into the aquifer. Across the Border, dams are built so more people in more sun cities can water more green grass.

El Camino del Diablo, the Devil's Highway, was a trail along the Border traveled by the thirsty a century ago. From Sonoyta it was comparatively easy going to springs at Quitobaquito, but then came the waterless stretch from Agua Salada to Tule Tank or the Tinajas Altas, where water might be found in natural rock tanks, *tinajas*, on the mountain slopes. The aborigines ambushed bighorn sheep at the high tanks. Forty-niners may have seen their bones, as some of these travelers sought and failed to find the higher, more inaccessible, and per-

manent *tinajas*. Human bones and graves were scattered about Edgar
Mearns's campsite here in 1894.[21]

It is difficult to appreciate those days, as I drive to the Tinajas
Altas from Wellton in a few hours. I do not wait for water to come to me
in the manner of a quiescent *sapo*, a toad, particularly Couch's spadefoot toad. Some years, like these last ones in the Sierra del Rosario,
spadefoots feel no raindrop vibrations at all, and they need this cue to
emerge from deep burrows in the sand.[22] In other years a brief rain
may fill a pool in a rocky wash or similar *charco* ("pool") at the base of
some dunes, and spadefoots may emerge from their burrows for a few
nights of reproductive splendor. Imagine this three-inch amphibian,
waiting, simply waiting, for most of its life, buried in the sand.

We wonder how far down we will have to dig as we treasure-hunt
for spadefoots among roots and dry sand. They are here along the
wash, perhaps beneath the ironwood trees. Couch's spadefoots can
burrow at least two feet. In the San Simon Valley, Arizona, western
spadefoots may dig to a depth of three feet. They burrow less than
three inches in the monsoon season but average ten inches when the
rains stop, twenty-two inches in winter, and are back up to around seventeen inches the following spring. At the Algodones Dunes, California, there is a permanently moist layer one to two feet beneath the surface, and Couch's spadefoots may live in it.[23]

The same amphibian skin that transmits water so freely to the air
absorbs it just as quickly from burrow walls. An inactive spadefoot
stores nitrogenous wastes (urea) in its tissues, which then draw water
out of the underground environment. Water always moves from regions of greater to lesser concentration, and urea-rich tissues are water
poor comparatively. Although water may transfer from a wet toad to
dry sand or soil, a burrowed Couch's spadefoot sheds several layers of
skin that adhere to its body as a presumed water-conserving cocoon. At

---

[21] E. A. Mearns, *Mammals of the Mexican Boundary of the United States*, U.S.
Natl. Mus. Bull. 56 (1907), p. 122.

[22] M. A. Dimmitt and R. Ruibal, "Environmental Correlates of Emergence in
Spadefoot Toads (*Scaphiopus*)," *J. Herpetol.* 14 (1980):21–29.

[23] R. Ruibal, L. Tevis, Jr., and V. Roig, "The Terrestrial Ecology of the Spadefoot
Toad, *Scaphiopus hammondi*," *Copeia* (1969):571–584; W. W. Mayhew, "Adaptations of
the Amphibian, *Scaphiopus couchi*, to Desert Conditions," *Amer. Midl. Natur.* 74
(1965):95–109.

least this adaptive strategy resembles that of the burrowing, cocoon-encased lesser siren in dry resacas of the lower Rio Grande.

Nevertheless, Couch's spadefoots must reproduce in the archaic egg-tadpole fashion, despite the fact that some kindred toads can lay eggs on land or carry eggs with them and "give birth" to small editions of themselves. Two important questions are suggested. First, how do spadefoots get their eggs laid and tads transformed into burrowing toadlets, when water temperatures may reach ninety-five degrees Fahrenheit in an evaporating pond that lasts but a few weeks? And why haven't they adopted some terrestrial mode of reproduction, given the limited water supply?

The last question is answered partly by answers to the first, since Couch's spadefoots have the highest temperature tolerances and fastest hatching and tadpole growth rates of any local amphibian.[24] Water temperature is the major controlling factor, of course. The hotter it is, the faster things happen. Over a typical sixty-eight- to ninety-five-degree daily regime, the species' eggs hatch in twelve to twenty-four hours, and the tads grow to transformation in ten to fifteen days. Two other species of spadefoots can do as well, yet the Couch's is alone in the Gran Desierto, perhaps simply by chance.

Additional features of spadefoot tadpole life are equally important. The earliest tads hatched produce some sort of growth inhibitor against others. Presumably this frees food and space for fuller utilization by a few individuals, allowing them to grow to transformation size before the pond dries up. Also, these older, larger tads may cannibalize their smaller siblings in the manner of large tiger salamander larvae along the Jornada del Muerto in New Mexico. Because of the additional protein food, cannibalism may hasten growth to the largest hence most favorable size for dry-land life.

So the Couch's spadefoot lives in this abject desert, doing basically what it has always done, which is the spadefoot mode. That suggests it hasn't been here long. At least its desert hasn't been here long, geologically speaking—no more than eight to eleven thousand years. Is it

[24] H. A. Brown, "The Heat Resistance of Some Anuran Tadpoles (Hylidae and Pelobatidae)," *Copeia* (1969):138–147; R. G. Zweifel, *Reproductive Biology of Anurans of the Arid Southwest: With Emphasis on Adaptation of Embryos to Temperature*, Bull. Amer. Mus. Nat. Hist. 140 (1968).

Couch's Spadefoot Toad (Emory)

possible that the Couch's spadefoot and other desert dwellers lived here but in very different communities at the close of the last glacio-pluvial age? Or were they displaced southward, together with their deserts, only to return with the hotter, dryer postpluvial climate?

In the northern Sonoran desert region, prehistoric woodrat dens contain answers in the form of amphibian, reptile, and plant fossils.[25] Either the early den makers were as adept at caching bones as their modern descendants, or the original bone owners were boarders that died in the dens five to fifteen thousand years ago. At least twenty-five species of thermally instructive reptiles and amphibians are represented, including Couch's spadefoot toad. It lived here in the Wellton Hills in shrub desert, but no earlier than that community's inception. Western banded geckos, brush lizards, and sidewinders have similar histories among modern desert associates, although twice as many cohabitants occupied evergreen woodland in the same region prehistorically.

Clearly, the desert creatures come from different backgrounds. No single scenario of community expansion and retreat suffices to tell their tales. Furthermore, true shrub-desert animals are relatively few

[25] T. R. Van Devender and J. I. Mead, "Early Holocene and Late Pleistocene Amphibians and Reptiles in Sonoran Desert Packrat Middens," *Copeia* (1978):464–475.

in the Borderlands. I think, for instance, of fringe-toed lizards that occur nowhere else, as opposed to Couch's spadefoot toads that burrow in Texas and Oklahoma grasslands much as they do here. Eric Pianka recorded only nine to eleven lizard species in this area, compared with twelve to eighteen in the Kalahari Desert of Africa and eighteen to forty in the Western Australian Desert.[26] This desert is just too new and perhaps too small to have been colonized by many species.

It is nearly Easter weekend, April, 1971, a poor time to visit the "national desecration area" of southern California. But I must rendezvous with the destructive reality of off-road vehicles. Enroute I cross the Wellton Canal, carrying irrigation water from the Colorado River, and am myself diverted by more subtle transformations of the desert. Do any native creatures benefit from irrigation agriculture? I can find an answer, because snakes have been studied in the Imperial Valley, California, near the western limit of the Sonoran desert region, where irrigation began in 1902.

In the 1920's and 1930's, Laurence Klauber drove along roadways of the Imperial Valley and found 2.7 times as many snakes in irrigated areas as in the wild desert.[27] Diurnal species made the difference—gopher, coachwhip, and western patch-nosed snakes especially. Because they are active in the daytime, when it is hottest, they may lose more water and hence require more than nocturnal snakes. Furthermore, the diurnal species are broadly distributed in habitats other than deserts, and such snakes generally lose more water than strictly desert forms.[28]

Among common nocturnal snakes only the glossy and long-nosed were more numerous around irrigated cropland. The others, spotted leaf-nosed and western shovel-nosed snakes plus the proverbial sidewinder, were absent or nearly so in these areas. But the latter three are

[26] E. R. Pianka, "The Structure of Lizard Communities," *Ann. Rev. Ecol. and Syst.* 4 (1973):53–74.

[27] L. M. Klauber, "Studies of Reptile Life in the Arid Southwest. Pt. 1: Night Collecting on the Desert with Ecological Statistics," *Bull. Zool. Soc. San Diego* 14 (1939): 7–64.

[28] C. Gans, T. Krakauer, and C. V. Paganelli, "Water Loss in Snakes: Interspecific and Intraspecific Variability," *Comp. Biochem. Physiol.* 27 (1968):757–761.

obligate desert dwellers with restricted distribution, whereas the glossy and long-nosed snakes are widespread in grassland, including that of the southern Great Plains. Am I to believe that irrigation agriculture benefits these two plus the diurnal snakes because they are secondary desert species, recent inhabitants perhaps, that require more water?

Klauber's pioneering has provided the basis for an analysis of temporal change in the community structure of serpents. If the same roads are resurveyed now, I wonder whether the glossy and long-nosed snakes, species with the broadest niches here a half-century ago, will have even bigger roles in the modern evolutionary play. Niche width was most highly correlated with diversity of habitat use in the 1920's and 1930's. The five nocturnal species overlapped least on this spatial basis.[29] Today, however, monocultural simplicity sweeps the desert, and the spatial factor may bow to others in the allocation of the stage space among snakes.

I was familiar with the tracks of off-road vehicles decades old yet little different from others but a few hours of age. And I knew the dune buggies and motorcycles directly. Once, after a slow, hot drive of many miles over a dirt track, I parked a few hundred yards from a fan palm oasis, walked in, and was admiring the trees' tenacity when a dozen motorcycles roared out of nowhere, dug through the grove, and left me in a cloud of dust and delirium. Did it matter to them that only about fifty such oases remain, relics of the Miocene birth of this land, arranged along the western perimeter of the Sonoran desert region?[30]

But I was not prepared for the awesome devastation of the off-road vehicle races that Easter weekend in 1971. The mindless noise and weaving headlights, dust and smog haze, mauled shrubs and mashed creatures were hellish. Certainly I believe in alloting some desert for destruction if it is replaced by construction in the service of

[29] From data in tables 2, 3, 10, and 13 in Klauber, "Studies of Reptile Life," niche width and overlap are computed as in footnote 7. Partial correlations of habitat, monthly appearance, temperature, and time niche widths with total niche width are 0.36, 0.23, 0.19, and 0.15, respectively ($P>0.05$, 4 $d.f.$).

[30] D. E. Brown, N. B. Carmony, C. H. Lowe, and R. M. Turner, "A Second Locality for Native California Fan Palms (*Washingtonia filifera*) in Arizona," *J. Arizona Acad. Sci.* 11 (1976):37–41.

man or beast. But 150-mile, 3,000-vehicle races between Barstow, California, and Las Vegas, Nevada, whose effects sift through the air for untold distance and time outside the primary path of destruction, are simply beyond my ken. Destruction for pleasure. . . .

The nature of damage due to off-road vehicles has been documented. For instance, consider a minor but nonetheless significant fact that during those Easter races of 1971 I found ten dead and three live serpents on twenty miles of highway in the area, whereas the same transect yielded two dead and five live snakes two days later. Or ponder the more fundamental fact that in one eight-hour period in April, 1973, some 700 motorcycles destroyed all vegetation along a path up to six feet wide and three miles long in the midst of a proposed desert tortoise preserve.[31]

Add to this the travesty perpetrated by off-road vehicles near Barstow in 1974–1975. What remained of that living desert could be categorized according to intensity of destruction. Moderately affected areas held almost the usual number of creosote bushes typical of natural areas, whereas heavily used sites contained but 60 percent, and camping and staging areas had only 35 percent. Numbers of terrestrial vertebrates declined in direct proportion to the incidence of mangled shrubs—reptiles 35 to 73 percent, mammals 39 to 86 percent.[32]

Now reconsider the motorcycle race from Barstow to Las Vegas, during which each rider could destroy 130 animals. Albeit crude, this estimate is based on the average of moderate and heavy impact and the assumption that the riders together cut a square-mile swath. Granted that the nearly one dead critter per mile can be matched on certain highways, landscape kill is really the critical factor. The broken shrubbery will not regrow completely in this century, and soil compaction plus erosion will alter things permanently. Some plants and animals might never come back. Native creatures don't live on highways; now they may not live in the desert either. Only man can choose to return.

[31] $\chi^2 = 4.4$, $P<0.05$, in a 2×2 tabular comparison of dead versus live snakes during and after the race weekend. The 1973 observation is from a mimeographed statement to the Bureau of Land Management by the staff of the Museum of Vertebrate Zoology, University of California, September 25, 1973.

[32] R. B. Bury, R. A. Luckenbach, and S. D. Busack, *Effects of Off-road Vehicles on Vertebrates in the California Desert*, U.S. Fish and Wildl. Serv. Res. Rept. 8 (1977). See also R. C. Stebbins, "Off-road-vehicles and the Fragile Desert," *Amer. Biol. Teacher* 36 (1974):203–208, 294–304.

It is welcome relief to sit in the shade of a huge Fremont cotton-wood. With this symbol of survival, I reflect in the sun-dappled surface of the pond at Quitobaquito, Arizona, the "place of little springs." Small birds feed above the *represa*, while desert pupfish dig pits in its silty bottom, eat diatoms in the process, and defend their luncheon territories. Do the finished pits become settling basins for diatoms in a manner similar to the ant-trapping pits of terrestrial ant lions?[33] Quito-baquito is a tranquilly instructive scene, albeit an unnatural one. The pond, a part of Organ Pipe Cactus National Monument, was enlarged in 1962 from an irrigation reservoir dug a century earlier.

Nearly a mile to the south, the Río Sonoyta tells a painfully famil-iar story. Once this river was served by natural reservoirs, its cienegas, and ran smoothly through desert plains grazed by livestock and farmed by adding irrigation water. But in August, 1891, the river flooded and entrenched itself below irrigation level, resetting the ecologic stage for a different play. Mesquite *bosques* replaced desert grassland, the cie-negas disappeared, Pueblo Sonoyta was forced downstream, wells were dug, and native creatures like the Gila topminnow and desert pupfish declined concurrently with the reduced flow of surface water and the introduction of common mosquitofish.[34]

Meanwhile, the pond at Quitobaquito was a boon to its resident desert pupfish and Sonoran mud turtles, for it represented expanded living facilities. Yet these natives are now threatened even here. In 1970, for instance, misguided fishermen dumped golden shiners into a community already inhabited by slider turtles of dime-store deriva-tion. Fearing adverse consequences for the pupfish, because it had dis-appeared from most of its natural range, the Park Service removed live specimens, drained the pond, bulldozed its bulrush marsh, and poi-soned it with rotenone. A dozen mud turtles were saved, but at least an equal number succumbed.

When the pond was refilled and pupfishes replaced several weeks

[33] Cf. W. L. Minckley and E. T. Arnold, "Pit-digging: A Behavioral Feeding Adap-tation in Pupfishes (Genus *Cyprinodon*)," *J. Arizona Acad. Sci.* 5 (1969):254–257.

[34] U.S. Boundary Commission, *Report of the Boundary Commission upon the Sur-vey and Remarking of the Boundary between the United States and Mexico West of the Rio Grande, 1891–1896*, pt. 2, 55th Cong., 2nd sess., 1898, Sen. Doc. 247, p. 23, and facing figure; Mearns, *Mammals of the Mexican Boundary*, p. 116; C. Lumholtz, *New Trails in Mexico* (New York: C. Scribner's Sons, 1912), pp. 178–180, 199.

later, I was most concerned about the mud turtles. No one knew what had become of the "fortunate dozen." Because of its isolation, I was especially interested in the Quitobaquito population. How large was it, and what was its potential for recovery? Could I discern population features in common with Sonoran mud turtles in the species' continuous range to the east? What about the similarly small population of rough-footed mud turtles in Alamito Creek, Texas? Are such relicts viable in man-made and oft-altered environments?

My survey technique was the same for the Sonorans as for roughfoots, and I observed a similar dominance hierarchy for them. The mark-recapture procedure, cumulated over three periods in April–May, 1971, suggested that between 76 and 162 individuals inhabited the pond. What a pleasant surprise. Considering that their livelihood had been removed temporarily and their lives poisoned only a year earlier, the little *tortugas* seemed remarkably resilient. Some must have buried out of danger in the pond bottom, and migrating cousins from the Río Sonoyta may have bolstered their forces.

Nevertheless, I could not find any *tortugas* the following July, when pond water was 88 to 102 degrees Fahrenheit at maximum, some 12 to 22 degrees hotter than in April–May. Since another summer survey at Quitobaquito failed to mention Sonoran mud turtles, I suspect they are inactive under unfavorably hot conditions, just as yellow mud turtles are.[35] Therefore they might not grow as rapidly as kindred living at more moderate temperatures. But this is not so, for I found that Sonoran mud turtles in O'Donnell Creek, Arizona, grew no faster.[36] The generally warm water of Quitobaquito's pond may foster rapid growth during most of the year, and this could compensate for lost time in the summer.

Interestingly, I discovered that two- to four-year-old juveniles rep-

---

[35] G. A. Cole and M. C. Whiteside, "An Ecological Reconnaissance of Quitobaquito Spring, Arizona," *J. Arizona Acad. Sci.* 3 (1965): 159–163. Two yellow mud turtles were taken from the pond at Quitobaquito, July, 1957 (P. W. Smith and M. M. Hensley, "The Mud Turtle *Kinosternon flavescens steijnegeri* Hartweg in the United States," *Proc. Biol. Soc. Washington* 70 [1957]: 201–204), but I did not find the species there. Was it introduced?

[36] Slopes of regressions of pastron length on age (data log transformed) for the Quitobaquito (0.596) and O'Donnell Creek (0.801), Arizona, populations are alike ($t = 1.6$, $P > 0.05$, 23 $d.f.$). Cf. A. C. Hulse, "Growth and Morphometrics of *Kinosternon sonoriense* (Reptilia, Testudines, Kinosternidae)," *J. Herpetol.* 10 (1976): 341–348.

resented about half of the Quito population. This suggested stability, as in the rough-footed mud turtles of the Texas Borderlands. I caught one adult eight or nine years of age. The rest were five to seven, based on counts of their annuli, or growth rings, on scutes of the lower shell. Seasonal cessation of growth apparent in those rings supported my contention of summer inactivity while confounding age determinations. Above all, I was impressed by the resemblances between my rough-foots and these Sonoran mud turtles. As long as both species have water, I think they will survive.

15. The Lessons

No doubt about it, water is the ultimate limiting resource of the Borderlands. In reflecting on my years of personal discovery here, I see
that water puts everything in its place—sooner or later. Natural limitations imposed by the lack of water or its seasonal delivery are complex
enough. But man's cultural modifications of water, his subtractions
from the limited surface supply and transfers from underground reservoirs, complicate the region's life-support systems. Essentially all I
have learned from this landscape carpet reveals its shrinks and swells,
its dynamism in the context of the natural and unnatural history of
water.[1]

To begin with, the natural landscape features moisture gradients
between dry desert seas and wetter mountain islands. The islands
themselves are transitional between the cooler-wetter Rockies and
warmer-dryer Sierra Madres; the Chihuahuan seas are wetter hence
grassier, and the Sonoran are much dryer. Species reach their natural
range limits in these moisture gradients, expanding and contracting
with the natural cyclic flux of water, although man seems determined
to put and take water unnaturally, sending plants and animals on one-
way journeys. His ponds promote hybridization toward extinction, for
example, and his irrigated plantings spread species on northward
invasions.

Dramatic seasonal, historic, and prehistoric changes in the avail-

---

[1] In reaffirming that one can learn from nature while learning about it, I reread
Aldo Leopold and especially J. W. Krutch, *The Twelve Seasons* (New York: W. Sloan
Assoc., 1949), p. 125. Krutch's warning is important: "The distinction between learning
about and learning *from* is, I am sure, the crucial one, and any science which proposes
for itself nothing but the first is dead; can be no more than a branch of practical mechan-
ics; can accomplish none but utilitarian purposes. It furnishes no subject for contem-
plation; it contracts rather than enlarges the understanding; it impoverishes rather than
enriches the emotional life of man. *From* Nature we learn what we are a part of and how
we may participate in the whole; we gain a perspective on ourselves, which serves, not
to set us aside from, but to put us in relation with, a complete scheme."

ability of water typify the region. Natural community stability does not exist where flood, drought, and consequent fire are frequent stresses. Yet a certain structural integrity of both terrestrial and aquatic communities is fostered by the resiliency of dominant species in the midst of seasonal upsets or the substitution of their close competitors during longer cyclic swings.[2] Man's major problem in this orchestration of allegros and largos is that he proceeds a la forte against the natural course of water. So determined, does he hasten his own substitution?

Native creatures cope with the natural stresses by employing avoidance and reproductive tactics like cocoons and monsoon-timed egg laying. Or they may switch between the single- and multiple-use approaches to resources, depending on the availability of water—the tiger-salamander strategy. Still another answer is to share the scarcest resources, those most directly dependent on water. Desert rodents, for example, converge upon a limited variety of food types but diverge in space. I expect closely related species' niches to overlap on the rare resources by segregating on common ones like space, whether rarity is absolute as in deserts or periodic as during drought cycles in any natural community.

Space, food, and then time differences separate potential competitors unless man's desertification changes the structural nature of space and brings species together. The natural partitioning is vertical, up-canyon versus down-canyon, for instance, or patchy at a given elevation, in accord with variations in vegetative structure. Vertebrates with the most vertical mobility, the birds, are most strongly controlled by vegetative diversity, whereas the plants themselves and earth- and water-bound animals are more constrained by the dimensions and diversity of horizontal space.

Once large body size was an advantage that promoted energy and water conservation plus the mobility to avoid temporary water shortages and excesses. But large size became a liability when man arrived. Extinction or local extirpation often followed, then reintroduction for some species deemed worthwhile. Along with induced competition,

[2] Borderlands communities are resilient while fluctuating, in the sense of C. S. Holling, "Resilience and Stability of Ecological Systems," *Ann. Rev. Ecol. and Syst.* 4 (1973):1–21. See also G. H. Orians, "Diversity, Stability, and Maturity in Natural Ecosystems," in *Unifying Concepts in Ecology*, ed. W. H. vanDobben and R. H. Lowe-McConnell, pp. 139–150 (The Hague: W. Junk, 1975).

such retrospective behavior seems to typify the arch predator. Furthermore, the vanishing of large, natural predators may mean fewer, smaller animals in man's future since predators control the numbers of smaller species by eating abundant ones, hence reduce competition among prey and promote a diversity of coexisting species.[3]

While small-bodied creatures survive better in man-altered landscapes, culture relegates all organisms to islandlike populations, in which their genetic diversity may be demoted. A major question, therefore, concerns survival of the genetically simplified in the face of unnaturally sudden, culturally induced, environmental changes. Naturalists suspect that genetic hence adaptive diversity of species' populations is directly proportional to size of the area inhabited, as well as population size, and proximity of that area to sources of colonists that may contribute new adaptive traits.

Thus naturalists know something about the design of living museums.[4] They must be large in order to retain maximum spatial and resulting biotic diversity and rounded in outline to minimize the cultural attrition that increases with border area. Furthermore, they should be linked to one another by wild, green corridors to permit colonization in concert with climatic flux. Despite arguments for many small preserves instead of fewer large ones, in my opinion the overriding consideration is man, whose unnatural history is least intrusive on large preserves.

Living museums are necessary to retain the kind of natural genetic diversity that man cannot afford to lose because of its potential for both domestication and insights into hydrologic integrity.[5] Only in such museums can wise men understand the water cycles that govern the actor's guild of life and by comparing processes there with those in

[3]Theoretical and empirical evidence is in H. G. Hairston, F. E. Smith, and L. B. Slobodkin, "Community Structure, Population Control, and Competition," *Amer. Natur.* 94 (1960):421–426; and R. T. Paine, "Food Web Complexity and Species Diversity," *Amer. Natur.* 100 (1966):65–76.

[4]Compare J. M. Diamond, "The Island Dilemma: Lessons of Modern Biogeographic Studies for the Design of Natural Reserves," *Biol. Conserv.* 7 (1975):129–146, with D. S. Simberloff and L. G. Abele, "Island Biogeography Theory and Conservation Practice," *Science* 191 (1975):285–286.

[5]W. R. Van Dersal, "Why Living Organisms Should Not Be Exterminated," *Atlantic Natur.* 27 (1972):7–10; R. I. Miller, "Conserving the Genetic Integrity of Faunal Populations and Communities," *Environ. Conserv.* 6 (1979):297–304.

cultural settings, learn which human activities are supportable and which must be discarded as too expensive hydrologically.[6] Also, living museums boost local economies by furnishing nonconsumptive recreation—the Santa Ana Refuge example—while freely recharging man's underground water supplies. By no means are they idle lands, a common accusation, for their services in behalf of life are legion.

But how much acreage is needed? Some space must go for urban-industrial systems, certainly, and more for food and fiber production. What balance is necessary for survival? Eugene and Howard Odum suggest that 40 percent of the acreage per person in Georgia must be wild, which translates into five acres per person.[7] Georgia is an appropriate model for the Borderlands, because its thermal regime is similar. Major differences in precipitation can be adjusted for by subdividing the Border country into four climatically distinct sectors and considering them separately.[8]

By dividing the average annual precipitation of each sector into that of water-rich Georgia (fifty inches) and multiplying the quotient by the five-acre Georgian allotment, I can begin to extrapolate. Since year-to-year variations in precipitation along the Border are 1.5 to 2.1 times Georgia's, I multiply the first set of correction factors by regionally specific ones for average flux and thus build safety into my the-

[6]W. H. Moir, "Natural Areas," *Science* 1977 (1972):396–400; R. E. Jenkins and W. B. Bedford, "The Use of Natural Areas To Establish Environmental Baselines," *Biol. Conserv.* 5 (1973):168–174. On specific expense, see R. J. Becker, "Non-conservation in Arizona: Estimates of Some Costs," *J. Arizona Acad. Sci.* 10 (1975):90–97.

[7]E. P. Odum and H. T. Odum, "Natural Areas as Necessary Components of Man's Total Environment," *Trans. 37th N. Amer. Wildl. Nat. Res. Confer.* (1972):178–189. See also W. E. Westman, "How Much Are Nature's Services Worth?" *Science* 197 (1977): 960–964.

[8]The frost-free or major biotic water-cycling period averages 234 days annually in both Georgia and the Borderlands (data reduced from *Climate and Man*, Yearbook U.S. Dept. Agricult., 1941). One-way analysis of variance (ANOVA) of frost-free days ($F = 41$, $P < 0.001$) and annual precipitation in inches ($F = 96$, $P < 0.001$) followed by Tukey-HSD tests of homogeneous subsets, identify four sectors: Boca Chica to Bordas Scarp ($N =$ seven twenty-year or longer records; 305 ± 17, 25 ± 2 are mean $\pm$ 2 standard deviations of annual frost-free days and precipitation inches respectively), Bordas Scarp to Big Bend ($N = 10$, 287 ± 11, 20 ± 2), Big Bend through Baboquivari Mountains, Arizona ($N = 17$, 218 ± 18, 14 ± 3), rest of Arizona through Sonoran desert, California ($N = 11$, 264 ± 13, 6 ± 3). On water cycles and organism support see M. L. Rosenzweig, "Net Primary Productivity of Terrestrial Communities: Prediction from Climatological Data." *Amer. Natur.* 102 (1968):67–74.

oretical per-capita acreages. And I figure the needed wildland of each
sector by designating 40 percent of the space necessary to sustain the
1970 population and compare this with the acreage saved through the
1970's.[9]

Finally, my observations identify some overpopulated sectors on
the basis of local water supplies. I do not account for man's ability to
increase his present options by using fossil water or to persist temporarily by persuading an extraregional populace to contribute their
water through treaty and taxation. I simply relate existing human occu-
pancy to the support capacity of local landscapes, a necessity once the
groundwater is gone and transport from the outside becomes so costly
that landscape evaluation and planning are mandated.

Now I travel one last time from Boca Chica to the western edge of
the Colorado River Basin. As I focus on land per capita and the remaining natural history, I revive treasured memories of special landscapes
that contributed most to my education and should serve all of man-
kind. Again I am reminded that man is only a momentary actor, not an
owner of these wild stages. The duration of his theater run depends on
his acceptance of hydrologic limitations. The land owns man.

In the lower Rio Grande Valley, the wettest of all sectors, sixteen
acres per person is the hypothetical requirement for survival, but I
find only twelve available in Texas. Adding the Mexican population in
the equivalent area of Tamaulipas actually subtracts one acre per inhabitant. Clearly, overpopulation is suggested. And so it seems in the
second sector, the region from the Bordas Scarp to the Big Bend, with
sixty-seven acres per capita in Texas but only sixteen overall, whereas
nineteen per person is the requirement. Monterrey and Nuevo Laredo, Nuevo León, are the major problem spots.

By comparison, man is widely dispersed in the Big Bend country
of Texas and neighboring Mexico; twenty-seven acres are needed to
support each inhabitant here and seventy-four are available in 1970.
But this third sector stretches to the Baboquivari Mountains in Ari-

[9]Populations and acreages of counties in the U.S. border region are from J. N.
Kane, *The American Counties* (Metschen, N.J.: Scarecrow Press, 1972); equivalent in-
formation on Mexico is from S. A. Arbingast et al., *Atlas of Mexico* (Austin: Bur. Bus.
Res. Univ. Texas, 1975).

zona, so I find it illuminating to consider certain of its portions separately. For instance, greater El Paso–Juárez has a land-to-man ratio of nine acres, although thirty-eight are required. Should the Big Bend and wild Coahuila-Chihuahua support this fourfold excess? Can any adjoining landscape with comparable climate sustain an apparently unnatural concentration of humans and still retain its necessary wildlands?

Perhaps southwestern New Mexico and adjoining Chihuahua offer a buffer to the west. Here 31 acres per person are needed, and 121 exist in 1970. Similarly, 23 acres is the survival figure in southeastern Arizona–northeastern Sonora, and 50 remain. Interior Chihuahua-Sonora furnishes additional recompense, although I note a growing colonization of sector three as I survey the declining waters and undescribed pupfishes of Palomas Spring, Chihuahua, in 1971. By 1978 the spring is dry.

West of the Baboquivari Mountains and in northwestern Sonora I read the cultural landscape with equal foreboding. First, I find that 53 acres per person are essential, but only 24 remain near this fourth sector's eastern edge. Tucson and Phoenix, Arizona, account for most of the overpopulation in the second-fastest-growing U.S. state (New Mexico is ninth, Texas tenth, California eighteenth during the 1970's). In southeastern California 131 acres per person are necessary, and only 37 are available. The addition of equal space in Baja California and its inhabitants drops the land-to-man ratio to 12 acres, the greatest regional discrepancy between actual and hypothetically sustainable populations I observe.

On the assumption that wildlands can support such overpopulation within major watersheds, the net difference between real and postulated survival acreage is cumulated across the Borderlands. The value increases from negative 5 to positive 39 between Boca Chica and the Big Bend but declines to 10 in the Rio Grande Basin near El Paso. Westward, a positive net of 90 to 117 acres per person across the Gila River Basin seems encouraging, but the value drops to negative 29 near the Colorado River and then minus 148 at the western edge of the Sonoran desert region.

Fifty-five percent of the original natural vegetation persists in these thirsty California Borderlands. Twenty-six percent of it is protected, although 23 million wild acres are needed here and in northern Baja California. Eastward, sector four retains 89 percent of its native

Colorado River and Pilot Knob below Yuma (Emory)

landscapes, but only 7 percent is preserved in Arizona. Thirty-one million acres are necessary for the natural servicing of this area. Unfortunately, there are no formal preserves in the Mexican Borderlands like the U.S. state and national parks, wildlife refuges, and wilderness areas that I assay. Nor is there any assessment of remaining natural acreage similar to that of the United States in the 1970's.[10]

Sector three has 95 percent of its native vegetation intact but only 7 percent is protected west of the Big Bend. Twenty-five million acres are required, including 11 million just to sustain El Paso–Juárez. Considered alone, the Big Bend possesses twice its natural landscape requirement in designated preserves, but think of the pressure from bordering sectors and unprotected Mexico. Sector two on the east retains 93 percent of its heritage vegetation, sector one only 82 percent, and they have designated less than 1 and 4 percent, respectively, of the 12 and 5 million natural acres they require.

While preserve planning must accord with regionally specific hydrology, protecting aquifer-recharge zones in particular, it must also respond to the historical proportions of each natural community and attend to the most threatened ones first if genetic diversity is to be

[10] J. M. Klopatek, R. J. Olson, C. J. Emerson, and J. L. Jones, "Land-use Conflicts with Natural Vegetation in the United States," *Environ. Conserv.* 6 (1979): 191–199.

maintained. Setting aside 40 percent of an untrammeled landscape is only a general rule. The critical part is deciding which "back forty." Of necessity naturalists scramble to stay ahead of bulldozers, so they must plan the survival of natural history on a priority basis. But the scrambling has led to site-specific evaluations, a logical second step behind the regional appraisals that remain to be accomplished.[11]

Luckily for the Borderlands, most options on preservation are not lost, because the destruction of natural history is focused in the lower Rio Grande and Colorado River basins. Thus, shrub desert clothed 43 percent of the historical landscape, and 87 percent of it remains. Desert grassland covered another 26 percent originally, of which 90 percent survives. Succulent desert, 18 percent of the historical carpet, has 97 percent remaining. Plains grassland occupied 10 percent, and 89 percent of that still lives. Finally, deciduous woodland, evergreen woodland, and coniferous forest together accounted for a mere 3 percent of the postpluvial countryside, but 96 percent of that is available today.[12]

To simplify my understanding of original and surviving carpet coverage, the latter sometimes due to regeneration, according to the Boundary-monument evidence, I multiply the two percentages that characterize each community and list resulting products from smallest to largest. This results in a priority scale for preservation versus development. From the broad perspective, woodlands, forest, and plains grassland are in shortest supply, shrub desert and desert grassland abundantly available. Accordingly, my prescription for a model preserve includes two or more of the largest mountain islands joined by wooded draws across grassy seas or a rounded plains grassland traced by deciduous woodland or studded with clumps of evergreen oaks.

When similarly calculated, regional variations follow the Borderlands perspective, but with some surprises. Riparian woodland is at

[11] For example see F. R. Gehlbach, "Investigation, Evaluation, and Priority Ranking of Natural Areas," *Biol. Conserv.* 8 (1975):79–88; D. F. Wright, "A Site Evaluation Scheme for Use in the Assessment of Potential Nature Reserves," *Biol. Conserv.* 11 (1977):293–305.

[12] The historical acreage of each natural community is computed from planimeter measurements of the map in A. W. Kuchler, *Potential Natural Vegetation of the Conterminous United States*, Amer. Geogr. Soc. Spec. Publ. 36 (1964), and modern comparisons are in county-level data sent by Jeffrey Klopatek (see fig. 2 in Klopatek, Olson, Emerson, and Jones, "Land-use Conflicts").

a premium, as is plains grassland in the lower Rio Grande Basin. Upriver, however, shrub desert dominated by ceniza and associates is first in priority for museum status. Tree-dominated communities plus plains grassland again become critical concerns in the Big Bend and remain so until plains grassland naturally runs out of the carpet pattern in south-central Arizona. Thereafter succulent desert is most threatened, followed by desert grassland in the lower Colorado River Basin.

Withal, I conclude that all tree-dominated communities must be respected, especially those flanking the lower Rio Grande. A lineal preserve, an International Riparian Corridor, must extend from at least Falcon Reservoir to the palm jungles below Brownsville. Existing small preserves in Texas may be interconnected and counterparts in Mexico constituted to form the corridor. Similarly, an International Coastal Corridor can be designated along the Gulf of Mexico, joining the Rancho Nuevo area of Tamaulipas with coastal preserves in Texas north to the King Ranch. It would contact the riparian corridor's eastern end in coastal plains grassland.

Plains grassland and woodlands on the King and adjacent ranches could be protected by explicit agreement to manage privately in favor of all natives in addition to livestock. I think properly managed stock can be viewed as simply replacing the lost large grazers of the last glaciopluvial.[13] These wildlands could continue in private hands, since they serve the public, providing that malpractices are eliminated. Indiscriminate varmint control is one such procedure that may be averted by requiring selective removal of livestock-conditioned predators, asking the public to reimburse stock owners for certified kills, and practicing aversive conditioning.

I would designate the entire Devils River Basin as a national scientific preserve. I include the extensive ceniza-dominated shrub desert of the dry Devils as well as the free-flowing river with its riparian woodland remnants. There is no reason to wrest this landscape from private ownership, but there is good reason to publicly guarantee its protection through restraints on overstocking, especially with sheep and goats. As a southern counterpart, Mexico's living museum could

---

[13] On the introduction of exotic ungulates in this regard, see P. S. Martin, "Vanishings and Future of the Prairie," *Geosci. and Man* 10 (1975):39–49.

be the Cuatro Ciénegas Bolsón, Coahuila, with prohibitions against continued diversion of its water.[14] Instead of expanding irrigation agriculture, why not expand winter tourism?

The same I suggest for the southern Toyah Basin in Texas, since there is demonstrated recreation here. I recommend state preserve status because of the existing state park, comparatively small area, and consequent lower diversity of organisms. Increasing population and irrigation cannot continue, as the declining spring waters document. But seasonal tourism that features instructive spring fishes, sport fishing, and abundant sunshine is functional. Eventually, croplands might be turned back into the original plains grassland and connected with natural communities of the nearby Davis Mountains, which offer the potential of integrated hydrologic management.

Western slopes of the Davis Mountains are equally important, because the Marfa-Valentine grassland and Alamito Creek watershed furnish exemplary natural history. These areas can become state scientific preserves, remain in private use, but receive public guidance relative to protection. A nearby dream is a Big Bend–Sierra del Carmen International Park linked with a Rio Grande–Río Conchos International Riparian Corridor that would incorporate the normally dry Rio Grande and the wet Conchos in addition to the established wild river. Thus protected would be a unique drainageway lined by cliffs, remnant marshes, hot springs, and unique places like Capote Falls.

For the sustenance of El Paso–Juárez and the Borderlands generally, I describe a rectangular preserve, tying the Guadalupe Mountains with the Franklin–Organ–San Andres cordillera through intervening salt flats, sand dunes, lava beds, and both desert and plains grassland. Landscape and hence genetic links with the Big Bend can be secured by a connection to the Rio Grande–Río Conchos Corridor. Present military, municipal, private, state, and federal jurisdictions could remain if a consortium for the coordinated conservation of life were formed. I hope for a U.S. ecosystem authority in this region.

New Mexico's panhandle and adjacent areas offer more outstanding opportunities to protect forested sierras within their desert and

---

[14]W. L. Minckley (*Environments of the Bolsón of Cuatro Ciénegas, Coahuila, México, with Special Reference to the Aquatic Biota*, Sci. Ser. 2 [El Paso: Texas Western Press, 1969]) describes this unique area, which I have not seen.

Rio Grande and Sierra del Carmen (Emory)

grassland seas, to consecrate hydrologic units called ecosystems. The Hatchet, Animas, San Luis, and Peloncillo-Guadalupe islands, plus the Playas, Animas, San Bernardino, and San Simon valleys, are favored with instructive maze dwellers that merit more than a fragmented museum system. Disparate groups that presume to own this land must coordinate efforts, although the international scope of the endeavor makes stewardship difficult. Perhaps more easily, a U.S. ecosystem authority could protect the Huachuca, Whetstone, Mustang, Santa Rita, and Patagonia ranges and the Empire and San Rafael valleys in Arizona.

Smaller museums are easier to acquire, and their prompt protection averts resource depletion that may accompany the years of political haggling over large museums. Audacious frontiersmanship—"git in and git it while the gittin's good"—too often prevails on private lands projected for public service. In the New Mexico panhandle, therefore, the Animas–San Luis and Peloncillo-Guadalupe sierras plus the Animas Valley would comprise a viable, smaller preserve. Similarly, the reduced Huachuca–Patagonia–San Rafael combination would be sustainable, providing the thread of the Canelo Hills were woven into the carpet pattern. These should be U.S. national scientific preserves.

The Sierra Madre Occidental of Chihuahua-Sonora furnishes raw material for what I project to be the largest national park in the Border-lands. I see a sanctuary rivaling Yellowstone in protecting grand geo-logic flooring covered by big-scale biota and unique Tarahumara and extinct Anasazi Indian lifeways. I think of at least fifteen thousand square miles of sanctuary, headquartered near the Río Yaqui–Río Gavilán region in the north and given life support via a forested cor-ridor to a similar, expanded portion at the Barranca del Cobre in the south. Such a national park could bring Mexico the economic advan-tage of international tourism like that pioneered by the U.S. national parks and duplicated in east Africa.[15]

But this cannot be accomplished by poisoning grizzly bears and gray wolves, hunting down jaguars and cougars, and clear-cutting the mature pines required by imperial woodpeckers, followed by thick-billed parrots in nesting. Nor can it be done by damming streams and piping off more groundwater for *ejido* development. I would be less than frank if I did not predict that Mexico will lose much more in the long run by overusing such renewable resources than it gains tem-porarily through *campesino* productivity. Tourism is a viable alterna-tive to the present patterns of resource depletion in the magnificent Sierra Madre.

Along the way, hard decisions must be made about small but spe-cial places that deserve single-use status within the multiple-use framework of a larger preserve. For example, Fresno Canyon in the Big Bend and Aravaipa, Cave Creek, Guadalupe, and Sycamore canyons, Arizona, appear submerged on this last journey over desert seas, but they are ideal research sanctuaries. Each houses unique natural history that contributes to enlightening studies of community persistence de-spite environmental change. Why not close them entirely to settle-ment, grazing, and even recreation, for there is plenty of landscape to support these activities elsewhere in the mountain islands.

Near the end of my travels I recommend combining the Imperial Refuge east to the Kofa Mountains, Arizona, into a single ecosystem authority and expanding Anza Borrego Desert State Park to the Salton

<hr>

[15] F. R. Gehlbach, "Wildlands Recreation: A Theme for the Future of the U.S.–Mexico Borderlands," in *Abstracts of the Conference, Science and Man in the Americas*, pp. 34–35, Con. Nac. Cienc. Tecnol. and Amer. Assoc. Advanc. Sci. (1973). See also P. A. Jewell, "Problems of Wildlife Conservation and Tourist Development in East Africa," *J. South Africa Wildl. Mgmt. Assoc.* 4 (1974):59–62.

Sea in California. Above all, I support a Gran Desierto International Park, connecting the Organ Pipe Cactus and Cabeza Prieta preserves with the Gila and Tinajas Altas ranges in Arizona and the extraordinary wilderness southward, the Desierto de Altar, Sonora. This oft-mentioned but untried wildland could be North America's greatest desert museum, at least twelve thousand square miles in extent, matched only by the Sierra Madre in its vastness.

Yet recreational man prefers woodlands and forests near culture, rather than remote desert landscapes, so it is difficult to muster public sentiment in favor of such a park. By studying the determinants of visitor use in eighteen primitive and wilderness areas of southwestern parks and monuments, I find that area of tree-dominated vegetation accounts for the most recreational use, and proximity of the nearest large city is the only other significant factor.[16] The latter may become another value in the calculus of designating and protecting natural preserves, as increased leisure time and the decline in fossil fuels place more pressure on nearby wild space.

While I advocate expanded tourism and wildlands recreation to counter the quick water loss that accompanies expanding agricultural and urban-industrial systems, I must add that new management is a necessity. I support the common calling for advanced reservations, perimeter lodging, internal bipedal and mass transport, and sliding-scale fees, which foster the least human impact on living museums. But the most crucial issues are determination of the human carrying capacity of each preserve, which will dictate its use, and environmental education prior to that use.[17]

Why not training in land ethics as a public-school requirement? This would improve each visitor's understanding of functional synchrony in the carpet pattern, and appropriate use tactics would be more common knowledge. For example, small fires fueled by dead

[16] A multiple stepwise regression of man-use days in designated primitive and wilderness areas (1966–1971 data from U.S. Natl. Park Service) gives the following r^2 values for presumed causative factors: woodland and forest area = 0.24 ($F = 15$, $P<0.05$), distance from nearest city larger than 50,000 = 0.23 ($F = 12$, $P<0.05$), grassland and desert area = 0.13 (n.s.), total wild area = 0.05 (n.s.); multiple correlation (R) = 0.81 ($P<0.001$, 16 d.f.).

[17] R. Cahn, "Future of the Parks: 2," in *Research in the Parks*, pp. 213–220, Natl. Park Serv. Symposium Ser. 1 (1976).

branches gleaned from the ground could replace the unnecessary chopping of trees and the dangerously blazing extravaganzas I see at campgrounds and could provide an alternative to natural litter control by burning. Man who hacks live trees with axes, tramples vegetation in the onrush of bird-listing, and questions "What good is it?" can learn to survive without such discord.

Always I am aware of maintaining a harmonious, natural-cultural mosaic throughout the Borderlands, a landscape diversity managed by the controlled growth of culture. Alternatively, I visualize an unending, man-made desert on border trips of the twenty-first century. Whereas those intrepid surveyors and naturalists of the nineteenth century gave man his first glimpse of the Border's diverse physical and biotic resources and twentieth-century naturalists have documented what fraction remains and how it harmonizes in the arid context, travelers henceforth must be concerned primarily with the interplay of resource keeping and using—the rapprochement of man and nature. The most difficult stewardship is yet to come.

Index